Arnulfo L. Oliveira Memorial Library

GOD'S
HARVARD

GOD'S HARVARD

A CHRISTIAN COLLEGE ON A MISSION TO SAVE AMERICA

Hanna Rosin

Harcourt, Inc.

Orlando   Austin   New York   San Diego   London

Requests for permission to make copies of any part of the work
should be submitted online at www.harcourt.com/contact or mailed
to the following address: Permissions Department, Harcourt, Inc.,
6277 Sea Harbor Drive, Orlando, Florida 32887-6777.

www.HarcourtBooks.com

Grateful acknowledgment is made to the *New Yorker,*
where portions of this book originated.

Library of Congress Cataloging-in-Publication Data
Rosin, Hanna.
God's Harvard: a Christian college on a mission to save America/
Hanna Rosin.
p.   cm.
1. Patrick Henry Community College.   2. College students—Religious
life—Virginia—Martinsville.   3. College students—Virginia—
Martinsville—Conduct of life.   4. Christian education—Virginia—
Martinsville.   5. Community colleges—Virginia—Martinsville.
I. Title.
LD6501.P39R67   2007
378.755'692—dc22   2007015215
ISBN 978-0-15-101262-6

Text set in Perpetua
Designed by Lydia D'moch

Printed in the United States of America
First edition
A C E G I K J H F D B

To David,
my favorite and my best

CONTENTS

INTRODUCTION

When I first began covering religion for the *Washington Post,* more than ten years ago, deflecting conversion attempts became a routine part of my work. Although they are unfailingly gracious, evangelicals are not so good at respecting professional boundaries. What did it matter that I was a reporter doing my job if I was headed for eternal damnation? To a population of domestic missionaries, I presented as a prime target: a friendly non-Christian who was deeply interested in learning more about their beliefs.

The first time someone tried to share the gospel with me, I naively explained that I was Jewish and born in Israel, thank you, thinking this would end the conversation. This was a big mistake. In certain parts of Christian America, admitting I was an Israeli-born Jew turned me into walking catnip. Because God's own chosen people had so conspicuously rejected Jesus, winning one over was an irresistible challenge. And the Holy Land glamour of Israel only added to the allure. Preachers told me they loved me, half an hour after we met. Godly women asked if they could take home a piece of my clothing and pray over it. A pastor's wife once confided to my husband, "You're so lucky. She looks so . . . Biblical." Once, at a Waffle House in Colorado with some associates of the influential Christian activist James Dobson, a woman in our company stared at me so hard it became uncomfortable for me to eat. Finally, I looked up at her. "When I look at you, I see the blood of our Savior coursing through your veins," she said.

"Thank you," I gulped. "More maple syrup?"

Explaining that my family had been Jewish for many generations and that, by converting, I'd be breaking a deep, rich tradition only encouraged them to break out the big gun. I've heard it so many times that I can recite it by heart. Matthew 10:36: "For I have come to turn a man against his father, a daughter against her mother, a daughter-in-law against her mother-in-law—a man's enemies will be the members of his own household. Anyone who loves his father or mother more than me is not worthy of me." This didn't stick with me, either. Clearly they had not met my mother, or any Jewish mother for that matter. The Jews haven't endured for nearly 4,000 years by giving their cubs up so easy.

Biblical verses, like turtlenecks go in and out of style. During the nineties I heard Matthew 10:36 on nearly every reporting trip. This was a paradoxical decade for evangelicals. The Christian right had become a fixture in American politics and the nation was about to elect George W. Bush, the closest thing American evangelicals have had to a pope. At the same time the Christian home-school movement was booming—a relic of the age of separatism and retreat. Evangelicals were poised to move from the fringe to the elite power circles of American society, but they just couldn't seem to make the jump. Unless they learned to polish their act and stop telling people to renounce their own mothers, they would never make it.

I first visited Patrick Henry College in September 1999, a year before the school opened its doors. The "school," that afternoon, consisted of founder Michael Farris, a Christian homeschooling activist, manning an excavator on a construction site just off a Virginia highway exit. Farris was affable, his usual manner with reporters, as he laid out the plans for his revolution. The school would enlist the purest of born-again Christians in a war to "transform America" by training them to occupy the "highest offices in the land." Year after year, it would churn out future congressmen, governors, and federal judges, until they finally had the majority. "Few students will know more about the political ramifications of reinforcing homosexuality through special rights than ours," he told me. One day, he bragged, he would introduce the ultimate graduation-day speaker: "President So and So, an alumnus of Patrick Henry."

It all sounded a little far-fetched. After all, he hadn't even laid the first brick.

Then Bush ran for president as a born-again former alcoholic, and won. Suddenly Farris seemed much less delusional. In the early winter of 2005 I visited again. The central building, Founders Hall, was now an impressive Federalist structure. Inside, the walls were covered with posters for an upcoming production of Oscar Wilde's *An Ideal Husband*. A Whiffenpoofs-style singing group occupied the grand staircase. After talking to some kids having lunch, I concluded they were some of the most anal, competitive teenagers I had every come across. They input their daily schedules into Palm Pilots in fifteen-minute increments—*read*

Bible, do crunches, take shower, study for Latin quiz, write debate briefs. After Jesus Christ they bowed down to the "1600s"—the handful of kids each year who'd gotten perfect scores on the SAT. The atmosphere was much more Harvard than Bob Jones.

They resembled the overambitious junior executives who populate the Ivy League these days—only without the political apathy. Hardly a dorm window, car bumper, bathroom mirror, or laptop went unsullied by some campaign slogan—for George Bush, John Thune, Bobby Jindal, or one of the many Christian conservatives who won during the 2004 campaign. Many students had taken a sanctioned two weeks off classes to volunteer for campaigns, and they were giddy with victory. One senior told me how she'd sacrificed a couple of weekends helping out Bush adviser Karl Rove. One Saturday afternoon, he stopped by to give her a thank-you present. "Good thing it was an ice-cream sandwich or I would have kept it forever!"

"You are the tip of the spear," Farris likes to tell his students at morning chapel, drawing on his limitless arsenal of military metaphors. Polls would place them among the 29 percent of Christian teens who attend church weekly, pray, read the Bible, and describe religion as "extremely important" in their lives. Sociologically speaking, they are a parent's dream. They are less likely than most teenagers to cut classes, do drugs, have sex, get depressed, feel alone or misunderstood, talk back, or lie. Within the third of Americans who call themselves "evangelical" or "born again" they make up an elite corps, focused, disciplined, and not prone to distraction.

When they use the word "Christian," they are speaking their own special language. To them, a Catholic or Mormon, with some exceptions, is not really a Christian. Someone who goes to church three times a year and sings hymns is not a Christian. Someone who goes to church every Sunday and calls themselves "evangelical" is not even necessarily a Christian. "She thought I was nice and Jesus was a great guy and she went to church a lot, but she wasn't a *Christian*," Farris once told a group of students about an acquaintance, and they understood exactly what he meant. To them, a "Christian" keeps a running conversation with God in his or her head *always*, Monday through Sunday, on subjects big and small, and believes that at any moment God might in some palpable way step in and show He either cares or disapproves.

On the issues that have come to define the modern Christian right, the students at Patrick Henry generally cleave to orthodoxy. During my year and a half on campus, I never heard any student argue that homosexuality is not a sin, or that abortion should be allowed in any circumstances. I heard people criticize Bush, but only from the right. After the 2004 campaign, I heard a rumor that someone had voted for John Kerry. I chased down many leads. All dead ends. If it was true, no one would admit it publicly. At Baylor University in Waco, Texas, a much older Baptist institution that's lately been trying to modernize, the student newspaper defended gay marriage in 2004. Such a transgression is unthinkable at Patrick Henry—so beyond the pale that the possibility is mentioned only in passing in the otherwise-very-thorough student code of conduct.

Yet a Patrick Henry student is unlikely to be caught on camera giving a loony Jerry Falwell–style rant about gays and lesbians causing September 11. They worry about gay rights, but they worry just as much about mainstream culture's thinking they're homophobic. "Yes, it's a sin, but so are a hundred other things," one of the students told me, in a self-conscious nod to the "whatever" cadence of his peers. One day a CNN crew came to film a feature story on the school on the same day some students had made two snowmen holding wooden paddles. The snow sculpture was an inside joke about the students' fratlike ritual, recently criticized in the school newspaper, of paddling newly engaged boys. But Farris was mortified. "Do you really want a story to develop that suggests a connection between PHC and those that have beaten homosexuals, etc.?" he wrote in an e-mail to some students who had defended the snowmen as a harmless prank. "PHC 'a school for vigilante justice.' Is that the image you want?"

At first, when I encountered students who were wary about being interviewed by me, I assumed it was because of the usual evangelicals' suspicion of outsiders. After a while I realized it wasn't that at all. Mostly, they were protecting their résumés. "If I want to get into politics, no history is a good history," class president Aaron Carlson told me. "I want to be prudent that nothing I say is ever misconstrued." The Patrick Henry generation will not repeat the mistakes of their fathers. They are not the reckless, fuming, fed-up generation that left Egypt—evangelical code for the modern world. They are the "Joshua Generation," as Farris likes to say, the first ones savvy enough to "take back the land."

Patrick Henry students are supposed to be lights unto the world, an example to the unsaved. And yet, there I was, blind as can be, and no one on campus tried to convert me, at least not outright. I never once heard Matthew 10:36. No one told me to turn against my mother, and no one told me I looked like Jesus. Once Sarah Chambers, a PHC student I knew well, left me a note about a book I'd loaned her, a memoir by a former evangelical. She said the book was charming and funny and astutely observed but ultimately unsatisfying because the author fundamentally did not understand what it meant to have a close personal relationship with God. ("If you don't have it yourself it's hard to understand what motivates these 'crazy fanatics,'" she wrote.) I took this note personally. Months into my reporting, I still didn't understand.

I began to ask around: What does it mean to keep up a running conversation with Jesus in your head, and at the same time to function in the modern world? I asked as a reporter, but the question kept striking people in a way I didn't intend. To Farris and many of the students I knew, I seemed to be sending out the signal that I was open to hearing The Word. Farris loaned me Dallas Willard's *Hearing God* and one afternoon pulled a splinter out of my hand, which at the moment felt close to bathing the feet of the sinner. He prayed "that things come up to help me really show her what it means to have a relationship with God. I feel so inadequate. This is so strange." One sweet freshman told me, "Uhm, well, I like you and I'd just feel really bad if you died and you weren't sure."

Farris must have known I'd be a hard case. I am Jewish, and most of my family lives in Israel; I spent my teenage years in Queens, New York, in the eighties, where my idea of a dress code was matching my miniskirt to my handball gloves. I work and leave my children for several hours a week in the charge of a babysitter who is (gasp!) not related to me. I firmly believe the earth is 4.5 billion years old, or whatever the current scientific consensus says. I have many beloved gay friends and have never once suggested to any of them that they enter into reparative therapy to "cure their disease."

I am naturally democratic almost to a fault. (I've always been grateful that I don't live in a country ruled by a despot, since I could have ended up the one to "humanize" him.) So, despite our differences, I had no trouble letting them in.

For a few weeks during the summer of 2005, Sarah Chambers lived with my family. She'd gotten an internship at a national magazine based in Washington, D.C., and needed a place to stay. When I told my friends this, most of them would give me a quizzical why-are-you-harboring-Nazis-in-your-attic look. Once they met her, they were even more worried. Sarah is charismatic, funny, and adventurous. She climbs, snowboards, and plays the guitar. Her musical tastes range from Jack Johnson to Puff Daddy. She's a terrific writer and was the only intern in her class hired for a full-time job. She could be one of those power girls in a Nike ad, looking glamorous even at the end of a marathon. On top of that, she's an astute judge of character with an introspective side. Sometimes in the mornings I'd find her upstairs in her bed, reading her Bible and taking notes. "If they're all like this," one of my friends said, "we're in trouble."

Often, in the evenings, we would sit around and talk about what she believes. One night my husband finally asked her the question: "So, are we going to Hell?" The Patrick Henry statement of faith, which Sarah and all the other students have to sign, is quite explicit on this question. Satan is real, it says, so is Hell. "All who die outside of Christ shall be confined in conscious torment for eternity." Barring the Second Coming, chances are quite high that my husband and I and our two young children are going to die outside of Christ.

At this point, Sarah had been living with us for almost a month. She'd bathed our children and read them bedtime stories. She'd given my five-year-old daughter a magnificent white model horse, Snow White, that she herself had loved as a child.

"Yes," she answered. "But I'm not jumping up and down with joy about it."

CHAPTER I

Welcome, Surfer Ninjas and Knights

Many seventeen-year-olds brag or exaggerate on their college applications. Not Derek Archer. Even when he wrote to Patrick Henry College about the year that had set the course of his life—the year when he, a homeschooled missionary's kid from a depressed suburb of Akron, got to see President George W. Bush *in person*—Derek kept his hubris in check. "I would be a fool to believe I made it through the past few months by my might and my power, for truly it was by the Lord's grace and His Spirit alone!"

Derek was not one of the school's usual incoming freshman stars known as "the 1600s"—the handful of kids each year who get perfect scores on their SATs and ignore courting letters from Harvard and Stanford to come to Patrick Henry. What he had was not something the six-year-old college could easily boast about in press releases, but what it valued much more: a near-perfect balance of ambition and humility, the one impulse pushing him toward the White House and the other always reminding him Who was really in charge.

In a few heady months during the fall of 2004, the Bush campaign had served as one endless, amazing high school field trip—better than going to Europe or Disneyland or Papua, New Guinea, where his family once lived in a house on stilts. He had made phone calls and knocked on doors in the critical swing districts in Ohio, near where he lived. He had won a contest for registering more than 100 voters. He had learned to take verbal abuse with grace. He had created a minor local celebrity by writing articles and flyers under the fogyish nom de plume "Franz Holbein" who complained about "some of the most appalling displays of disrespect this nation has ever seen." Twenty minutes before the polls closed, a car full of rowdies whizzed by him, screaming "Kerry won! Kerry won!" He prayed it couldn't be true, and his prayers were answered. In the battle between the "forces of righteousness and unrighteousness," the right side had won.

"Those few months have had a powerful impact on my life in preparing me for the ministry of political activism," he wrote to Patrick Henry. "If in any matter I can bring glory to my God and King, may He grant me the grace to do just that."

It's not just that Derek was a missionary's kid and knew how to say the right things. Patrick Henry prides itself on not being your run-of-the-mill Bible college: It doesn't give automatic preference to MKs, who can be just as rotten as any kids. Instead the school takes the measure of its students constantly, probing the nature of each individual's personal relationship with Jesus Christ with the care and trepidation of a parent monitoring a fever, or a schoolgirl checking whether you're still her best friend. Under that microscope, Derek glowed.

God's voice was like the sound track to the movie of Derek's life, lending texture and meaning to every action. In return, Derek thanked God for everything. He thanked Him when a seemingly chance meeting led to a great internship at the local Republican headquarters. "The Lord just dropped that one into my lap!" He thanked Him for his mom sending his favorite granola bars, for his sister passing her driving test, for the extra cheese on his turkey sub. He thanked Him for his new used car, although it was dark purple and the AC didn't work and the windows seemed to be glued shut. He thanked Him for his after-school job at Leach's Meats and Sweets down the road, where he worked in the chilly back room hacking up raw chickens and grinding up beef to stuff into their "famous" sausages while tolerating the boss's son's endless tracks of AC/DC ("the worst band in the whole wide world").

"It's really been a blessing," he told me one day as he wiped his knife on an apron streaked with bloodstains.

In the year before he left for college, Derek had moved down to the basement of his parents' house in Barberton, six miles south of Akron. In the evenings, his mom, Donna Archer, would go down there to drop off his clean laundry "and see if he's ready to hit the hay, and I'd find him down on his knees praying. As a Christian mom, nothing thrills me more. Nobody was watching him; it's the real thing. He doesn't do it to please us. You can see God's spirit at work in him."

"Because of that," his mom added, "I'm not worried if he heads into politics."

For Patrick Henry College, Derek was a white sheep, the son you were pretty sure wouldn't roll his eyes at you the minute you turned your head or sneak a cigarette outside his dorm window at night. The school thought of itself as a training ground for political missionaries; its founder, Michael Farris, traveled the country recruiting conservative Christian kids like Derek who were bright, politically minded, and itching to be near the president. Farris was aware of the risks of launching them into the cutthroat and dirty world of politics: He could unwittingly turn out to be the agent of their corruption, involving them in what Derek had once heard described by a pastor as "an innately wicked endeavor." So Derek was a particular gem, a boy who, as much as anyone this side of heaven, seemed incorruptible.

"Okay. Here goes," Derek said, as he spotted the Welcome Students sign hanging in Founders Hall. Like most of the kids who go to Patrick Henry, Derek was homeschooled by his parents all the way through high school, so college could be a shock. But during orientation week the campus still felt warm and familiar, like a big homeschool family reunion. The central buildings and dorms were packed with typically oversized homeschooling families— ten-year-old girls pushing strollers, toddlers scrambling after their pregnant moms like baby ducks. The little kids were eerily independent and well behaved; they sat in circles on the grass or outside the cafeteria, playing games or reading the campus maps for fun. The incoming freshmen boys, meanwhile, looked like children playing the role of adults in a high school play, with crisp white polo shirts, new leather computer bags, and their last bits of acne. The girls wore twin sets over their khakis or black slacks, which surprised Derek's mom. "Okay, this is going to be more casual dress for the girls than I thought," said Donna, whose daughter goes to a Christian school where skirts are required. But, she added, "I'm happy for the lack of tattoos and piercings."

A handful of families looked like reenactors lost on their way to Colonial Williamsburg: mothers in braids carrying babies in bonnets, girls in their best Laura Ingalls Wilder white-collared dresses taking a stroll around the lake—a tableau that made the campus feel a century—not an hour—away from downtown Washington, D.C. The parking lot was jammed with vans bearing messages on their bumpers: TRUTH, or BUSH/CHENEY, or LIFE. One license plate read MOMOF8.

Derek, who has blue eyes and sharply parted blond hair, already had business casual down. He was wearing an oxford shirt and khakis and sneakers that looked recently cleaned. Like many homeschooled boys, Derek seemed both old and young for his age. If he was in a good mood, he bounced more than walked and whistled, like Dennis without the menace, or an old contented preacher lost in happy thoughts. With his tall frame, gangly arms, and big grin, he was built for stand-up comedy but he was more often straining to seem more serious. He was polite and sometimes absurdly formal, and when he was talking to an adult and feeling nervous, he used constructions more appropriate for the witness stand. ("Yes, ma'am, I have been to this campus on two prior occasions.")

The campus is tiny, less like an Ivy League college than like a Hollywood set of an old Ivy League school, with one main building and several dorms grouped around a lake, all in Federalist style. The art in Founders Hall is designed to remind the students that America was founded as a Christian nation—a gallery of portraits of the Founding Fathers, all copies, leads up the staircase to the picture of Patrick Henry at the second Virginia convention, a shaft of light from Heaven guiding his speech. "Harvard for Homeschoolers," founder Michael Farris likes to call it, invoking the Harvard of earlier days, whose laws instructed students to "know God and Jesus Christ."

The last time Derek was on campus, his assigned dorm hadn't been built yet, and when he saw it, he was impressed. "So stately," he said, noting the chandelier in the entranceway and the winding staircase leading up to his room on the second floor. But the first thing that struck me about the boys' dorms was what was missing. Even during moving week, there were no flip-flops and shorts, because the dress code encourages "glorifying God with your appearance." There were no iPod speakers perched on anyone's windows, shuffling from Beyoncé to Coldplay, because iTunes lists are monitored and headphones are encouraged. There were no movie posters zeroing in on Scarlett Johansson's cleavage, and no live cleavage either, because girls are required to cover their chests and, in any event, girls aren't allowed in boys' dorms. There was no impatient "Mom, aren't you guys going somewhere for dinner?" and no sneaking around to figure out where the rush parties were because at Patrick Henry there are hardly ever parties, and drinking and dancing are not allowed. There were no heaps of clothes on the floor, or open bags of Cheetos. The only thing left blocking the hallway for any amount of time was an ironing board—an ironing board, in a boys' dorm!

Throughout the year, school administrators conduct room checks to monitor cleanliness, but Derek did not really need that incentive. Without any prodding, he set up his room like a Republican Felix Unger. Above his desk he hung a signed Bush/Cheney poster ("To Mr. Archer, with deepest appreciation for your support"), a promotional calendar from the Bush campaign, and a postcard of Ronald Reagan ("If we ever forget that we are one nation under God then we will be a nation gone under."). He unpacked his favorite authors—Joshua Harris, Rush Limbaugh, John Owen—and his prize possession, a Bible bound in black leather that he got when he was twelve, its front cover so worn from use that you have to divine the once-gold monogram with your finger, like the Shroud of Turin. Above his desk sat a wood-block I've seen in many a Republican congressman's office. It read: TRUST ME.

Although Patrick Henry has rules about movie watching, some students keep secret stashes of DVDs in their bottom drawers, but Derek brought only one—*Surf Ninjas,* a martial arts spoof about two surfer brothers who discover they are long-lost princes from a South China Sea island kingdom and use their newly discovered special powers to overthrow an evil madman dictator. ("I enjoy the kind of humor it presents.") He'd seen some movies in theaters, but not very many. "You really have to be careful about how much you consume," he said. "Watch one movie now and again with a bad message, and it will help you know what's going on in the culture. But if you have a constant diet of that, that's where it gets destructive."

He brought only a handful of CDs by contemporary Christian artists such as Steven Curtis Chapman and Mercy Me—the kind of syrupy Christian ballads about which the AC/DC-loving boys at Leach's had given him endless grief.

"You don't have to be careful when you listen to them," said Donna.

"Yes," Derek added, "the gospel message is clear. Unlike some secular songs, which leave you with an empty feeling."

Derek indulged in excess in only one area, and this, too, he could trace back to his mom. His closet was bulging with clothes— suit pants and jackets and dress shirts and T-shirts and ties. But this display was not exactly what it seemed. These were hand-me-downs, collected from an aunt "with fashionable inklings" and various church-run thrift stores. And while most teenage boys might find it annoying to be sent to school with plaid vests and suit jackets to "grow into" and dozens of shirts and ties collected from church sales, Derek did not see it this way. To him, it was an embarrassment of riches, so much so that he decided to bring it up with his mom.

"I feel it's a bit flashy, if you will," he said. "I mean, you don't have to wear something different every single day," he added, in a tone that from him counted as defiance.

"Well, I'm glad you don't have a lack," she said. "It's better not to wear the same thing over and over. Girls notice that kind of thing—that kind of lack of hygiene—more than guys."

OUTSIDE, THE KIDS were comparing schedules—something new for homeschoolers used to learning at their family's pace. Over and over they recited the freshman routine—"Latin, History, Logic, Lit"—a litany meant to calm them down. Derek had been warned that students at Patrick Henry "study, like, fifteen hours a day," that they stay up all night or wake up at 4 A.M. and are generally tightly wound and type A, much more so than he is. He was pretty sure he could keep up, but some other freshmen already seemed on the verge of snapping under the pressure.

"I've been planning my classes for the last year, and now the schedule's not going to work," said one girl with a very tight ponytail, emerging from a meeting with her adviser.

Homeschoolers are not the most obvious raw material for a college whose main mission is to train a new generation of Christian politicians. Politics, after all, is the most chaotic and social of professions, and many students arrive at Patrick Henry having never shared a classroom with anyone other than their siblings. In conservative circles, however, homeschoolers are considered to be something of an elite group—rough around the edges but pure in their focus, capacity for work, and ideological clarity. The kids at Patrick Henry were raised advocating for the rights of homeschoolers; during orientation week, they shared stories of lobbying congressmen sympathetic to their cause or volunteering for campaigns. Most homeschoolers take field trips to the statehouse the way public school kids visit the zoo or the pumpkin patch.

Their parents raised them tenderly, not with the intention of sheltering them forever, but of grooming them for their ultimate mission: to "shape the culture and take back the nation." It's a phrase repeated in homeschooling circles like a prayer, or a chant, or a company slogan. It shows up in homeschoolers' textbooks and essays and church youth groups; their parents whisper it in their ears like a secret destiny: *There's a world out there, a lost and fallen world, and you alone can rescue it.* Derek said it to a reporter who profiled him in the *Akron Beacon Journal* during his senior year of high school. His father, Mark Archer, read Deuteronomy to him and explained how Moses never got to enter the Promised Land; it's the young Joshua who would lead the way to salvation.

"If there's any hope in this country, it's from you kids," his dad told him. "Morally, there is so much bad going on in this country. It will be you kids coming out of the homeschooling movement, your generation, who will do it."

"Homeschooling does give a hope," his mother said, more gently.

At school the upperclassmen echoed their parent's voices: "We're the salt of the earth and it's no good if the salt is kept in a shaker," said Matthew du Mee, one of the school's star graduates.

"It's like training knights," said a junior. "We wear thick armor to make the battle easier. We're not saying we're closer to Heaven, but we go above and beyond the call of duty."

The world out there, this enemy, was something the freshmen had seen only in bits and pieces—at summer jobs at 7-Elevens, playing sports at the local high school, or while changing channels. Their parents might have told them horror stories of drugs and date rape and gay-pride parades, but most of them could hardly imagine what those things might look like. But the Patrick Henry freshmen, like nerdy teenage boys everywhere, loved science fiction and its cinematic equivalent—*Star Wars* and *Star Trek* and *Ender's Game* and *Surf Ninjas*—stories in which a race of morally and intellectually superior boys must leave their childhood home prematurely to go fight enemies who want to destroy an already-mostly-destroyed nation. And the boys always won in the end. Substitute Hillary Clinton for Darth Vader or the Klingons, and their destiny suddenly made sense to them.

Campus in the first few days of orientation week felt like Jedi Academy or Battle School in the Belt or Hogwarts School of Witchcraft and Wizardry (if they'd been allowed to read *Harry Potter*). The boys were suddenly faced with an army of other Chosen Ones just like them, and they found it discomfiting. They knew the adults around them were looking for the next Napoleon, the next Alexander, or at the very least the next Antonin Scalia, and they wanted to be It. At the endless series of lunches and dinners under the big white tent, they sized each other up, jockeying for position, and flexing their muscles in crude and awkward ways. They bragged about their special powers in ways that they would cringe to remember a couple of months later.

"I'd like to be a senator," said one acne-faced boy who'd been chewing on a pencil.

"I'm thinking more of starting with a state office first," answered one with a bow tie. "I've already been introduced to several state legislators."

"I'm more interested in the judiciary. Perhaps a Supreme Court clerking might be a way to start. After law school, of course," said the one who liked soft jazz.

"I want to be president of the United States, so I wasn't certain if I would be better off at the Naval Academy or here," said another, who seemed only six months past holding his mother's hand.

"Not to brag, but I got a perfect SAT." This from a boy wearing a bow tie and cowboy boots. "I guess that's bragging."

There were concert pianists, and opera singers, and kids who read the Bible in Latin. There was a kid who was convinced the Lord had used him to save his parents from getting divorced, so he felt invincible. Derek had done his share of political work, but he was competing with kids who cut pictures of senators out of the newspaper so that they could quiz each other on who was who. Suddenly, having spent nearly half his life away on missions in Papua, New Guinea, didn't seem like such an advantage.

"I'm sorry, what's 'P.C.'?" Derek said, showing a fatal lack of intimacy with the enemy.

"Jon Stewart? I've not heard that name."

At the talent show, kids played Brahms and Rachmaninoff, sang arias, and played violin suites. "No personal talents, sorry," Derek had written in his application, so he created a skit: He interviewed four upperclassmen from his dorm, on the premise that it was thirty years in the future. All of them had turned out to be utter failures except one, who was a Supreme Court Justice about to provide the critical vote in overturning *Roe v. Wade*. The skit was the first hint of anxiety creeping into the plan to shape the culture and take back the nation. For the newly arrived freshmen, that mission suddenly felt more like a lottery than a certain destiny; a lucky few would make it, but others might not.

Orientation week crescendoed in a special chapel service with Patrick Henry's founder and president, Michael Farris. Many of the kids had ended up here because they'd heard him speak at a local homeschool conference, where he'd convinced them of their particular destiny. Now here he was, ready to start the training. They begin with their own version of a battle hymn.

> *Take my heart and form it*
> *Take my mind and transform it*
> *Take my will and conform it——to yours, to yours*

Chapel at Patrick Henry is held in a modest space on the bottom floor of a dorm building. With its folding chairs, white board, and raised stage, it often doubles as a conference room or a classroom. But this is the place where every morning the nail biting and gossiping are put on hold for fifty minutes, while the kids sing and sit through a sermon. Today the atmosphere was especially charged, as Farris gave a welcome-to-the-school address that spoke as much to the ambitions of the parents as to their children.

"This nation desperately needs leaders to shape its beliefs," he said, echoing what they already believed. He laid out the basics (lots of schoolwork, no racial discrimination), and school rules.

"Some we believe are commanded by word of God—like sexual purity—and some are simply our organizational preferences, like the dress code. The Bible doesn't say you can't wear jeans to class, and it wouldn't be a sin. But we want to create an orderly atmosphere, give you a sense that you are being trained on the job."

Patrick Henry bills itself as a classic liberal arts college, but Farris told the parents not to worry when their kids come home talking about the Greeks. "I don't care what Plato says. We don't need the world's knowledge and information to *guide* us. This is basically what's called opposition research," he said. "We need to understand where we are in this time; we want to understand history, the flow of ideas, and great literature. These are all things that are important to us so we can create a Christian image that is winsome."

Derek, his parents, and his three siblings sat near the front. After Farris's talk Donna had one thought running through her mind: "This is him! This is where he belongs!" She felt good about leaving her son in somebody else's care for the first time.

His backpack was weighted down with new books and a neat row of yellow highlighters hooked on for easy access. With no help from his mom, he had freshly combed hair, like a schoolboy's, or a senator's.

"I stand here and say good-bye to the only life I've ever known," he said. "I'm blown away by the fact that you guys are so incredible." He hugged his mom and then his two little brothers.

Donna held herself together for the six-hour drive home, for the first steps into the little two-story tract house, now empty of her firstborn. She walked into the downstairs bathroom and saw Derek's old yellow towel still hanging in its place.

"I guess we won't be needing that anymore," she said to no one in particular. And then she finally let herself cry.

THE ARCHERS MOVED TO Barberton when Mark became pastor at the Valley Community Church, a tiny place with a mostly elderly congregation. Their house belongs to the church—a two-story cream bungalow on a street with lots of identical houses; a few of which have had FOR SALE signs out for over a year. The inside is tidy and cozy; the kitchen is decorated with Christmas tins and a small piano dominates the living room. The house centers around the oval kitchen table where Donna gets dinner ready or homeschools Derek's two younger brothers, Justin, eight, and Jared, five.

On one afternoon when I visited just before Christmas 2006, Justin and Jared had just finished their lessons for the day and were sitting on the living room floor playing with Legos. They were both blond and fair like Derek and wore identical striped shirts and jeans. There were no bleeping toys or superheroes or handhelds around. There was no noise, either. The boys played quietly, and when they needed their mother's attention they came and whispered in her ear. Once the boys clowned around by tumbling over the couch—silently—and she put a stop to that with a glance. Donna is exceedingly gentle, even with telemarketers who call in the middle of dinner.

Like their brother, Justin and Jared have a weakness for video games. When they were done with Legos, Justin pulled out an old eighties Atari set and put on a grainy black-and-white Tom and Jerry game. The aim was to get Tom to the top of the maze before some little goblins ate him. Justin almost made it before Tom got wiped out. A little halo appeared over the cat's head, and a Tom-shaped spirit floated up from his body. To me this seemed a nice Christian touch—a soul rising up to Heaven—but Donna found it too wizards and warlocks.

"Uh-oh, that's not good." She looked at me conspiratorially and turned the game off.

Homeschool culture is awash in nostalgia, but it's sometimes difficult to exactly place the source of the longing. The emphasis on female modesty, parent-sanctioned courtship, strong sibling ties, and the moral value of thrift are all ideas borrowed from the nineteenth century. Homeschool girls idolize Jane Austen and the most romantic of them keeps a stash of hand-sewn "Lizzy gowns" in her closet for upcoming contra dances—old-fashioned line dances involving a caller that are popular among homeschoolers. In pop culture, however, homeschool families tend to romanticize the forties and fifties, a prelapsarian age before the Pill, when the "TV and movie censors were doing their jobs," as the parents will often say. In homeschool households I've seen complete boxed sets of *The Andy Griffith Show* and *Leave It to Beaver;* I've met ten-year-olds who know *Casablanca* by heart and can name every movie in which Fred Astaire didn't dance with Ginger Rogers. If they allow video games, parents permit only the oldest ones they can find, which usually places them somewhere in the early eighties.

Some have suggested that homeschool families, in choosing a radically different lifestyle, share something with the sixties counterculture they are supposedly reacting against. Like some of the Patrick Henry parents I've met, Mark Archer grew up as a hippie. Although he is "born again," some parts of his new self would be recognizable to the old: his aversion to name brands and plastic junk, his missionary hunger for a nomadic existence, his desire to overhaul the settled, decaying culture. When Paul Weyrich, a founder of the Christian right, wrote a famous 1999 letter urging Christians to drop out of the culture, he knew his audience well; in a conscious echo of the famous sixties phrase, he urged them to "turn off, tune out, and drop out."

Mostly, however, the routines of a homeschool life seem to take place out of time. Ten minutes away, a new bubble tea bar is the buzz of downtown Akron; along with the new martini bar, it's trying to efface this little strip's seedy reputation as the home of Heaven and Hell Tattoos & Body Piercing. But Donna has never been to the strip or to the local mall. She and the boys leave the house only to go to the library or to pick up their sister at school. Justin and Jared's whole world, every day, is this little house, from upstairs in their parent's bedroom where the computer is, to downstairs where the TV and their schoolbooks are. Sometimes they wander out to the patch of grass at the side of the house where they turn sticks into light sabers and pretend-duel. Mostly they stick close to each other and to their mom.

For the Archers, homeschooling was a natural extension of their missionary life in New Guinea, where they had no choice but to teach Derek and his sister Bethany at home. By the time they settled back in the States, in the mid-nineties, the major legal battles giving parents the right to homeschool had been fought and won, mainly by Michael Farris. Now competing companies offer prepackaged curricula, making schooling at home a breeze. "I thank the Lord for Christian Liberty Academy," says Donna, referring to the company that provides most of the textbooks she uses.

In the homeschooling curriculum, theology is not a distinct subject, a little Sunday school thrown in at the end of each day.

God and Jesus' life are integrated into every subject—science, history, literature, and math: One Pharisee plus two Pharisees equals how many Pharisees? Jared has just started his first science book, *Exploring God's Creation*. One page looks like your average science book—*Write the names of the different body parts of an insect*. On the next page—*Write the day of creation on which God created the following things: the land, the sky, etc.* Justin's workbook—*History for Little Pilgrims*—is a child's-eye version of the American Manifest Destiny that Derek will learn about during his freshman year at Patrick Henry, moving seamlessly from Adam and Eve to the Alamo, and everything in between ("Christ Builds His Church," "America Moves West"). Test questions include *God saved Noah and his family from the* _____ and *Congress is held in a building called the* _____.

By high school, the message gets more explicit. Derek's favorite textbook, *God and Government*, states, "Those who say religion and politics do not mix fail to realize two essential points," and advises that "Christians should be working to elect distinctively Christian leaders."

Derek dates his conversion to the age of six. The family was living in a timber house they had built in New Britain, an island off the northern coast of Papua, New Guinea. He remembers the experience now with fresh emotion and even a bit of fear; when he told it to me, he created a kind of hush in the noisy Patrick Henry cafeteria. One afternoon at naptime, his dad was reading him and Bethany a story from *The Bible in Pictures for Little Eyes*. The story was about Absalom, who was stabbed to death by Joab after his long hair got caught in the thick branches of an oak tree. Derek recalled feeling "a great sense of dread."

"Will he go to heaven?" Derek asked.

"No, I don't think he will."

"Dad, will I go to heaven?"

"Well, no. Not unless you accept Jesus Christ as your messiah."

Derek and his dad knelt and recited together the sinner's prayer: "*Heavenly Father, I know that I am a sinner and that I deserve to go to hell . . .*" Afterward Derek felt a "great sense of peace and joy," and then went to tell his mom.

Mark Archer was not raised a Christian, far from it. When he was Derek's age, he was chanting with street-corner Hare Krishnas and worrying about scoring some great Colombian weed. One summer he took a bus from California to the Dayton Art Institute, where he was supposed to take classes. During the trip, he came upon a homeless-looking man haunting a bus terminal. "All you have to do is ask Jesus Christ to come into your heart," the man told him. At the time, Mark thought of the Bible as a "fairy tale," but that man jumpstarted Mark's stoner paranoia. He hid under an overpass in case lightning should strike. Eventually what the man said stuck. Mark told his friends, but they laughed at him, so he gave up sleeping on their mattresses. A few years later, on a mission trip in Brazil, he met Donna, who had grown up in a Christian family in Albany, New York. They were married in 1981 in Cobleskill, New York.

Derek was born in 1986 in New Guinea, where Donna and Mark had moved with the support of New Tribes Mission. The Asengseng tribe on the island of New Britain hadn't interacted with many Westerners outside of "anthropologists with atheistic thinking" who had looked at the tribes and saw, in Mark's view, the ideal life they wished they had found in Haight-Ashbury—free love, no sexual possession or rules. But Mark felt the Margaret Meads of the world had misread them. At heart, he thought, they were a God-fearing culture that understood the concept of sacrifice and just needed to learn about the ultimate one. The Archers spent a couple of years learning the language and then began their real work: telling the tribes the history of the world, from Creation to Resurrection.

In photos, their life looks like a grand adventure, two blond kids playing with bats, eating cassava root, Mark tan and still sort of hippie-scruffy, but happy. In the village, the retelling of the Bible served as the equivalent of a soap opera involving death, destruction, and plays for power that unfolded in daily episodes under a lean-to. Derek and his sister argued about who would get to play the role of Isaac. After three months they got to the final episode—the crucifixion—and it was like who shot JR. The gathered crowd gasped—"They didn't expect him to die." They were silent for a while. Mark stayed quiet, too, to let it sink in. Then he did the reveal. "He died for our sins," he explained. "He took our place, took our sins away." He waited again. "It was the most cliffhanger moment of our lives," he recalled.

"Then Pete, an older man, stood up, and he said, 'I believe, I believe that Jesus took my place. I can go and be with God when I die because Jesus took my place.' His eyes were just wide open, like two lightbulbs."

Keeunla, a tribal warrior, was next to speak: "I've killed a man. Now I know the blood of Christ will forgive me."

The Archers settled in a few more villages until they needed a change and they came back to the States, to Sacramento, California, and to Bill Clinton's presidency. Now it was Mark's turn to be "Shocked! There was so much sin in society." This wasn't like the sixties for Mark, because this time he was seeing it from a parent's perspective. The president was a degenerate. His semen was discussed on the evening news. Every time they turned on the television they saw a new sitcom with "every off-color joke and sexual innuendo you could imagine. Even on the ones meant for kids!" Derek was interested in superheroes, and that, too, horrified them. "The kids would play with these action figures, these Power Rangers or whatever, who would go up to the top of the mountain and summon lightning. Where did they think these kinds of powers come from?"

Derek told me a story from that period that shows his enormous superego already at work. It was his twelfth birthday and a few days before Christmas. Derek desperately wanted a video game—the sequel to *Age of Empire*—and he'd let his dad know more than once. The afternoon of his birthday the presents were piled in the kitchen, and there was one box that looked just the right size. "I was jazzed," he recalled. "I really wanted that game, and I knew Dad was a great gift-giver."

He reached for the package first and opened it. It was . . . a Bible, a new leather-bound King James edition. "I was pretty put out, but I tried not to show it." What came into Derek's head was, ironically, something from Scripture: "Hope deferred makes the heart sick." Derek turned it over and over in his head, but he didn't complain. Video games were a "poor use of time," he decided. He turned it over again, and then just accepted it. "That Bible is more precious to me than any video game," he concluded.

Over many years of writing about evangelicals I've heard dozens of testimonials—stories of how people really came to have a personal relationship with Jesus Christ. The stories follow the same formula as a VH1 special: false pride, the fall, and blazing recovery. Unless someone was really a drug addict or murderer, the stories always feel a little thin to me, perfectly ordinary vicissitudes shoehorned into a tidy drama. But when Derek told me his, I felt that he really meant it, that he experienced the events as crashingly as if he had been William Burroughs redeemed.

I asked Derek one day if he'd always been a Christian and he said no, he hadn't, which surprised me. I'd known him for a year and had never seen him do anything remotely sinful, even gossip. "There came a point in my life between the ages of eleven and fourteen. There was an outward Christian walk, but it wasn't inward. I read the Bible and memorized the verses and acted like a good little Christian kid. But there was sin in my life. Issues in my life that led me astray from the Lord."

His family was still in California. Derek had a crush on a girl, or as he puts it, "I was involved in an emotional relationship with a young lady." He didn't really talk to his parents about it or even tell them when he was seeing her. When his parents teased him about the girl—"Oh, is she your girlfriend?"—he shut down the conversation. He was never outwardly rude to them, not once, but in his head "things were going on secretly without their knowledge."

"My thought life," as he puts it, "definitely was not very pure."

Evangelicals do not really believe in adolescence. They believe that teenage angst is an invention of some liberal educational philosopher or maybe James Dean. When their teenagers act up the parents will call them "grumpy" or "testy," but refuse to acknowledge it as time-honored rebellion. If a crush is the roughest problem I have with my kids during their teenage years, I will be thrilled, but to Derek it was monumental, the pivotal moment of his life. You can think of it like one of those child loves that chill you forever—Annabel Lee, only in reverse, remembered not in longing but in revulsion.

Derek was miserable, and couldn't find a way out. His family had moved to North Carolina so his dad could pastor a church there, but he still couldn't get the girl, or the rebellious thoughts, out of his head. Homeschoolers don't have teachers, coaches, or peers to give them guidance when they feel out of sync with their parents. What they have is "sound teaching." Derek's dad had dozens of Christian books lying around the house, and in one slim paperback Derek found his salvation: a reprint of the *The Mortification of Sin* by John Owen, originally published in 1656.

The text is arcane, full of heavy aphorisms:

It is a sad thing for man to deceive his own soul herein.
    When God comes home to speak peace in a sure covenant of it, it fills the soul with shame for all the ways whereby it hath been alienated from him.

These quotes are both from the last chapters. When Derek talks about the night he read it, he comes closest to sounding like a regular teenager. "It was, like, wow. I don't even have to try. It's just a matter of trusting God. I was, like, wow, walking on clouds. It was the Christmas service that night, and this just added that little bit of ecstasy."

With his "days of mediocrity, of spiritual darkness, of apathetic lethargy" gone forever, Derek developed the sense of mission that defines him today. His mother read about something called a "constitutional law" camp in Virginia. It didn't sound all that exciting to Derek, but he loved his *God and Government* textbook, so he decided to try it. He went, heard Farris speak during that week, and discovered his calling: the "ministry of political activism." He followed up with a weeklong "political activism camp." The counselors, who were Patrick Henry students, took the kids on field trips to Monticello and Mount Vernon, and to Congress to learn how to lobby. "They took a bunch of students who knew nothing about campaigning or activism and showed us everything we needed to know," recalled Derek.

His parents were somewhat surprised. "I would have thought he'd do ministry directly, or missionary work, but he just started heading this way," said his dad. "I guess it became Derek's desire to impact the culture for Christ through political means."

"When he got interested in politics I just started grasping at what the Lord has in that for him," his mom remembered thinking at the time.

The truth is, in any other generation, Derek probably would have been a missionary or a pastor. But in this generation, he found a place to easily plug that evangelizing instinct into politics. The older people in his dad's church still warned the family that this was a wicked endeavor. But the older people are pushing against a tidal wave. The days when politics was a dirty business for evangelicals are long gone. Derek's family was in New Guinea during the rise of the Christian Coalition, so he missed the whole period when Christians broke through to the mainstream. His parents may tell him Christians are discriminated against, kept out of the public sphere, but his experience tells him otherwise. According to what he learned at political activism camp, Christians are crucial players on the political scene. They are the base, the army on the ground, and if Derek wants to work on a campaign or intern with a congressman, someone at camp just has to make a phone call and *poof,* when can you start?

Derek helped run a voter-registration drive at the Alive Festival—the "Christian equivalent of Woodstock," his mother called it. He met a fellow homeschooler whose dad worked with the Christian Coalition. "Then door after door after door opened up," his mother recalled. There were Republican dinners and voter-registration drives and lobby days at the statehouse. His sister, who still thought of him as her best friend, had to get used to his being away all the time, campaigning. His mother had to get used to the backseat of her minivan piled with voter guides and lawn signs.

During the height of campaign season, Derek's alter ego, Franz Holbein, was born. The mysterious Holbein wrote about the "disgraceful" performance of Whoopi Goldberg at the Kerry fundraiser, "when we, as decent American citizens, [watched them] speak of our elected officials as the scum of the earth." He wrote about Kerry voting "time and time again in favor of abortion laws," about "the fictitious separation of church and state," about the "appalling lack of patriotism in the 'peace' riots." He wrote a screed against marijuana: "Will our mothers and fathers become addicts to an otherwise destructive drug just because they've been diagnosed with cancer? Shall our hospices become places where insane laughter echoes through the halls?"

He wrote urging Christians to help elect godly men to government. "Patrick Henry's words ring true. The war is actually begun . . . Why do we stand here idle? . . . I implore you, my fellow Christians. Do not stand here idle."

Derek began to seem older, far away, and more Holbeinish by the day. He asked if he could drive the car on the highway, instead of just on back streets. His mom became self-conscious if she nagged him. "You know, Derek, I'd do that even if you were president. I'd call and ask 'Did you brush your teeth?'"

Mark, too, marveled at his son's burning ambition. By Derek's age, the only "job" he'd ever had was hanging around the head shop where his friends worked. His son has already shaken hands with two senators. "He's had a lot of experiences we'll never have, working on campaigns and meeting people. I don't want to say he's worldly-wise, but he's broadened." The Archers found themselves in a position like that of many immigrants: They prepare their children for great things and then have to adjust when one day the children float away to a higher plane.

The brochure for Patrick Henry promised the school would prepare the students for "careers of influence." It boasted of graduates working on Capitol Hill, in the White House, at Republican think tanks. It featured an endorsement from President Bush: "The College holds a vision for the future of America, a vision which, when fully realized, will have a profound impact upon the course of our nation."

"It's like they take the best and the brightest, the cream of the cream, and they plug them in," said his dad.

"And, it's just an extension of Mom and Dad!" added his mom, hopeful that she could still hang on to some part of him.

They prayed on it, but they didn't much need to. They knew it was right for Derek. With the $18,000 he had earned over the years at Leach's, scholarship money ("Missionaries! Very poor!" his mother wrote on the financial-aid application), and a campus job, they could just make it work.

THIS WAS A DRY RUN at taking back the culture, and so far it wasn't going too well. The Patrick Henry boys were standing on a Washington Metro platform they would later remember as "church something" (it was West Falls Church), and looking slightly confused. They were ten freshmen in suits carrying red folders, and a leader, a burly sophomore named Josh Dispenza with a barking coach personality. They got lost maybe ten times driving over here, and they'd already missed their 8:30 briefing. On the Metro platform, they looked like interns who had misplaced something—their badge, their wallet? Still, they exuded the unmistakable eagerness of the typical PHC freshman.

The boys had been dispatched as lobbyists by Freedom Works, one of several conservative groups that teach young people to push their pet issues on the Hill. Derek had lobbied before in the Ohio statehouse for the Christian Coalition, but this was different. Back then he had lobbied for issues he could easily get his head around: banning abortion and supporting traditional marriage. This time he'd be pushing the agenda of the Republican establishment: Social Security reform (privatization, personal investment accounts), telecom laws (deregulation), and the asbestos bill (tighter regulation on lawsuits). To do that, he had to turn himself into a young Ralph Reed, using Scripture to justify the standard Republican platform, sounding certain but making little sense. "Of course we have to repeal the estate tax," he said. "The Earth is the Lord's, not the government's."

The boys took the exotically long escalator out of the Capitol South station. Derek, with his excess kid energy, ran up the stairs. As soon as they got outside, the boys took pictures of everything: strolling senators, plaques on doors, the Capitol elevators, the Capitol mail trucks, the ornate winding staircases. They behaved like tourists with an acquisitive mind-set who know they will one day be back.

"We got game! We got game! Let's go," shouted Josh when he spotted the Capitol, and he divided the boys into teams. The men at PHC take the concepts of leadership and authority deeply seriously, and they all wanted to prove themselves worthy. Josh talked importantly on his cell phone the whole time ("Yeah, I'm in D.C. I'm in D.C. right now."). He referred frequently to "my boys." The boys meanwhile elbowed each other to become one of Josh's "point guys."

Derek was paired with Jacob Holt, a Texan who'd scored 1600 on his SATs, and one of the guys who used to cut out pictures of senators from the newspaper. When it came to Texas politics, Jacob knew enough facts to challenge Karl Rove to a trivia game. But he had yet to put his head knowledge to any good, practical use.

"Look him in the eye," Josh explained. "Don't read from the script, but don't go off on tangents." He doesn't for a moment let them believe their mission isn't real. "Cosponsor is a big word," he explained. "If you can't get them to cosponsor one of our bills, then get them on record saying they'd be willing to debate it. That will work for us in the election."

"Okay, Derek, Jacob, I need you to plot, then execute."

At the first couple of stops, the boys got a lot of rejections. Most senators had left for the swearing-in ceremony for John Roberts, who had just been confirmed as chief justice of the Supreme Court.

"Do you have an appointment?"

"No, but I think my associates sent out a fax," said Josh.

By the fourth stop, however, things warmed up for them. They got to the office of the late Representative Charlie Norwood, a conservative from Georgia—the first office with a Patrick Henry graduate on staff. "Leanne, these are my boys," said Josh, introducing them to a young woman who had graduated the previous year. "She's a cool person. A lot cooler than any of you will ever be." Josh followed her into her office while the boys sat outside and munched on free peanuts. Lesson 1: Networking is key.

Now everywhere they went they had an in. Senator George Allen's office had just hired another PHC graduate. "How's Dr. Farris doing?" asked the chief of staff. "Oh, Patrick Henry, I love that college," said Senator Lindsey Graham, and invited them into his office for a chat. "But aren't you guys a little young for politics?" After some chitchat, Graham grabbed some popcorn, dropped some, and stepped on it. Lesson 2: Senators eat popcorn, and they step on it. They are just people, no more, no less.

Walking between buildings, they passed the steps of the Supreme Court, where some students their age were protesting against abortion rights by taping their mouths shut with red tape—the "silent scream" was intended to represents the pain of an aborted fetus. It was a scruffy crew—a girl wearing headphones and ripped jeans, swaying to some tune only she could hear, boys with unruly near-Afros. The Patrick Henry boys walked on by, barely looking; their future was inside that building sitting next to Roberts, not protesting on the front steps. Lesson 3: Always wear a suit.

In the next building, they stopped by Hillary Clinton's office, conjuring in their minds the next episode in the culture war. "Let's see the lions eat the Christians. That'll be fun," said Josh. They convinced themselves they were being watched by her Secret Service and stayed for a bit, for the thrill of it. She never materialized, so they moved on. Next stop was Senator John Thune, a Republican from South Dakota. Thune was the epitome of what they wanted to be, a conservative evangelical who is a successful member of leadership, a handsome young ex-basketball player with a beauty-queen wife and two Bush twin–like girls, and the JFK for this young generation of Christian conservatives. They rested there for a while, until Josh spotted something outside.

"Charley, go see who that is. He's kind of weird-looking."

Charles was jumpy when he came back. "Whoa, it's Ted Kennedy."

The boys sat up, alert. The enemy was in their sights. Young Luke and Darth Vader were about to face off, and not for the last time.

"Storm, what are you doing? Nothing? Good. Go, boy. This is yours."

Kennedy was walking with his arm around the shoulder of Senator Dodd.

"Excuse me, Senator Kennedy?"

"Yes, son. I'm talking to this other senator right now. Come along with me," Kennedy said, and pulled Storm along.

"Would you support Social Security reform?"

"You mean Bush's bill? No, I don't think I'm for that."

"Well, would you be interested in a debate about it?"

"Sure, sure."

The Patrick Henry kids almost never speak disrespectfully about adults. But later, when they told this story (over and over) in the cafeteria, they would describe Kennedy as "gravelly," "fat," "sweaty." "He looked like he was about to keel over." "He looked like there was nothing holding that guy together."

At the time, Storm came back with a big grin on his face: "Hey, guys, guess what I just did!"

At the end of the long day, Josh asked Jacob and Derek if they could see themselves walking the halls as a senator one day.

"Perhaps I'd like to think so," said Jacob, and he broke into a huge smile. "I'm sure I'll be back here in some capacity, someday."

Derek, however, was feeling shaky, disoriented. "Despite all the glamour that surrounds Washington, D.C., and all the important decisions taking place here, I was just kinda really struck with the fact that I don't know if I want to work in the Capitol Building or in D.C. itself," he said. "I think I'd enjoy something maybe a little bit more laid back. It's so uptight and so professional. There seems to be sort of a, a, gloomy air about the Capitol." On the ride back, he fell asleep, temporarily drained of his usual energy and certainty.

A week later, I caught up with Derek at an evening "town hall" meeting on campus. That day the speaker was David Kupelian, author of *The Marketing of Evil* and editor of WorldNetDaily.com. I knew Kupelian only from the WorldNetDaily e-mails he sends out. If there is a Larry Flynt of the Christian world, Kupelian is it. WorldNetDaily is like a gruesome tabloid in reverse. Typical headlines include QUEERLY BELOVED and THE BLOODY LIFE AND VICIOUS TEACHINGS OF MUHAMMAD.

Kupelian was talking about some of his favorite subjects: homosexuality, Alfred Kinsey, and homosexuality. "Homosexual men are regarded today as the equivalent of modern-day lepers. They've turned that into a positive play for victim status. I'm not making this stuff up. I call it desensitization. You say something over and over again and eventually people start to believe it. You get straight people to believe that homosexuality is just another thing. I like vanilla, they like chocolate. If everyone around you is behaving this way, it must be the right thing."

Derek was nodding, taking notes.

"I'm betting the next movement coming down the pike: normalization of adult-child sex."

One of the kids in the audience stopped him to ask a question: "So you're saying not to compromise your principles?"

"Oh, absolutely. They say politics is the art of compromise, but you have to be careful. Pretty soon you're working against the very thing you believe in most. This is typically what happens in politics in Washington. Now, I hear some of you want to join those ranks and breathe some fresh air in there. Well, Godspeed."

Derek was sobered by the talk. He thought of Kupelian as someone who had been to the heart of darkness and come back alive, a prophet calling him and his fellow Christians back to their urgent duty. Like a soldier heading into Fallujah, Derek knew what he must do. Now he saw the trip to the Capitol in a whole new light.

"I realize Washington, D.C., isn't a place of virtue and moral character. Storm was shaking Kennedy's hand, and maybe that was a thrill. Yet Ted Kennedy is one of the most immoral men in a political position. You are shaking hands with an evil man, and he is maybe symbolic of maybe where we are as a nation. To see such an ungodly man in such a high position, it's grievous."

"But it's not beyond the Lord to turn that around. If that's where the Lord wants me to be a light, that's where I want to be. It's in gloomy places where light is needed the most."

CHAPTER 2

Harvard
for Homeschoolers

The drive from Patrick Henry College to Michael Farris's takes you past all the landmarks of a rapidly changing Loudon County: a McDonald's, a Subway, a few tiny strip malls, and a creamy new subdivision ("Quaker Village"). At some point along Route 7, a sign pokes out—BROWN EGGS, $2 DOZEN—a relic of the kind of place Purcellville used to be when Farris moved there twenty years ago. His place is still past the end of the blacktop, down a dirt road. A profile in the *Washington Post* implied that the dirt road was Farris's private driveway, tarring him with the showy materialism of his new neighbors. The mistake so irritated Farris that he once drove me to the road in the middle of lunch to prove it wasn't true.

Tech-boom money has put Jaguars and BMWs in the local high school parking lots. The few barns left around town are destined for "reclaimed" wood benches in somebody's new mudroom. Only a thin line of trees separates Farris from yet another new subdivision going up across the road. But on his side the view is still mostly pure. On the March day I visited, the neighbor's horses grazed by a white picket fence as a couple of rabbits hopped by. It was quiet enough to hear squirrels scratching bark or the first songbirds of spring—the perfect sound track to Farris's fantasy of protected wholesome living, of the kind of life where barefoot children chase butterflies on the grass while their father supervises from a nearby hammock, a C. S. Lewis hardback resting on his chest.

When you hang around the paternalistic culture of Patrick Henry long enough, some part of you comes to believe that Farris really does control everything. As I pulled up to the house just before 8 A.M., NPR was airing an item about the White House drug-policy office's latest finding that, out of thirty teenagers, seven use drugs, thirteen drink, six smoke, and ten are sexually active. "Believe it or not, officials call that an improvement," said the host. *Touché,* I thought to myself. Could such timing of a story that puts NPR to the *right* of the Bush White House, and that happens to justify everything Farris believes, be mere coincidence?

At this time in the morning, most kids would be getting ready for school, but at Farris's house he was the only one up and about. Homeschooling families set their own schedules, and many start their day at a much more reasonable hour. The house was orderly but not fancy, with evidence of ten children and various grandchildren in every room—high chairs and a Barbie graveyard and piles of schoolbooks and the verse of the day on the blackboard in the sunken living room where Farris's wife, Vickie, still homeschooled the three youngest of their kids: *Blessed is the nation whose God is the Lord.*

Farris was in the habit of taking advantage of this quiet time every morning to commune with God. More specifically, he sat down at the oak desk in his study—a halfhearted replica of a Victorian library, with a Persian rug and Christian bestsellers lining the shelves—and copied out a passage of the Bible by hand. He was writing out the whole thing, in longhand, on plain loose-leaf paper, on a surface cluttered with other papers, stray acorns and wires from unplugged gadgets; his golden retriever, Sunny, lay down behind his chair. He was doing it because it says in Deuteronomy that this is what the head of a nation must do. The people are to choose a King whom the Lord in turn has chosen. The King shall not enrich himself with either gold or wives or horses. He "shall write him a copy of this law in a book," which in Farris's case means some cheap-looking plastic binders from Office Depot.

In this prophecy, Farris does not get to be King. He had his moment in 1993, when he ran for lieutenant governor of Virginia and lost; the following year he declined to run for the senate. Instead, he views himself as God's consigliere, or recruiter, or anointed messenger, St. Gabriel of the Beltway. His job now is to teach himself "by what standards we should measure political leaders, and how to recognize one," he says. "We want to train leaders to be the way God wants them to be. I've encouraged people at the school to think that if you want to be a godly leader, don't deviate from God's standards." The Bible's command not to take too many wives translates into: Don't get a divorce. The injunction not to accumulate lots of silver and gold means: Don't use your public office for personal gain. Don't lead your people back to Egypt means: Don't use the world's way, use God's.

Farris took out a few sheets of paper and began to write in the same careless handwriting he might use to write a note to his secretary or a Post-it to himself. I Corinthians 14:2: "For anyone who speaks in a tongue does not speak to men but to God." This verse is used by more charismatic denominations such as Pentecostals as the justification for speaking in tongues. If Farris were one of his students, he might have cursed his bad luck to have come upon this verse in the presence of an NPR-listening reporter such as me. The average Patrick Henry student may have attended a charismatic church in his youth, or even been overcome by ecstatic moaning now and again. But the student, especially if he had any serious political ambitions, would not want to leave me with that image of his ten-year-old self lost in religious ecstasy. However, Mike was from a different generation, and he was unfazed. "There are phonies out there but I think it's real," he says about speaking in tongues, "because God can do anything."

By 9 A.M. the house started coming to life. Michael Farris's youngest son Peter, then nine, played scales on their piano. His nineteen-year-old daughter, Angie, turned on the computer in the hall behind him.

"Dad, what's that site that reviews movies?"

"Google 'Ted Baehr.' I think it's 'movieguide.com.' Why? What movie are you looking at?"

"I was thinking of going out with Lydia Sunday night, and she was suggesting several movies and one that looks kinda iffy."

Movieguide.org is a Christian parent's best friend; it rates movies from "EXEMPLARY: Biblical, usually Christian, worldview, with no questionable elements whatsoever" to "ABHORRENT: Intentional blasphemy, evil, gross immorality, falsehood, evil worldviews, and/or destructive, horrendous worldview problems."

Angie scrolled down to *Date Movie*.

"What's it say?" Farris asked.

"'Abhorrent,'" she read. A red warning box. "'Strong Romantic worldview in which morality is reduced to pursuit of individual desires, and a flamboyant homosexual character; 12 profanities and 29 obscenities, many of them strong, several vulgar gestures, and crude bathroom humor. Media-wise families will avoid this detestable movie targeted at teenagers.'"

"Okay," her father said, "I guess that's a no."

Farris is a constitutional lawyer and Baptist minister who has worked in Christian causes for decades. When I met him he was fifty-three, but he seemed younger, with thick, sandy brown hair and a slightly amused expression. In his writing Farris can sound morose, warning parents about the land of "MTV, Internet, porn, abortion, homosexuality, greed, and accomplished selfishness." But in person, and especially with the media, he aims for charm and even irreverence; he sees very few movies or television shows, but he absorbs just enough decadent culture to talk about "chick flicks" or joke about some woman he met who looked like a "very expensive prostitute" and turned out to be a Republican Party chairwoman.

He loves to tell stories that put him at the centers of power, arguing before the Supreme Court, having dinner with Clarence Thomas, making Justice John Paul Stevens laugh so hard his bow tie shook. But his favorites are tales out of school: standing on the floor at the 1996 Republican National Convention after Bob Dole's speech, watching Senator George Allen throw a foam football forty yards to hit Sam Donaldson in the head, or challenging the constitutionality of parking tickets as a law student in Spokane.

Farris founded Patrick Henry in 2000 after fielding requests from two constituencies: homeschooling parents and conservative congressmen. The parents, who looked up to him for his work with the Homeschool Legal Defense Association, would ask him where they could find a Christian college with a "courtship" atmosphere, meaning one where dating is regulated and subject to parental approval. The congressmen asked him where they could find homeschoolers as interns, "which I took to mean someone who 'shares my values.' And I knew they didn't want a fourteen-year-old kid." So he set out to build what he calls an Evangelical Ivy League, and what the kids call Harvard for Homeschoolers.

Farris bought the land for the Patrick Henry campus with $400,000 from the Home School Legal Defense Association's reserves; he raised the rest of the money for the college—$9 million—from parents and such donors as Tim LaHaye and James Leininger, a San Antonio businessman who is a part owner of the Spurs and is known in Texas as the "sugar daddy" of the religious right. Farris decided the school would not accept any federal funding.

In *The Joshua Generation,* his manifesto for the school, Farris places himself in the "Moses generation" that "celebrates the fact that it left Egypt." But "leaving Egypt is not the end goal." The homeschooling movement will be counted successful only if the kids—the Joshua Generation—"engage wholeheartedly in the battle to take back the land." They are the nation's future senators, governors, residents, and Supreme Court justices, he writes. "The goal is not a political coup or the establishment of a new Israel . . . It is about raising men and women of faith who, because they love God, refuse to sit silently by while their nation hates what He loves and loves what He hates."

The problem was, when homeschoolers graduated from high school, they faced a résumé dilemma. Elite universities are "pathways to power," but for Christians they are full of pitfalls, places where knowledge of God is considered "unenlightened" while "homosexuality and other perverse forms of sexual behavior" are "pronounced good and celebrated." Places where you take classes on "sex and gender" and learn that America is the real terrorist state ("Yes, we should shudder," he writes).

"You cannot fight something with nothing," Farris writes. "For us, to give the top Christian students the best possible opportunities, there must be a Christian equivalent of the Ivy League."

At Patrick Henry, Farris tried to re-create the education of the Founding Fathers. In their first two years, Patrick Henry students take a "classics" core with a Biblical slant; they read Plato, Aristotle, Locke, Virgil, Shakespeare, and Milton, and analyze them through a Christian lens. They suffer through Euclidean geometry. Latin is not required, but many students take it as a sign of their commitment to rarefied intellectual pursuits. They are encouraged to form tight bonds with their professors, who make themselves available after classes and even at home. For the second two years, especially for government majors, school turns into a kind of Beltway training camp. Students take practical courses in state government, polling, and statistics. They find internships in the offices of Republican politicians or conservative think tanks. All seniors do a directed research and writing project that is designed to mimic the work that an entry-level staffer would do because "a whole lot of elected members of Congress started out as Hill staffers," Farris said. "If you want to train a new generation of leaders, you have to get in on the ground floor."

The school is too young to turn many students away, but the applicants are fairly self-selecting. The average SAT score is a tier below Ivy League—1230–1410, the equivalent of the University of Virginia or Rice. The atmosphere is very much pressure-cooker—the first time I visited, the students had just petitioned the library to open before 6 A.M. so they could get in earlier to study. "Everyone here is going for the same prize," said Sarah Chambers. "Nothing here is chill."

The best students are offered full or near full scholarships, and for everyone else tuition and board costs around $20,000. The students are mostly white; about 15 percent qualify as multiracial and a handful are Asian or Hispanic. Derek's freshman class included a Korean American, an Indian American, and someone from Taiwan. There was also a student who was legally blind. In Derek's class there were no African Americans, although the following year there was one. They come from all over the country, and about 8 percent come from conservative military families. By its own insular terms, the school considers itself theologically diverse because it attracts a wide range of evangelical denominations. But because it bills itself as a pipeline to official Republican Washington, political viewpoints vary little. When Farris travels to homeschooling conferences and Christian-education seminars to recruit new students, he often emphasizes the school's "vast network of political connections." One day, Farris tells them at chapel, "An Academy Award–winner will walk down the aisle. He'll get a cell-phone call congratulating him. It happens to be the president of the United States, his old roommate from Patrick Henry." So far, his students are working hard to prove that he's not delusional.

Three times a year, the White House chooses about one hundred students for a three-month internship. Patrick Henry, with only three hundred students, has taken between one and five of those spots in each of the past five years—roughly the same as

Georgetown. Other Patrick Henry students volunteer at the White House. Tim Goeglein, the Bush administration's liaison to the evangelical community, told me the numbers reflect the talents of the Patrick Henry students, who "have learned a way to integrate faith and action." For the White House, it's also a way to reach out to the base while helping to build a generation of young political operatives.

Of the nearly two hundred fifty graduates so far, eight or so have had jobs at the White House (one in Karl Rove's office), dozens of others have been at various federal agencies. Nearly every conservative Republican senator or congressman has had a Patrick Henry student work on his or her staff or campaign. Farris used to call his friends in Washington to recommend his students individually; this year, he said, he no longer had to. Patrick Henry interns were well known enough that the internship program was running on "autopilot." Every year two students were invited on a trip to Israel sponsored by the Foundation for the Defense for Democracies, a group founded after 9/11 to promote American values abroad. The other students came from Harvard, Yale, Princeton, and other better-known colleges, but Patrick Henry was included because, as the trip's organizer told the students, "We hear you guys are good at getting into the White House."

One year there were five White House interns from Patrick Henry and four volunteers; so many that the *Patrick Henry Herald* ran a weekly column called "Inside the White House." Students wrote dispatches that ranged in tone from reverent ("I finally realize I'm working for and meeting the very people I've always emulated") to cheeky (overhearing Bush say, "I stepped on Laura's foot"), but never disrespectful. After four columns, the White House asked the students to stop, and of course they did.

In 2003 the college began offering a major in strategic intelligence—students in the program learn the history of covert operations and take internships that allow them to graduate with a security clearance. In their junior year, they write "open-source" intelligence reports as free research for the CIA and dream of becoming spies. "Thou shalt not lie" hangs heavy over these majors, but they balance it with God's commanding Moses to send spies to the land of Canaan. In the hierarchy of campus cool, SI majors consider themselves on top; to guard their secrecy, they're not allowed to be quoted in the student paper or even to tell fellow students their major, a warning they take very, very seriously. Several graduates have landed at the FBI and the CIA, and one worked for the Coalition Provisional Authority in Iraq. One person working in military intelligence sent Farris an e-mail saying a Patrick Henry student was the best intern he'd seen in sixteen years.

On paper, the great majority of students supported the Iraq war—at least in 2005. But many harbored a Vietnam-era ambivalence about actually signing up, lest it interfere with law school. So students were always thankful when the handful that was patriotic or reckless or just not cut out for politics announced they were joining the forces.

A cross section of Patrick Henry on a typical day looks like a microcosm of the Beltway, with every sector of official conservative Washington life represented; one girl had just finished running a state legislator's campaign, another starred in campaign commercials for her father. One crew had returned from a Blogs4Life convention, another was collecting petitions for a marriage amendment in their home state. One student was running for local office in Loudon County. Someone else had just gone overseas with the State Department; another was applying to intern at the Supreme Court. One student was fund-raising for a group that supports privatizing Social Security; another was headed to Senator Sam Brownback's weekly meeting of social conservatives.

This year several students started a new blogring "for all those who aspire to run for Political Office one day (or become a First Lady), whether it be Senator, Governor, Congressman/Congresswoman, or PRESIDENT!!!" Within a week, a quarter of the campus had signed up. If you could live anywhere in the whole world where would it be, one student asked. "Washington, D.C. OF COURSE!!!!!!!," another answered. Their online names included christandcountry, futureprez, and elect35.

During election season, the school excuses students from classes on the days that coincide with the Republican Party's 72 Hour Task Force—the on-ground blitz to get out the vote. Students say things like, "We played a major part in George Bush winning Ohio"—and they believe it.

You can divide the student body by different Washington character types, too. Some are front men likely to run for office—tall, clean cut, respectable, charismatic yet cautious. Others are Karl Rove types, behind-the-scenes operators who possess a wickedly clever sense of strategy but have trouble sustaining eye contact. There are shiny, happy Bush administration press-secretary types who smile and speak in empty sound bites. There are protest warriors who infiltrate antiwar rallies with cleverly obnoxious signs, and who would wear their hair longer if they were allowed to. There are self-important secrecy freaks who will only tell you their class schedules "off the record." There are political junkies who've been working campaigns since they were eight years old and by junior year sound totally burned out. Most common are the kids who seem like ambitious kids from Georgetown or Harvard or any other place where being twenty-one and working near power gives you a high.

"So he was kinda bored, distracted, glancing down my résumé and I was saying stupid stuff like 'I definitely support the president,'" one of the graduates was telling her friend at a party at the beginning of the year. "And then he cut in with: 'Oh, you're from Patrick Henry? Why didn't you say so? That's all I needed to hear.'"

"Psych!" and they high-fived. (She got the job, at the Department of Labor.)

For Farris's generation of conservative Christians, political power came as a giddy surprise. Farris barreled into politics in the eighties and early nineties with the Moral Majority, delighted at rocking the establishment. He and his cohorts never expected to be invited into official Washington, so they behaved as if they had nothing to lose; Jerry Falwell, founder of the Moral Majority, used to roll firecrackers in the aisle of his private jet, or knock on random hotel doors and disappear, giggling.

The Joshua Generation is different. They came of age with George Bush as their president, reaching out to them, speaking their language—Bush identifying Christ as his favorite political philosopher in a 1999 campaign debate is a perfect encapsulation of Patrick Henry. Most saw C-SPAN before they watched their first cartoon, and they got their first suit before they turned ten. They are the spiritual children of Ralph Reed: ambitious, entitled, and fearful, above all, of being irrelevant.

Unlike their parents, they don't have the stomach for marginality. "I'll do my DRW," said one, using the shorthand for the final paper, "and then I'll probably go work at the White House." Another told his best friend: "We always joke, he'll be my legal adviser when I'm the president." In this atmosphere what counts as humility is this, from Aaron Carlson, student-body president: "It would be great to be president, but it's not up to me. It's up to God."

The getting-into-politics part they have covered. As the school grows up, they are slowly moving to conquer the culture, too. The first few graduates are starting to get jobs at prestigious magazines and in Hollywood. Mark Shane got an internship at a major network. He got adopted by a top executive and was rewarded with a stream of celebrities to shepherd around. Now he has a job at the network reading scripts, preparing himself for the day when he finds the perfect one to produce.

This is what Farris dreamed of—the president, the Academy Award–winner—and what he brags about to the stream of reporters from all over the world who come to see the odd little experiment he's conducting. And yet, and yet. *Hath not God made foolish the wisdom of the world?* It came up again and again in his chapel talks. There was a price to pay for all this head knowledge, all this ambition. He had to see kids in his office who cheated on the morning-chapel enforcement, kids who snuck out at night, kid after kid who drank. He had too many students who were just "fawning over their intellect," as he put it; they seemed to like reading Kant more than they liked reading the Bible, they thought they were too good for some Holy Roller church so they wanted structure, history, ritual, in one case even Catholicism. He didn't like to think of it this way, but sometimes it was hard not to notice a pattern: On one side were the devout kids who were not quite so successful. On the other were the smart, successful ones who were shaky in their faith. A kid got an internship at the White House or with some Republican congressman. He started out idealistic, and then he just followed along with the herd, hanging out at the Capitol City Brewery Company or at Oktoberfest, getting wasted. If they were the spiritual children of Ralph Reed, did that mean they would end up like he did, tainted by power and money?

Farris told himself over and over: *It's not my role. We could put these kids anywhere, and there's some risk they will turn away from what they were taught. These are not my three hundred children. I don't have charge over all their souls. I am not a preschool teacher. I am not their parent. I have to give myself the freedom to fail or I'll go crazy in my job. If they go a different way, they go a different way.*

"But we just need to ask ourselves honestly," he said, "are we doing anything to cause it?"

The history of American evangelicals goes something like this: In the beginning they controlled everything, and then suddenly they didn't. And ever since, they've been beating their heads against their stone tablets, wondering why. Whether or not America was founded as a Christian nation, the point is, saying so would not have prevented you from becoming a very important person as late as the 1870s. In fact, you could say, as one prominent Methodist did, that America would soon become a nation "without an adulterer, or a swearer, or a Sabbath-breaker," and not become a circus act like perennial candidate Alan Keyes. Rather, you might have become an eminent senator, or president of one of the nation's elite seminaries from which all cultural dominance radiated: Yale or Princeton, the Patrick Henrys of their day.

Then, pretty quickly, God-fearing fell out of fashion. The culprits were immense, and there were too many to resist: Darwin, progressive social reformers, German biblical critics who treated the Bible more as a historical document than as God's inspired word. Overnight, universities were crawling with the earliest incarnations of Farris's nightmares: scientific rationalists, clove-smoking coeds going on about the "Social Gospel," the nineteenth-century version of a sit-in. For a while, universities tried to reconcile Darwin's observations with God's creation. But it didn't work. In 1909 James Leuba, a psychology professor at Bryn Mawr, posed a statement to the nation's leading scientists: "I believe in a God to whom one may pray in the expectation of receiving an answer." Among the ones he classified as the "greater" scientists, only 27.7 percent agreed. That same year, *Cosmopolitan* (not the *Cosmo* of today) published an exposé of higher learning that reads like a first draft of Farris's *Joshua Generation*. "In hundreds of classrooms, it is being taught daily that the Decalogue is no more sacred than a syllabus; that the home as an institution is doomed; that there are no absolute evils." The Farrises of the day were reduced to the usual stereotype of deposed monarchs: at best, hopeless nostalgics, and at worst, power-hungry lunatics.

Like all ruling classes in crisis, the Protestant establishment split and turned on itself. Some argued for riding out the changes, others for fighting back against the assault on Christian truth. Between 1910 and 1915, the fighters published a series of pamphlets called "The Fundamentals," the source of the epithet "fundamentalist." Their main goals were to save the major denominations from liberal influence and to stop the teaching of Darwinism in schools. In 1926 fundamentalists in Tennessee succeeded in convicting biology teacher John Scopes for teaching evolution, but they lost the war. In the press they became the butt of jokes still popular among late-night comedians: no drinking, no dancing, no swearing, no playing cards, no full set of teeth; in short, no fun and no money. Two years later, the Scopes conviction was overturned.

In the following years, the fundamentalists retreated, conforming to their own worst stereotype by growing ever more isolated and paranoid. In the forties they were captive to separatism, the idea of dropping out of society that later fueled the home-schooling movement. They stayed out of the mainstream intentionally and instead created a parallel culture with alternative schools, art, and science. Their theology became dominated by premillennial dispensationalism, a reading of the Bible that argues that history is a death march toward ever more chaos and decay until one day, Christ will return to scoop up the faithful and leave the rest behind—the inspiration for the bestselling Left Behind book series written by Jerry B. Jenkins and Tim LaHaye, Farris's mentor and a major donor to Patrick Henry. (LaHaye's wife Beverly sits on the board, and the portraits of the couple, who endow a prize for a graduating senior each year, hang in the main hallway.)

In the late forties, a group of young moderate fundamentalists tried to put an end to the paranoia. In *The Uneasy Conscience of Modern Fundamentalism,* theologian Carl Henry argued that fundamentalists had become trapped in their own antagonism toward the world; in order to win over souls, they had to create a new culture, new politics, and new institutions of higher learning. This movement of neo-evangelicals produced Harold Ockenga, one of the founders of the National Association of Evangelicals, and, most famously, Billy Graham.

The feud continued for most of the century unresolved. Evangelicals began earning more money, going to college, opening their own colleges. Yet like embarrassing uncles who always show up at the wrong moment, the fundamentalist branch of the family refused to go away. For every Billy Graham shaking hands with the president, a Jimmy Swaggart popped up to mock him. "We've gotten on the right side of the tracks now, and that's what's ruined us. They used to throw rotten eggs at us, and laugh at us, but now, you know, we can go to those old movies and we can drink our wine with our meals. Am I bothering you? Am I offending you? Don't rock the boat, that's what they say now," Swaggart preached. "I don't fit in."

In the eighties, what's now known as the Christian right came knocking at the door, and all these distinctions got papered over. Nobody cared who was a fundamentalist and who was a neo-evangelical. They had more pressing enemies: *Roe v. Wade,* "the antimoral activism of the homosexuals, feminists, and other so-called human-rights advocates," as LaHaye wrote in his famous 1980 call to arms, *The Battle for the Mind.* Why they should bother saving a world that was supposed to be self-destructing is a question they would debate later; for now (and we might as well get used to their beloved military metaphors straight away), they had a war to fight.

In 1976 LaHaye and a group of Christian leaders went to a White House breakfast with President Jimmy Carter, who was an evangelical Christian and talked openly about it. Waiting for his limo to take him back to the hotel, LaHaye felt depressed, out of sorts. If Carter was a Christian, why was he so mealymouthed on abortion, why did he support the Equal Rights Amendment, why wouldn't he speak out against gay rights? Still waiting, LaHaye said a prayer: "God, we have got to get this man out of the White House." Later, he and the others made a commitment: "For the first time in our lives, we were going to get involved in the political process and do everything we could to wake up the Christians to be participating citizens."

Farris met LaHaye in 1980. The young Christian activist and lawyer had organized an event called "America, You're Too Young to Die" in Richland, Washington, and he invited LaHaye to speak. Afterward, Farris talked to him about "raising an army of Christian lawyers to defend Christians," LaHaye recalled. The LaHayes became mentors to Farris. He was in their living room when LaHaye hatched the idea for the Council for National Policy, a secret group of conservative leaders that meets twice a year to plot a unified strategy, and the source of many conspiracy theories about theocrats taking over America.

In confessional moments, Farris will admit to his flaws. By all accounts, he has a very bad temper; at Patrick Henry he's been known to yell and scream at his employees and slam doors, and sometimes fire people in a fit of rage, only to try and win them back later. "I have the human capacity to grab someone by the throat and rip them up," he says. "It's my greatest weakness in battle." He is also a showman; when he's in front of cameras, Farris can spin and joke and verbally crucify his opponents to a degree that skirts the un-Christian.

During the eighties Farris lost his temper publicly and said many outrageous things. He once railed in a debate that allowing abortion would create a future in which we "kill off old people to save money for sex-education films." Later, when he was running for public office in Virginia, he apologized for some of those things. Some of these apologies seemed heartfelt and others seemed flip and dismissive. Who but Farris himself knows what he truly regretted and what he merely discarded in the more sober political moment? In any case, it's easy to see how it all happened. The eighties were an intoxicating time for a young Christian activist. In an era of pointless excess, these zealots in gray flannel suits had a certain rebel glamour—Black Panthers for the Jesus Freaks.

Farris grew up as the son of a devout public-school principal in eastern Washington State who had been saved by a Christian janitor who put Farris's dad in the path of an evangelist. Throughout the fifties and sixties, as the Supreme Court was ruling against teaching creationism in the schools, his father would come home and tell Farris and his three siblings stories about the ACLU "robbing the schools of God." One day, Farris recalls, his father told them he'd seen a teacher pass by three kids who were kneeling down in a circle. The teacher looked down and saw that they were shooting dice. "'Oh, that's okay,'" his dad recalled the teacher saying, "'I thought you were praying.'" Farris knew from a young age he'd be a lawyer, and his father set him the goal of saving the public schools.

Like most good Christians, Farris went through a "spiritually miserable season" in his late teens, while he was at Whitman College. "The PG version of prodigal son," he calls it, "maybe PG-13 at times." This was in the late sixties and early seventies remember, so by most people's standards, Farris was a choirboy. He got drunk once. He smoked pot once. He swore and chased girls. "By the world's standards, I was a totally good kid, but I was ignoring God."

In his freshman year Farris met Vickie, a petite brunette and the only child of devout Lutherans. At three, Vickie had gotten some fingertips chopped off by the blades of an old-fashioned push mower; her father had prayed to God that if her finger could be saved, he'd start going more regularly to church. Her finger was saved. Vickie herself says she became a "Christian," as in born-again, at eighteen, around the time she met Farris.

At the end of their sophomore year, she and Farris got married and moved to student housing, which was a small unit in the basement of a converted hospital. One evening a week, they went door to door witnessing with a Christian program. His "wild" days were over.

In 1973 Farris went to Gonzaga University School of Law in Spokane and launched his first crusade. He heard the Spokane Opera House across the street from where he worked was about to open a tavern, so he started a group called Citizens Opposed to Opera House Liquor (COOL). No one in the press knew that the membership roster numbered two: Farris plus a nominally active eighty-year-old woman. The tavern's defenders tried to start a scandal when they dug up evidence that Mike Farris had a drunk-driving record, but it turned out to be a different Mike Farris. The crusader they were up against managed to block the tavern, and the opera house opened a part-time liquor outlet instead.

By now it was the late seventies, and Jerry Falwell was just getting the Moral Majority off the ground. Farris was made executive director of the Washington State branch, which he eventually turned into the organization's largest outpost. He set out to fight what he saw as the scum swept in by the sixties: sex education in public schools, the Equal Rights Amendment, abortion rights, pornography, prostitution, and gambling. Farris got to debate Kurt Vonnegut and, in 1981, at Whitman College, Timothy Leary.

"Jesus Christ was totally against the Moral Majority types," Leary told him. "He changed water to wine and said, 'Let the good times roll.' He didn't have time to hang around hotels checking for marriage licenses." Farris, then a twenty-nine-year-old in a three-piece pin-striped suit, called him "Dr. Leary" throughout the debate: "He says man is God. We believe God is God. Without God, man will sink further in depravity and is doomed." Soon after, Farris was named Asshole of the Month by *Hustler* magazine.

Nearly everything Farris did made for good copy. He pushed advertisers to boycott a Tacoma station that aired *The Deer Hunter* because it showed full frontal male nudity. He sued a community college for showing *The Last Temptation of Christ.* He hassled the Washington State Library to get the list of public schools that had checked out the sex-education film *Achieving Sexual Maturity.* That case fizzled; it turned out none had.

The LaHayes gave Farris a platform in Washington, D.C., as the first national field director of Concerned Women for America, founded by Beverly LaHaye to be the antidote to Betty Friedan feminism. Now he began to make national headlines, defending the rights of Christian parents. His clients included a student who was banned from singing Christmas carols in school, another whose teacher ripped up her Nativity scene, a third whose "Smile, God Loves You" stickers were confiscated by her teacher.

In a case the media called "Scopes II," Farris defended seven evangelical families in Tennessee who objected to a packet of assigned readings in public school. The packet included excerpts from science-fiction writer Isaac Asimov, fairy-tale author Hans Christian Andersen, and a passage calling Jesus a "long-legged white son of a bitch." The parents complained about *The Diary of Anne Frank* because it might make kids sympathetic to the notion that God favors all religions equally, and *The Wizard of Oz* because it portrayed some witches as good.

The parents did not want the books banned; they wanted to take their children out of school on the days those readings were taught and give them substitute selections. The lavish media attention only inflated Farris's bombast: He said a verdict against his clients would "mean blacks in South Africa would have more rights than Christians in the United States" and cause "the most strident political upheaval that this country has known since the Civil War." A federal district judge ruled in Farris's favor.

Farris also defended Betty Lou Batey, a Pentecostal mother accused of felony kidnapping for taking her son from her ex-husband. Batey claimed she'd taken him away because his father had become a homosexual, and she worried her son would be exposed to drugs, alcohol, and molestation in his house. Farris convinced a district judge to dismiss criminal charges of child-stealing and place the child in a foster home. Later a San Diego Superior Court judge awarded custody to the father, deeming his home a "stable and wholesome environment."

As part of their San Diego–based ministry, the LaHayes filmed a talk show for Christian television stations out of the Osmond studios in Utah. On the bleachers before a 1981 appearance, Farris met Raymond Moore, who had come to speak about home-schooling. Moore gave him his best twenty-minute pitch, recalled Farris. It was a hard sell, because only a few thousand families were homeschooling then, and mostly under the radar; in most states homeschooling was illegal. State laws required that teachers be certified, and parents who taught their kids themselves risked a daily fine. But homeschooling was catching on among Christian conservatives. Farris talked to Vickie, and they decided to give it a try.

They began homeschooling their children in 1982 (the same year Boy George hit *Billboard*'s top ten). The next year, Farris co-founded the Home School Legal Defense Association to challenge laws that made it difficult for parents to homeschool their children.

In 1993 he won a Michigan Supreme Court case that eliminated most of the obstacles, guaranteeing parents who teach their children at home First Amendment protection and ruling that they did not have to be certified as teachers.

As a homeschool pioneer and president of HSLDA, Farris helped create a countercultural movement as robust as any Timothy Leary had a hand in, and it lasted longer. In some twenty years, the number of homeschoolers jumped from 50,000 to an estimated 1–1.5 million, with 80 percent identifying themselves as evangelical Christians. Farris also organized the loner families into a political strike force. Whenever a bill threatened their interests, Farris sent out tens of thousands of fax alerts; once, homeschooling parents jammed the congressional phone lines, with some offices reporting having received hundreds of thousands of calls each.

In his books and speeches about homeschooling, Farris created a paper trail that would later make his political opponents very happy. He called the public-school system a "multibillion-dollar inculcation machine" promoting "secular humanism and New Age religions." He called the schools a "far more dangerous propaganda machine than existed in the Soviet Union." He accused the "humanists" in the schools of "destroying continuing generations of children" with sexually transmitted diseases and incest. He called public schools "per-se unconstitutional" and "godless monstrosities"—a quote he later told me an editor had inserted into one of his books. He mused about the problems caused by immunization and racial integration.

In 1993 Farris ran for lieutenant governor of Virginia as part of a first wave of Bible-quoting politicians. "We all know politicians who say to people like us, 'I understand your views,'" read his early fund-raising letters. "I'm here to tell you something different. I am one of you." That was a year after Pat Buchanan's famous "culture war" speech at the 1992 Republican National Convention, and around the same time that Ralph Reed prophesied a "huge wave of culturally conservative candidates that are going to hit the beaches of the political system."

The Virginia race resonated far out of proportion to its political importance. Farris turned a campaign for a largely ceremonial post into the most-watched race in the nation. Nationally, it became a test of the strength of the newly emerging Christian right. Farris kicked it off with some theatrics, storming the Virginia nominating convention with 4,500 homeschooling and anti-abortion activists. Bobbie Kilberg, his opponent in the primary, was pro-choice, and the Farris supporters yelled, "Killbaby! Killbaby!" Kilberg claims that Ralph Reed and Pat Robertson later apologized for this uncouth behavior.

The primary became a forum on Farris's radical views. Each time Kilberg quoted something Farris had said—that mothers are "sometimes unnecessarily hysterical," so fathers have to step in to solve problems; that daughters should be discouraged from "chasing the feminist dream of a two-career marriage"—Farris would back out of it, saying that the quotation had been taken out of context, or that it had been spoken in the heat of the moment, or a long time ago, or as a joke. Kilberg's pollsters discovered that voters didn't believe the quotes had come from Farris because they seemed too outrageous.

Farris won the nomination.

In the election, Farris preempted this fight. Early on, he presented himself as a mainstream "Reagan conservative" and talked about cutting taxes. He called his opponent, Democrat Don Beyer, "Big Debt Don," and did his best to keep his inner embarrassing uncle locked up. A few months before the race, however, with polls showing the candidates in a dead heat, Beyer changed tactics. He ran an ad that linked Farris to Jerry Falwell and Pat Robertson. He ran another that opened with a scene of Dorothy skipping down the yellow brick road. "Stop right there, Mike Farris," the voice-over said, and it accused Farris of trying to ban *The Wizard of Oz* and *Cinderella* from schools. Editorials complained that the ads were unfair; Farris had argued for letting parents read their children alternatives, not banning the books in general. Still, the aspersions stuck; in the end, not a single editorial page endorsed Farris, nor did very popular three-term Republican Senator John Warner.

Farris lost with 46 percent of the vote, at a time when Republicans everywhere else were winning easy victories. Even so, the press anointed him kingmaker for future elections, the "leader of the powerful conservative Christian wing of the Virginia Republican party." Thanks to him the *Washington Post* would never again call born-again Christians "poor, uneducated, and easily led," as they did the year he ran. Farris mused about running for Senate, but his career in politics was over. If anything, the race proved that it was no longer 1870. You could no longer rant about godless monstrosities and a Christian nation and be elected to public office; you could not associate with people who wanted to snuff out sweet little Dorothy and expect to advance your career. If you wanted America to return to its roots, you had to be more cunning and subtle in how you went about it. You had to temper your speech and learn to blend in. If you wanted to be accepted into the mainstream, you had to use a softer sell. Farris turned himself into the Joseph Kennedy of the Christian right. He faded from the political front line and began instead to pour his ambitions into the next generation.

Farris's loss notwithstanding, Ralph Reed's prediction was correct: a wave of culturally conservative candidates had hit the beaches of the political system. A couple more waves followed, and before long a Patrick Henry government major might be looking at an internship with one of 170 congressmen and senators—one third of the total—who defined themselves as evangelical. Candidates running for president, Republican or Democrat, were now obliged to talk about where they went to church and how often they prayed, and to come up with some version of what evangelicals would recognize as a testimony—a coherent narrative of why they embraced the spiritual beliefs they did.

The new evangelical elite sounded nothing like Farris had in 1993. They sounded like the kind of people Swaggart loved to make fun of. John Thune blanched when I asked if he was a tee-totaler. "I'll have a glass of wine every once in a while," he insisted. He wore cowboy boots and looked as chiseled as the pictures of Mount Rushmore around him; his wife, a former Miss South Dakota, smiled from high up on the walls. Sometimes Thune made Biblical references in his speeches but, he said, "I never want to exclude anyone." When Thune worked as a staffer in Congress in the eighties, he watched Mark D. Siljander, a Michigan Republican, lose a race for asking a group of ministers to help "break the back of Satan." Thune vowed he would not repeat that mistake. "You have to speak in the appropriate language," he said. "Since the eighties Christians have learned how to better communicate."

Representative Mike Pence from Indiana calls himself an evangelical Catholic. His colleagues see in him a future Speaker of the House. The forty-seven-year-old former radio talk-show host started Congress's first blog, where he jokes about his trips back home. "You do not demonize those who disagree with you," he told me. "If you believe in a woman's right to choose, you're not a bad person. We just disagree." His method is to subtly "season" his sentences with references to God, not to overwhelm his audience with Scripture. "I hope I never make people uncomfortable," he said.

In February 2005, during Derek's freshman year, *Time* magazine published a cover story on the twenty-five most influential evangelicals in America. Jerry Falwell, Pat Robertson, and Bob Jones III did not make the list. (The LaHayes did, thanks to the monumental success of the Left Behind series.) At the top was Rick Warren, a California pastor and author of *The Purpose-Driven Life,* the bestselling hardcover book in U.S. publishing history. Polled on the usual culture war issues, Farris and Warren would end up in exactly the same demographic: antiabortion, anti–gay rights. But the words "Christian nation" would never pass Warren's lips in public. To ensure widespread acceptance, Warren makes a point of going down easy: "You were made by God and for God, and until you understand that, life will never make sense," reads a quote of his that was printed on millions of Starbucks cups.

Evangelicals are finally starting to reverse their reputation as the guardians of "anti-intellectualism in American life," an epithet bestowed on them by Richard Hofstadter's 1964 Pulitzer Prize–winning book of that title. In "The Opening of the Evangelical Mind," published in 2000 in the *Atlantic Monthly,* sociologist Alan Wolfe traced a new "network of modernizers" at places like Wheaton College in Illinois, Calvin College in Michigan, Fuller Theological Seminary and Pepperdine in California, and Baylor University in Texas. These schools are graduating a record number of evangelical students. And they are mastering subjects their parents would have considered pollution of the mind: pop psychology, sociology, postmodern theory, film.

These graduates are the first generation with no baggage of cultural isolation; they move easily in and out of the mainstream. They love their iPods almost as much as they love Christ, and they don't see the need to choose. Skateboarders for Christ don't just stand there all day on the half-pipe bug-eyed and ranting about Revelation. They keep their headphones hidden behind appropriately shaggy hair, and when they're done they go home and play video games or spend hours on YouTube. You might spend a long time hanging out with them before you'd discover what they're really up to. If Christians want to take back the culture and shape the nation, this is the first generation that has a real shot at it.

For the first time, evangelicals are poised to follow the same model as German and Italian immigrants, and, more recently, Catholics in general: breaking out of the ghetto into the "knowledge elite," as John Schmalzbauer dubbed it in *People of Faith*. In exchange for accepting some aspects of modernity—the autonomy of scientific inquiry, feminism—those groups got to shed alienation and have an impact on the culture. At one time, Catholics at the *New York Times* couldn't aspire to rise above the rank of copy editor, writes Schmalzbauer. Now Maureen Dowd, a graduate of Catholic University, is a famous columnist.

But there's one hitch with this model: Many evangelicals, especially the older generation, are not like Catholics or German immigrants. Historically, they've had a much harder time leaving the ghetto. Farris does not want to make any compromises. He doesn't mind excluding people or making them uncomfortable. Patrick Henry's statement of faith spells it out in plain damnation English: anyone who is not us *shall be confined in conscious torment for eternity.* Conscious torment for eternity. Stew in that, Sam Harris. Biology classes make no concessions, either. Patrick Henry teaches that the earth was created in seven literal days and is about six thousand years old. Farris knows that in the sophisticated circles he wants his students to travel in, saying the earth is six thousand years old is the social equivalent of admitting you have two wives. But so be it. Better that than give the world another Maureen Dowd.

Farris is not interested in adapters who bend to the will of the mainstream. He wants shape-shifters who can move between two worlds with their essential natures intact. He wants updated versions of his twenty-year-old self, less hotheaded, more conscious of their paper trail. "You don't stand up in the public schools and say, 'We're going to bring prayer into your schools and we're going to do it with this bill right here right now,'" Farris told his constitutional law class, putting on his best faux Southern preacher delivery. "You do something smarter than that. You talk about intelligent design. You talk about teaching evolution and the facts that support it and the facts that negate it and pass a bill that says they shall both be presented in an evenhanded manner. And then you discipline your supporters to keep their stupid mouths shut."

Farris wants spies in the land of Canaan—although as anyone who's ever read a spy novel can tell you, Canaan leaves its mark, especially on the impressionable young. Farris may have his own particular vision for how the Joshua Generation will take over the world. But if he believed in modern adolescence, it might occur to him that the Joshua Generation might have their own ideas.

If ever there was an unreconstructed fundamentalist, Tim La-Haye is it. According to a recent study, 19 percent of Americans have read at least one of the books. Yet in all the time I spent at Patrick Henry, I never saw any of his books on anyone's shelf. I heard them referred to only as trash novels, the Christian equivalent of Nora Roberts. Once, in a rare Patrick Henry prank, some kids laid an empty suit of clothes in front of the portraits of LaHaye and his wife, a mockery of LaHaye's obsession with the Rapture and a gentle thumb in Farris's eye.

On that spring day I visited Farris at his home; his relationship with his usually adoring student body was just starting to fray. I followed him back to campus and stuck with him through most of the day. In every year there had been a small group of rebels who turned on him, but during that second semester, the campus was splitting more into a two-party system, the Farrises and the Anti-Farrises.

As he walked around campus Farris gave no indication that he noticed certain students were glaring at him or avoiding him. But at chapel that morning, he made a conscious effort to win them back. At his best, Farris makes the preacher/politician role seem natural. When he is up on stage speaking, he can make his young charges believe that they can be everything they want to be and sacrifice nothing, that they can be prankster, bully, comedian, celebrity, and still be right with God. Most importantly, he reminds them that they can win. Yes, he told them that morning, they have their wits and their Biblical principles. But their best weapon is one the other side lacks: "the supernatural."

At this point, he did not raise his arms heavenward and drop to his knees. He did not slip into a Southern preacher's cadence. He continued on cool, even ironic, both passionate and detached. Remember, he wanted them to understand that when they climbed the career ladder they shouldn't leave the supernatural behind, but rather use it to push themselves up faster.

He told ten stories about how God had intervened in his life at critical moments in visible, tangible ways—making a burst appendix vanish, keeping him from losing his temper on the Phil Donahue show, waking up several people at 3 A.M. to pray for him when he was being slandered on a radio show. "The God we serve is a mighty God," he concluded.

The students laughed at his stories and, at the end, stood on their feet and cheered. For that half hour, he had them under his spell. But then chapel was over and the supernatural was drowned out quickly by the petty and the mundane.

Coffee in hand, I followed Farris to his office, a large sunny space on the second floor of Founders Hall dominated by a giant stuffed elk head. His assistant ran down the list of people waiting for his attention. There was a parent outside, a nervous-looking woman who wanted to know whether her seventeen-year-old son could attend Patrick Henry as a distance-learning student because she felt he wasn't ready to leave home yet. The development people needed Farris's help packing a hall in Florida the following week for a fund-raiser featuring former attorney general John Ashcroft as the keynote speaker. (Janet Ashcroft, wife of the former attorney general, sits on the college's board of trustees.) A church group wanted to have Farris come talk about his run for Virginia lieutenant governor. Some lawyers from the Home School Legal Defense Association, which is housed in Patrick Henry's main building, wanted to report the results of their latest case.

But first, Farris had to attend to some personal business. His daughter Jessica was getting married in ten days, and the store had shipped the wrong wedding dress. She had ordered a cream dress with no design on the bodice, and they had sent one with a design. Vickie had gotten nowhere with them. So now Farris would get to test the advice in one of his books, *What a Daughter Needs from Her Dad,* updated for the Bridezilla generation. All I heard was his side of the conversation.

"I'm a college president and a lawyer and if you do that I'm going to sue you for breach of contract . . . If you let me talk and don't interrupt me . . . That's not a sufficient answer . . . Oh, so it's your policy to leave a girl hanging without a wedding dress?"

Pause.

"There's a *Washington Post* newspaper reporter here, and I can ask her if I'm yelling," he said, referring to me.

He hung up the phone, and the superego, or God, or whatever you want to call it, started explaining the situation to me.

"Did I cross the line?" he asked. "I was aware that I was getting close. I can treat individuals with a bit of a raw edge. I just hope it's not a full-blown sinful edge."

Eventually Jessica got the right dress. But some problems involving the younger generation are more easily fixed than others. When the dad and the daughter are on the same team, that's one thing. But when their interests diverge, evangelicals can find themselves at a loss.

Almost all the evangelical colleges that are trying to enter the academic elite have to cope with student rebellion. Baylor's administration was horrified over students' endorsement of gay marriage, and Vision 2012, a project intended to bring the college into the "top tier of American universities," crashed over disagreements in 2005. Such ventures tend to get tripped up by lingering fears about the intellect's sapping the soul. But Patrick Henry is so new and so captive to conservative homeschooling culture that the ice is especially thin.

When he was done fighting with the dress shop, Farris pulled out the three-page document that had been haunting him since he received it several weeks earlier. It was a letter from a Patrick Henry parent, a father of a freshman girl. In the winter the father had sat in on one of his daughter's classes taught by Erik Root, a professor of government, and apparently he didn't like what he had heard. His daughter, he wrote, was "discouraged by the lack of biblical perspective in some of her classes. She said that she feels as though she is getting conservative politics without a biblical worldview."

Farris could have rolled his eyes. He could have patiently and politely explained to this father that he had faith in his professors and yes, thank you, they would try their very best. He could have had an introspective moment and pondered the connection between conservative politics and a biblical worldview.

The professor in question had a cult following among the students and loyal allies on the faculty. Taking him on could shatter this tiny, fragile school, so young it had yet to be accredited. Still, Farris instinctively, fiercely, took the father's side. "I don't think he's like a secret agent coming in to do what he knows is evil," Farris said about Root. "He is just touched too much by the way he was trained."

All year, Farris was dropping hints that his experiment was disappointing him. It was proving quite difficult to train his children to take over the world and to shield them from it at the same time. What galled him most was that the corruption was coming from *within his own institution*. On that day he finally confided in me that he suspected some of the very professors he'd hired to protect and guide his young charges were instead leading them astray. "I have serious questions about whether they're being faithful to the Christian vision," he told me. "And I don't believe the students will be prepared properly to enter the world in battle if they are muddled in their thinking. If at Patrick Henry the trumpet does not sound a clear call, then who will get them ready for battle?"

CHAPTER 3

"Elisa Muench, Republican, for Idaho's Senator. She Will Make a Difference."

In the last days before the 2004 presidential election, Patrick Henry excused all its students from classes because so many of them were working on campaigns or wanted to go to the swing states to get out the vote for Bush. Elisa Muench, a twenty-one-year-old junior, was interning in the White House's Office of Strategic Initiatives, which was overseen by Karl Rove. On election day, she stood on the South Lawn with the rest of the White House staff to greet the president and Mrs. Bush as they returned from casting their votes in Texas. Elisa cheered along with everyone else, but in truth she felt "really down." Her office was "keeping up contact with Karl," and she knew that the early exit polls were worse than expected. Through the night, she watched the results shift with the rest of the interns on Capitol Hill. After Kerry conceded the next morning, she stood at the Bush campaign's victory party in the Ronald Reagan Building, in the same clothes she'd been wearing all night, and "cried and screamed and laughed, it was so overwhelming."

I met Elisa in the Patrick Henry cafeteria at lunchtime a few months later. She has clear, bright hazel eyes and sandy-brown hair that she straightens and then curls with an iron. Elisa loves Ann Taylor, the favorite brand of Washington professional women. She and her mom bought an Ann Taylor suit when she got her internship, and spring semester, Elisa took a weekend job at the Ann Taylor outlet near school. That day in the cafeteria she was wearing a navy skirt and a cardigan. The boys in the cafeteria all had neatly trimmed hair, and wore suits or khakis and button-down shirts; girls wore slacks or skirts just below the knee, and sweaters or blouses. Most said grace before eating, though they did it silently and discreetly, with a quick bow of the head. Except for the absence of more than a few older adults, we could easily have been in a Senate cafeteria.

Just as we sat down to talk, Elisa's cell phone rang. It was Dick Cheney's office, calling to thank her for volunteering for the vice president's Christmas party, and to ask if she would allow her name to be put on a list for future job openings. Elisa's internship with Rove had given her a reputation, much envied on campus, as someone worth knowing. After she hung up, a sophomore leaned across the table and sought her advice.

"How much do you make, starting salary, working on the Hill?"

"I'm not sure," Elisa said.

"I heard one of the graduates working for Joe Pitts is making, like, twenty-two thousand dollars. That's not that much." (Pitts is a Republican congressman.)

"Well, it's not too bad if you're a single person," Elisa told him, twisting her knife into a little cup of peanut butter.

"Do you have any intentions of running for office?" the sophomore asked.

"Yes," she said.

Elisa told me that she loved working for Rove—answering the phone and having a senator on the line, meeting Andrew Card, then chief of staff, who would come in every once in a while and say, "Hi, I'm Andy Card"—("He's a nice guy," she said), and Cheney ("He's really funny"). Elisa reads biographies of female politicians so she especially loved seeing Condi Rice ("always looks great") and Karen Hughes ("very down to earth and real") trot in and out of meetings. During her internship she woke up at five every morning and caught the Loudon County commuter bus at 6 A.M. to arrive at the White House by 7:30. Once she heard Rove pick up the phone and yell, "Bullshit!" Still, her work with Rove affirmed her belief that "he's just a political genius. He really understands what makes politics tick."

In her sophomore year, Elisa had become the first—and, so far, the only—woman at Patrick Henry to run for a student government executive office when she entered the race for vice president. Campaigns are unusually intense at Patrick Henry; candidates appoint campaign managers and run weekly polls on a campus of three hundred students. They advertise heavily and hold ice-cream socials or pancake breakfasts to woo voters. Elisa ran against a ticket that included fellow senior Matthew du Mee. Elisa remained close friends with Matthew's fiancée, Christy Ross, although the race got tense. Some students disapproved of a woman running for office, and her running mate calculated that it would cost them votes. Elisa comes from a military family and wasn't known as one of the campus party girls. Still, in public Matthew painted his opponents as the "unorthodox" ticket that wanted to fight the administration and loosen the school rules regulating curfew, movie watching, and dating; Matthew painted himself as the establishment candidate. In the end, a third, compromise candidate won.

Elisa would never describe herself as a feminist, which at Patrick Henry would be as shocking as admitting you were gay. Whatever girl-power instincts she possesses are more reflexive than intentional. She was annoyed one day when, in the midst of a campus tour she was conducting, one family asked her if Patrick Henry "arranges relationships." One day at Market Street, a coffee shop near campus where she and Sarah Chambers were the first Patrick Henry students to work, Elisa told me between making cappuccinos about something that had happened in chapel that week. A family of homeschoolers she called a "traveling minstrel show" had come to show off their talents. After playing some worship songs, a girl in the family who looked about ten was asked what she wanted to be when she grew up. The girl answered: "My dream is to go to Juilliard, but my place is at home." And inside, Elisa told me, she was screaming, "*NOOOOO!*"

Elisa is a senator in student government and once put in her name for chairman of a campus-affairs committee but then felt she had to withdraw it. "Then when it came time to nominate a secretary, and my name came up, their hands couldn't have shot up fast enough." Like all the professionally minded girls on campus, she keeps in her head a working woman's version of the dress code: *Don't* wear your hair in waist-length braids. *Don't* wear denim jumpers and ankle-length flannel dresses. *Don't* wear capes, ever. *Don't* faint at the thought of lip gloss.

She told me that at any other school she'd be considered a true conservative, which is what she considers herself, "but at Patrick Henry I'm more liberal." She was surprised to meet students who'd never been around any alcohol. "I like dancing, I don't think it's a sin to drink, but I think it's a sin to get drunk. And I don't think dating is necessarily wrong."

Above her bed hung a poster from *Rear Window,* with big binoculars reflecting a woman in her skivvies. She kept a stash of DVDs in her bottom drawer: *The Princess Bride, The Manchurian Candidate, Journeys with George,* and *Pillow Talk* with Rock Hudson and Doris Day, "even though it's considered a little racy." One Friday night we watched *Psycho* on her laptop in her dorm room. Elisa didn't blanch at the scene where Janet Leigh rolls around in bed with a man, even though "most people here would have turned it off after that." The *Glamour* magazine in her bathroom promised "Juicy Sex Answers from 109 Men!" Still, when her dorm wing made a CD compilation of their favorite songs, she thought to change the title of Avril Lavigne's "Damn Cold Night" on the song list to "Damp Cold Night."

Elisa knows that she is different from some of the other White House interns she worked with—they had fake IDs and slept with their boyfriends—but she told me that the kids in school who annoy her the most are the ones locked into their Bibles, like the one who, when they were studying Nietzsche, kept saying, "But God isn't dead!" She said, "It's frustrating they can't get past that. What happens when they meet people who don't even read the Bible?"

In the dorm lounge hangs the poster of Rosie the Riveter in a polka-dot bandanna, rolling up her sleeves, with the caption WE CAN DO IT! This just about summarizes Elisa's brand of gender equality. She had shaken hands with George Bush and noticed that his hands were soft, not real rancher's hands, like her dad's. "You meet him and think, 'He's just a man.' What's that expression? He puts on pants just like you."

At Patrick Henry men and women compete openly for grades, the chance to direct the school play, and spots on the prestigious moot-court team. When all the best papers in Farris's constitutional law class were turned in by girls—and not for the first time—Farris yelled at the boys to stop playing so many computer games and grow up: "You're supposed to be leaders!" A faction of homeschooling parents had lobbied Farris not to admit girls to the college on the grounds that it might steer them away from motherhood, but Farris told me that he considered that an "extreme" position. "All women, moms included, benefit from a great education," he said.

The new careerist code of the Joshua Generation can become a problem for the girls, however. Even the most ambitious ones—those who wake up at 3 A.M. to study, shine on the moot-court team, keep updated lists of White House and congressional contacts, and hire professional résumé designers—told me without reservation that as soon as they had children they would quit their jobs to raise them.

Farris has three married daughters who raise children and work part time out of their homes. They call themselves "empowered traditionalists," he said. "It's a way of saying they're not milquetoast and don't sit at home doing nothing, but they also believe there are seasons in life, and their best years are the ones they spend raising their kids." Once I was off campus with two professors, and we passed a group of preschool children out on a field trip. Just as I was about to display my maternal impulse and say, "How cute," one of them cut in: "So sad." (His own kids were home schooled.) When a female professor gets pregnant at Patrick Henry, she resigns, because it's an unspoken rule that no child care is allowed. Most people there assumed that when I was reporting, my children were in the care of a doting grandmother, or at least they told themselves that so that they wouldn't be complicit in my kids' abandonment. (For the record, my kids were in preschool, or with a babysitter who is not a relative.)

Forty years of feminism has done very little to budge conservative Christian notions of gender roles: Men are the leaders, and women play a critical but supportive role (hence the term "helpmeet," which has always sounded to me like a cold cut). Patrick Henry girls who are too loud, too eager for leadership roles, too political—no matter how appropriately they dress—are always kept at arm's length. Boys refer to them as the "red leather stiletto girls" or "political animals," and all but declare them unmarriageable. The administration would never say that such ambition is unseemly in a Christian woman. They will just pass over the Elisas for the resident-adviser spots they clearly deserve, and choose the quiet literature majors instead. Once a female student described to a visiting film crew the gender politics of Ultimate Frisbee on the campus lawn: If a girl tries to be one of the guys and just jump into the game, no one will ever throw her the Frisbee. Instead, she has to stand on the sidelines for a while, yelling, "Good job!" or "Great catch!" and eventually someone might toss the Frisbee her way.

Campus rules place great emphasis on female chastity, requiring girls to dress modestly and forbidding men, including workers, to enter female dorms without an escort. Resident advisers keep a close eye on their girls to make sure they don't wear shirts that show any bra or an accidental sliver of midriff. If they do, they'll get a friendly e-mail—"I think I saw you in dress code violation"—followed by a smiley emoticon. Smoking, drinking, and "public displays of affection in any campus building" are forbidden. Matthew du Mee, a graduate who'd been an RA, told me that if he saw a boy and girl sitting too close for too long, he would pull the boy aside and tell him to stop, because "the guy is supposed to be the leader in the relationship." I'd seen such a high degree of competence and devotion from the women that it took me months to realize that a woman was not allowed to lead morning chapel unless it was a separate service for women only.

"Reputation" is nearly as important here as it was in the Jane Austen novels many Patrick Henry girls have on their shelves. A girl can very easily bring suspicion on herself by dating a guy off campus or wearing skirts with high slits. In the afternoons, the dorms look like a scene from *Meet Me in St. Louis,* boys and girls talking to each other through open windows. Late at night they exchange longing but chaste good-byes at the downstairs door. Girls talk about not "stumbling" a guy, the equivalent of tempting him, "You must not lay a stumbling block in their way, nor blow up the fire of their lust," Dana Clay, the dean of women students, read at chapel one day, quoting from seventeenth-century clergyman Richard Baxter. "You must walk among sinful persons as you would do with a candle among straw or gunpowder; or else you may see the flame which you did not foresee, when it is too late to quench it."

During freshman orientation, I attended a sexual-harassment training session for the fifty or so female freshmen. The video featured leering male colleagues and sticky-fingered bosses who cornered secretaries in the law library and made their promotions contingent on dinner. Still, some of the freshmen displaced the blame. "Women have a part in helping a man not to lust," offered one of the Amish-looking girls who was wearing a homemade pale yellow frock dotted with flowers. "I think of Jesus' words, not to stumble. Our part is to watch what we look like and act like, if we are too flirtatious."

Dating is a theoretical proposition, much more talked about than practiced. Patrick Henry subscribes to the "courtship" model that has become popular among conservative Christians over the last fifteen years. "Courtship" discourages teenagers from any intimacy with someone they don't intend to marry and encourages them to involve their parents in all romantic decisions. In the first two years of Patrick Henry, the dean of students could call in any boy and girl he suspected of spending time alone together without telling the girl's parents. This turned out to be too wide a net. Now, the college will not get involved unless a parent requests it.

One professor likes to joke that the kids arrive freshman year "just past the pigtail-pulling phase." Much like the average American pre-teen, Patrick Henry coeds can conduct whole relationships, from infatuation to breakup, on instant message, hardly ever having spent time together outside of class. At the same time, they sometimes sound like your grandpa, baffled by all the longing and heartbreak that is the drama of dating life. "What's especially confusing, and something I noticed the day I arrived first semester, is that in some cases people actually look grumpier after they've started courting," blogged one student.

Those brave enough to try can enter a thicket of missed cues, scowling parents, and dull heartache. Men are expected to take the lead in the relationship, but women are cautious about responding, making it difficult to read the signals. If things do get off the ground, you might crash into one of the "freakazoid dads," as the boys call them, who quash the courtship for no discernible reason. Then, you are left feeling the pain of breakup from a relationship that technically never happened. The women, meanwhile, are stuck in the fairy-tale-princess role, waiting for God to drop the prince onto their path. ("If I were to wake up one day and find myself a wife and mother," is how one girl described her ideal future to me.)

In the girls' dorms, this dynamic unleashes a diffuse longing. Girls stay up late at night discussing whether they'll marry guys like their father, interjecting "My word!" if the conversation gets spicy. One dorm calls itself "Land of Lyonesse," with pictures of Lady Guinevere sending her knight off to battle, her cascading blond locks glistening in the sun. The "Courtly Rules of Love," hung on the wall in a tea-stained scroll, read, "Thou shalt keep thyself chaste for the sake of her whom thou lovest." In a different dorm, Sarah Chambers created a hidden collage across from her sink made of clothing and perfume ads torn out of fashion magazines, couples leaning against a wall or a tree or rising out of an aqua sea, frozen an instant before their lips meet. A handwritten caption read, "But he had found her lips at last and was drinking, unconscious of everything but the joy they gave him."

Still others find release in morning chapel, where they close their eyes and pour their hearts out singing modern Christian ballads that sound like displaced love songs: "I feel your arms around me/Your spirit moves right through me like a mighty rushing wind/So light the fire in my soul/Fan the flame." Or this one, from the giddy first days of spring: "There's no place I'd rather be than in your arms of love/In your arms of love/Holding me still/ Holding me near/In your arms of love."

Even the rumors recall a more innocent era. A student reports seeing a car in a parking lot with its signal lights flickering madly, a sure sign of two students making out in a cramped front seat. A boy engineers a removable pane for his dorm window so he can sneak back in long after midnight curfew without waking up his RA. A favorite escape is the Catholic church down the road, where students can kiss under protective but alien iconography.

The kids like to imagine they live in Austen's world, where elaborate decorum and idle-but-amiable fathers keep daughters with high sprits from straying. ("Pull your bodice up, for Christ's sake," was a big laugh line in this year's production of *Pride and Prejudice*.) But for a bright young woman with access to transportation, the rules are more flexible, and opportunity tips easily into danger. ("We're going clubbing in D.C." was the text message that showed up on one girl's cell phone halfway into the three-hour production on a Friday night. "U coming?")

Patrick Henry has to make room both for girls who are taught never to look a boy in the eye and for girls who stay up late in their off-campus apartments playing poker with boys who then ride off on their motorcycle ("Bye, sexy beast"). Every spring before the annual formal dance, Ben Adams, the campus thespian with the lounge-lizard sideburns, sends around a warning to his fellow female students. Anywhere else, someone who looks like Ben would be getting high in the black box theater every night, but at Patrick Henry, he plays the role of the scold. In a nine-page e-mail, he reminded his sisters in Christ to forgo those plunging necklines and bare arms at the formal. "Lust is sin," he writes. "It is sin for you to tempt us. It is . . . unloving. Unsisterly. Un-Christlike." Then a tall, funny girl with Olive Oyl eyes and divorced parents, forwarded Ben's e-mail to all of her friends under the headline: "This. Is. Amazing. You have to read this. I feel like barfing my guts out."

By junior year, the savvy girls hit the glass ceiling. It occurs to them that they are not getting anywhere eagerly volunteering for leadership spots, so they move off campus. In an apartment with friends, they can breathe a little more freely. Off campus there are no room checks, so you don't have to compete for future housewife of America; you can leave your hair clogging the sink for as long as your roommate will tolerate. You can stop pretending you sewed the quilt on your bed. You can wedge the Betty Crocker cookbook in the corner by the microwave, decoratively, next to yesterday's Giant brand guacamole. You can watch *Love Actually* and not have to panic during the scene where they show a porn movie being filmed. Off campus the rules are self-enforced, so they take on a less-oppressive flavor. The girls still kick the boys out around midnight, but when they do, the sexy beast, who is wearing an AC/DC shirt, flips them off.

Elisa thought about moving off campus but stayed in the dorms instead. I first visited her in her room the March after the 2004 election. Worship music was playing on her little portable radio, and her walls were decorated with pictures of the people she loved and admired: several large formal portraits of the first couple, George and Laura, at a ball or on the ranch, a picture she took of Karen Hughes during her White House internship, another of Dick Cheney, and also pictures of all her best girlfriends from school, arm in arm, smiling. Elisa still had a year of school left, but it seemed to her that school as she knew it was ending. One Friday a good friend got engaged. The next day, her roommate came back with a diamond-studded band. A week later, another friend turned up with a ring.

"It was insane," Elisa said. "That makes nine, no ten." She ticked down the couples one by one. "My mom wanted to know what's in the water."

"You've got plenty of time," her mom told her.

"I know, I know. I'm not in a hurry."

Elisa herself has courted twice at PHC, but neither time felt quite right. "I hate courtship," she said. "It makes everything move way too fast." She found herself in heavy conversations about birth control and medical insurance within two weeks, before the first kiss. In her latest relationship she found herself adapting too fast to his more conservative tastes—not watching movies she had liked, or listening to her favorite CDs. "I stopped doing things I was marginally okay with," she said. "I couldn't be me." He told her he didn't have a "moral" problem with women working, but then one conversation crystallized their differences: "He started realizing how much I really did love politics and wanted to be a part of it."

Elisa believes the Bible dictates that "there are different roles for men and women." As a White House intern she saw women with kids working "long, long hours" and she doesn't want that. Elisa wants to be the "wife of noble character" described in Proverbs 31. But the expectation of most of the guys she knows at Patrick Henry—that wives should just "fade out," that she should instantly take on the identity of a wife and mother "and consider it a blessing"—is not something that she's comfortable with. "You can't just say it's a blessing. It's a sacrifice! I just wish there was some way to have a family without it being your whole identity. I'll never be able to be at home doing nothing."

"I just think there's more that God called me to do, and that's a hard thing to say around here," she told me.

While in school, Elisa was trying to read the Bible every morning before working out at the gym. On one day I was talking to her, she was up to the part in Numbers where Joshua is getting ready to take over from Moses, the transfer of power that is

Farris's central metaphor for the school. Elisa didn't draw the same lesson from that generational transference of power that Farris did; instead she found it "very comforting to read that Jacob and Isaac and Joshua weren't perfect, but they still got to be God's chosen people."

IN THE SEVENTIES, Christian leaders started noticing their flocks drifting the way the rest of America was—more divorces, more women working, more little kids in day care. They were caught off guard, and they quickly sounded the alarm. "Come on, America. Enough is enough!" said James Dobson, a child-development expert turned family therapist turned culture warrior. "We've had our dance with divorce and we have a million broken homes to show for it." The right quickly built up an army of organizations to defend the family from modernity: Dobson's Focus on the Family, the Moral Majority, Concerned Women for America, and Family America, headed by the LaHayes.

The first step was to get back to what Dobson called "old-fashioned values." This meant reining in the women who were being seduced by the power and freedom offered by feminism. Leaders of the burgeoning Christian-advice industry hammered one message in unison: God assigned each sex a role in marriage. The man was ordained the head of the family, and he should reclaim his rightful position. The woman takes care of the domestic sphere.

Submit! Submit! Submit! On that the books were unanimous. If a wife works, "it breeds a feeling of independence and self-sufficiency which God did not intend a married woman to have," wrote Tim LaHaye in the brilliantly titled *How to be Happy Though*

Married. Mary Pride, a homeschooling advocate whose daughter attended Patrick Henry and one of the few female authors in this genre, presented a wink-wink happy-homemaker version of what she called the Biblical chain of command: God (Company Owner). Tarzan (CEO). Jane (Plant Manager). Boy (Trainee). "We can also pretty easily see what is wrong when Tarzan and Jane start battling over who should be boss. Alligators hang out below to eat whoever falls out of the tree."

For women, payback would come in the form of newly enlightened husbands who were full of praise and gratitude. Dobson would always say he drew his ideas from "ancient Judeo-Christian wisdom" but in fact he owed a great debt to seventies self-help culture. In *What Wives Wish Their Husbands Knew About Women,* Dobson took on an Oprah role, explaining to men how victimized women feel by their husbands' lack of attention. Buy her flowers. Take a shower. Rent a motel room and arrange for child care, he urged them. Detailed scenarios instructed men how to read their wife's every shift in mood, including those caused by her menstrual cycle.

The same Christian authors horrified by the Pill doled out advice to (God willing) inexperienced couples on how to spice up their sex life. Marabel Morgan, author of *The Total Woman,* enjoyed brief notoriety by advising wives to greet their husbands at the door wearing nothing but Saran Wrap. Now, in *How to be Happy Though Married* (his version of *The Joy of Sex,* minus the drawings), Tim LaHaye walked couples through the titillating details of the "marriage act." "When aroused, her nipples will often become hard and protrude slightly," and then, "A lubrication bathes the vulva area with a slippery mucous, easing the entrance of the penis into the vagina."

Using a mix of earth-mother imagery and Scripture, the authors promised women the satisfaction that comes with fulfilling their natural, godly roles, a lure sociologist W. Bradford Wilcox calls the "enchantment of inequality." "Don't you enjoy holding a sweet warm little baby and watching him nurse contentedly at your breast? Don't you treasure that first little smile as that baby drinks you in, the most important person in this world? Isn't it satisfying making a yucky little bottom all clean and sweet?"

The campaign worked. By the nineties, Christian conservatives had gelled into a culture heading in a different direction from the rest of America. Fifty-eight percent of conservative Christians think men should be breadwinners and women homemakers, compared to 35 percent of mainline Protestants. About the same number think preschool children suffer if their mothers work. At the same time, Christian conservative men report socializing with their wives far more often than their secular counterparts, and Christian women are much more likely to report that they are happy with the level of affection they get from their husbands. They also report by far the highest number of orgasms; 32 percent say they have one every time they do the "marriage act."

The Christian homeschooling movement grew out of this culture of reinvented domesticity. If women's roles were going to be so tightly scripted, homeschooling offered one of the few ways to improvise. Within her own four walls, a conservative Christian woman could find a way to be a "supermom" and fulfill the modern woman's entitlement to meaningful work. "Homeworking is the Biblical lifestyle for Christian wives," Mary Pride writes. "We are not called by God to *stay* at home, or to *sit* at home, but to *work* at home!"

I've encountered some version of this testimony several times. When her kids were of preschool age, a mom with a higher degree found herself picking up the blocks for the fifteenth time that day and thought, "Did God really put me on earth for this?" Then she decided to try homeschooling. Overnight she became a mother/teacher, juggling math and English workbooks in between lunch and dinner, keeping up with current events. The house was a little messy, but she was happy, fulfilled.

In the fight against the enemy, a homeschooling mom could play the critical role of first responder. Homeschool magazines warned of schools as the gateways to the corrupt culture, places where sex-ed classes introduced homosexuality and peers tried it out, along with drugs, nose rings, and yoga. It became the mother's job to save the next generation from contamination and prepare it to take back the land. Magazine covers showed determined mothers gathering their charges around the kitchen table, where under their fierce watch sin could not reach them. "Train up a child in the way he should go: and when he is old, he will not depart from it," is a favorite homeschooling verse from Proverbs. In theory, Dad was the head of the household, but in practice Mom did all the important work.

Sometimes I would visit homeschooling families expecting to find myself on alien territory, and instead I would encounter a scene that was all too familiar. The mothers would brag about their little prodigies and how well they'd scored on some standardized test. They would faux-complain about all the driving they had to do, from soccer practice to ballet to tai-chi. They sounded just like my overeducated, overinvolved mom friends from D.C. who had quit jobs to stay home full-time. When I asked why they started homeschooling, I heard the usual answers about ungodly schools. But the answers that truly animated them would be about the bureaucracy's failure to recognize the unique gifts of their children: a first-grade teacher who made a son do handwriting drills because his Rs were crooked, a principal who objected to a daughter bringing a turtle to school.

Homeschooling grew out of the era of intense progressive school reform in the sixties and seventies, the same era that brought us open classrooms and alternative schools. John Holt, an early homeschool advocate, urged parents to free children from the prison of desks and tests that crushed their natural love of learning. Raymond Moore, the Christian reformer who convinced Farris to homeschool, also complained about schools as factories that "tightened the noose and piled on the studies." But by the nineties, when the Christian homeschooling movement really exploded, these two branches diverged. The Farris wing asserted itself as independent of the progressive reformers. At home, Christian parents still worried about Jill and her turtle; but as a movement, they placed less emphasis on the child as an individual and more on his place in the family hierarchy. Children were not primarily free agents. They were subjects of parental authority who needed a firm hand to guide them.

Homeschooling families judge each other by their views on structure and authority; the Patrick Henry families tend to fall on the strict end of that scale. Homeschool families have no school communities or obvious support system, so they tend to group around gurus or schools of thought. When the Patrick Henry kids were growing up, one of the most popular gurus was Bill Gothard, who ran the Advanced Training Institute out of Oak Brook, Illinois. Gothard believes in running families like a military unit. He offers specific instructions on how kids should behave and dress, down to the length of their bangs. A few times a year, families would attend seminars around the country where the kids would learn "basic life principles," such as how to conquer an addiction to rock music. The bad kids would get in trouble for what the adults called "folly," which could mean listening to your clock radio in the hotel room or talking for too long to a member of the opposite sex. The good kids would go listen to the "reversal choir," made up entirely of kids born after their parents reversed a sterilization procedure.

Only a minority of Patrick Henry kids have families who were deep into ATI, although most went to a lecture or two by Bill Gothard. A few Patrick Henry girls keep his maroon leather–bound *Basic Principles for Life* books on their shelves alongside their copies of *Beyond Good and Evil*. They are not always the girls you'd expect; I borrowed my copy from someone I thought of as the campus riot grrrl, whose short hair, slouchy cords, and messenger bag screamed, "Get me away from these freaks." She and a guy friend drew witty cartoons for the campus paper.

When I read *Basic Principles for Life,* I could almost understand what someone like her might get out of it—almost. The two books, each about 350 pages, are filled with the kind of practical tips to a happy successful life you might get from a regular motivational speaker—how to be loyal to friends, avoid debt, keep your promises, learn to see difficult situations through the eyes of others. The overall message is standard self-help: avoid self-rejection and anger, "don't measure yourself with the outward standards of others in order to get approval."

But the bulk, well, it speaks for itself: "This may sound strange to you, but have you ever thought about dedicating your clothes to God?"

Uh, no.

The sketches make all the Biblical patriarchs look like Clint Eastwood and the matriarchs like June Cleaver, with an apron tied around her Barbie waist although she is supposed to have birthed ten children. There are earnest testimonies from couples who played their favorite rock records backwards and listened in horror as the "satanic words spilled forth." And fabulous conversation tips for a man and a woman who have just met and are interested in trying to deepen their friendship:

"Where were you born?"

"What special interests do you have?"

"Do you see any special significance in the Jewish race?"

"Would you say that you are mechanically inclined?"

"How much Scripture have you been able to memorize?"

"Have you ever had an experience where you almost died?"

In their advice to women, the books read like *sharia* law, with strict instructions on how to dress, date, and run a home, and with dire consequences for disobedience. Women are to avoid fashion trends and wear loose-fitting dresses in bland colors. They are to practice making "eyetraps," meaning accessories that draw attention to their eyes and not to other parts of their body— short necklaces, neck bows, big pilgrim collars. They are to avoid flirting, looking bold, or staring too long, all habits of "eyes that have not been brought into proper discipline."

Dating is submitting to "unwholesome sexual appetites." Instead, Gothard defines rules for courtship, which have been modified and loosened over time but basically became the standard for conservative Christian kids of that generation. "The proper way to get to know a young lady is by building a relationship with her father." Fathers and daughters sign covenants with each other: "I will protect you from unqualified men" for him, and "I will keep myself pure for my husband" for her.

Once a man is chosen, the engagement should be brief: "In courtship the young man has pulled the pin out of the 'hand grenade' of the young lady's emotions, and in a short time it will 'explode,'" he writes. "God has designed this 'explosion' to take place at the beginning of marriage, not while the woman is waiting for the man to prepare for marriage during an extended courtship."

Once they are married, the husband "gives the law" and the wife "works out the proper procedures to carry it out." Equal authority in marriage is "Satan's goal." The key to a happy marriage is "the wife's submission and the husband's sacrifice." "Reject the concept of working mother," the book advises. "When the scriptural functions of the home are restored, there will not be the time or the desire for the mother to work for someone else outside the home. God designed a wife to find her fulfillment by being a helpmeet to her husband."

For an ambitious Patrick Henry woman, this advice is difficult to reconcile with her current life of busily networking and applying for prestigious government jobs. Some do it by just ignoring the cognitive dissonance and giving themselves over to impossible dual fantasies. Rebekah Stargel is a tall blond athlete who wears tight Billabong T-shirts and exudes spazzy energy ("Where the frick were you???"). She was homeschooled and comes from a conservative family; her father is the state legislator who helped write the original Save Terri Schiavo bill in Florida. Rebekah told me she'd transferred to Patrick Henry from Florida State because she'd heard that "if you want to be a senator, this is the place to go. Everyone in D.C. loves us." But more powerful was her desire to be in the CIA, which she stated to her parents when she was two. ("I know, it's unbelievable.") In high school, her nickname was FBI.

She figured she couldn't pass for Arab because of her blond hair. So instead she'd settled for the Cold War, living in St. Petersburg for the summer and studying Russian during the school year.

This was during the height of the Schiavo debate, and as we talked, every half hour or so her phone would ring with updates from her mom on the situation. Rebekah was certain she didn't want a desk job in intelligence; she wanted to go undercover, for years and years. What about a family? "I don't like the idea of being someone's wife," she said. "But I do wanna have, like, fifteen kids." She waved her arms around. "And I want to homeschool them all." I didn't ask a follow-up. What was there to say?

Sometimes the girls veer from one extreme identity to another. When she first came to school, Samantha Walker looked like a typical California girl, with bright green eyes and cascades of sandy hair. During her freshman year, she met a guy, not from Patrick Henry, who belonged to a more conservative offshoot of ATI. Suddenly she started to dress, as she describes, like "I was from the backwoods of New Hampshire." At the time, Walker's roommate was moving in the opposite direction: The roommate used to dress like she was from the backwoods until she became intensely interested in politics, and she went to work for Karl Rove.

Samantha's then-fiancé made it clear that she would stay home after they were married. He also implied that there was no reason for her "to be literary or scholarly." So she dropped out of Patrick Henry. Instead of Plato, she began reading books with titles like *The Excellent Wife,* with advice on how to become the perfect helpmeet to her soon-to-be husband. She moved to Nashville, where he and his family lived. While she was making wedding plans, she started to see a therapist. "I felt like I didn't know myself," she said. She dug out her old schoolbooks, particularly Sophocles' *Antigone,* which is about a bold and rebellious daughter. Eventually she called off the engagement and came back to school.

The year I met her, Samantha was back to California girl. Her professors knew her as the "new and improved Samantha" ("Some would say 'gravely mistaken,'" she answered back) and a brilliant philosophy major. She dressed in the uniform of a 1940s liberated woman—tweed trousers and blouses—and wore her hair down, or loosely tied up. In the summer, she went backpacking in Spain with a boyfriend. Whenever something went wrong at school— her favorite professor got in trouble, she earned a bad grade—she consoled herself by saying, "Where could I be today? Pregnant, and in the middle of divorce proceedings."

"I foolishly gave up my identity once," she said. "I was one person to him and another at PHC. And I won't do it again."

At Patrick Henry, Bill Gothard is the punch line of many jokes. The few girls who still wear loose prairie dresses, no makeup, and their hair in hip-length braids are mockingly called the "Gothard girls," or the denim-jumper crew and, for the most part, fade into the background of the campus political frenzy. The rest of the girls, who call themselves "normal," look male professors in the eye, speak up boldly, and sometimes show up to class wearing what one girl calls "shockingly slutty conservative outfits." Still, somewhere in there is Gothard's warning voice from their youth: "Freedom is not the right to do what we want, but the power to do what we ought."

And if she does work?

"She blasphemes Scripture."

"She brings reproach to God."

"She fails the test of virtue."

"She endangers her marriage."

DURING SPRING BREAK of her junior year, I went to see Elisa Muench at her parents' ranch in Idaho, off a gravel road at the edge of Camas Prairie. The family had a few dozen cattle and three horses, which roamed free and galloped down the hill at the sound of Elisa's voice. It was April, but the ground was still frozen over in the morning, and the landscape looked bleak. But inside, the living room felt cozy, like a lodge, with antlers and an antique gun mounted over a piano. The wide windows looked out onto the prairie, and occasionally Elisa pointed out a rabbit or deer bounding away in the distance. In the afternoon Elisa's dad read the paper while she and her mom played duets on the piano. On the kitchen counter sat an article about Elisa—GRANGEVILLE RESIDENT INTERNS AT THE WHITE HOUSE—with pictures of her on the White House steps. "One thing Elisa realized was that she enjoyed the fast pace of Washington life," the story read.

I could see where Elisa got more egalitarian notions of gender roles. The day I arrived, Elisa's mother, Mary, who retired as a lieutenant colonel in the U.S. Army Reserve, was at her one-day-a-week job as a nurse anesthetist in Clarkston, an hour and a half away. Her father, Alan, who had been a surgeon in the army and retired as a colonel, was working full time on the ranch. When chores started at 6 A.M., or a calving call came in the middle of the night, Mary and Alan would take turns heading out into the cold. In the mudroom, Elisa's work boots and her Carter jacket hung on a hook alongside her brother's and sister's.

Her parents cooked a delicious dinner together, featuring steak from one of their own steers, and wine was poured all around. We began with a prayer for the food and for Terri Schiavo: "My plan for her is that God miraculously heals her somehow," her mother said. Alan was far from being the oppressive patriarch; his style was more chatty and jokey. He'd been on the receiving end of calls from guys wanting to court Elisa, and although he was happy to talk to them, he was a little mystified. "What do you mean by courting?" he asked them. "It's not entirely natural. It seems to me the heart has to come first, and then the rest of it will follow."

Like his daughter, Alan objected to being lumped into the "Christian right" movement, considering himself more independent than that. Still, the family had consumed the same ideological diet as other Christian conservatives. Around the house were scattered newsletters from Focus on the Family, a pile of Christian bestsellers and, in Elisa and her sister's rooms, posters of their favorite Christian singers. Their younger brother, Lee, then fifteen, was still being homeschooled, with mostly the same materials Elisa had used. On the day I visited he was up to the science lesson "The Lie of Evolutionists." In Elisa's old room he was watching a video of a class taught at Pensacola Christian Academy. (For older kids, lots of homeschooling is done by video.) The teacher, a battle-ax of a woman Elisa remembered well, listed the best evidence against evolution, including "the fact that no transitional fossils have ever been found." Lee's history book opened with "For the beginning of history the Bible is our only reliable record and it tells us that history begins with God's creation of the first man and woman."

As a child, Elisa lived on army bases in Italy and Alaska. When she was twelve, her parents left the military and moved the family to the ranch. They worried about the local public schools' test scores and about the "social atmosphere." So they ordered textbooks and videos from a Christian publisher, and taught Elisa and her brother and sister themselves. The Muenches told Elisa that she could go to the public high school, but she thought her education was better at home. She had no interest in partying and drinking, and "I liked having a Christian curriculum," she said. "I knew if I was in a biology class or something, I'd just start debating them on evolution."

Elisa took part in Idaho's mock legislative session for high school students, and was elected Speaker of the House. "She's always been fascinated by political personalities," her dad said, particularly women. She'd read Barbara Bush's memoirs, and a biography of Margaret Thatcher; they were still stacked in her closet, next to a copy of *Little Women, Jane Eyre,* and *Quo Vadis,* a novel about a Christian woman who falls in love with a Roman patrician. Leaning against the wall was a poster from *Star Trek Voyager,* which she loved as a kid partly because the Starfleet captain was a woman. On her desk was the latest *Parade* magazine interview with Laura Bush. Under it hung a poster that a friend made for her: ELISA MUENCH, REPUBLICAN, FOR IDAHO'S SENATOR. SHE WILL MAKE A DIFFERENCE.

When Elisa was about to graduate, her mother read about Patrick Henry in *World Magazine,* a Christian publication. The school appealed to Elisa because it seemed "not just Christian in name only." She knew kids from high school who partied and slept around, but were still going to what they considered a "Christian school." At the same time, it wasn't like Pensacola or Bob Jones, where, she'd heard, they do random checks on your CD collections and girls have to wear pantyhose every day. The family visited Patrick Henry and found it small and homey. When Elisa was offered a scholarship, they saw it as confirmation that the school was the right place for her.

Elisa loved her tiny hometown—the little coffee shop and the ice-cream place and the miles and miles of open prairie—but it was clear she'd outgrown it. "They know who the president is and the vice president, and that's about it," she sighed. Locals her age hung Mardi Gras beads on their mirrors; Elisa kept a leather Kenneth Cole organizer on the dashboard. A family friend we ran into at the coffee shop asked what she would do after college. "I might go back to Washington, to work at the White House," Elisa said, but tentatively, as if she was trying out an identity.

"Mom, I'm not really worried about getting married," she said later.

Her mother was supportive of whatever Elisa did. She mentioned, however, that she was twenty-seven when she had her first child, and regretted having waited so long.

I caught up with Elisa again when she came back to school her senior year. She was with some of her friends at the house of Erik Root, who lived five minutes from campus in a generic townhouse with wall-to-wall cream carpeting. Root was one of two divorced faculty members, and his two young children were visiting that week, so he and his new wife held a small party for them. Root lounged around in his shorts and leaned up against one of the three surfboards he'd brought with him from North Carolina while the students played board games with his kids.

Later, after Root's kids went to bed, the students sat around talking about the only thing anyone was talking about that week: the new student rules. Because Patrick Henry is only six years old, each year feels like a new historical epoch. The forty-page student handbook serves as a constitution in progress; each year directors tweak and shift certain rules. This year's rules had just come out, and students were poring over every change, highlighting and drawing emphatic red circles and giving voice to their anxieties about the school drifting in a more-or-less fundamentalist direction.

As usual, the rules instructed students not to drink or curse or have sex; they mandated morning chapel and instructed students to find a home church for Sundays. They set the on-campus curfew (midnight on weekdays, 1 A.M. on weekends), after which dorm doors would be locked. They laid out the specific definition of the required school code: for men, collared shirts, tucked in, "nice" sweaters and vests, no sweatshirts, no cargo pants or denim, no pants with pocket stitching on the outside, no tennis shoes or sandals; for women, blouses and nice tops, skirts or dress slacks, no tennis shoes, flip-flops, excessive or gaudy jewelry or makeup. They forbid gambling and public displays of affection. As usual, the courting rules had shifted a bit; this year the rules only said the college would make "every reasonable effort" to enforce the parents' position.

But that was small comfort to this crowd at Root's house, who had located plenty of newly oppressive restrictions. The entertainment guidelines had expanded to more than a page, instructing students to check on movieguide.org to make sure any film they were considering viewing had a rating of −2 or higher. No nudity (which ruled out *Braveheart,* a Christian favorite). No crude humor (*Austin Powers*), no sexually explicit situations (*Charlie's Angels*), profanity (*Bruce Almighty*), no phantasmagoric horror, violence, or gore (*Scream* and *Texas Chainsaw Massacre*).

But what really got them was a late addition, tacked on to the very end of the rules. "Any student who witnesses a violation of the College's rules or policies by students, faculty, administrators, or staff is obligated to inform those with care over the offending party." A new schedule of fines and punishments reinforced the point: students who failed to turn in others for breaking the rules would be punished at the same level as those who broke the rules. The idea came out of the Christian concept of "tyranny of the weaker brother," which warns righteous Christians to hold their brothers who stumble accountable, lest their ungodly habits dominate the community. But the students failed to appreciate this bit of Biblical wisdom.

"We're going to turn into a campus of snitches," said one girl leaning up against her boyfriend.

"I came here because I didn't want to go to Bob Jones," another said.

"Why can't you be Christian and be smart and just be cool?" sighed Rebekah Stargel, who was splayed out on the floor in another Billabong T-shirt, reading her Plato.

Elisa's mood was antsy, too. "I really want to get out of here," she said, meaning out of school. But she was not a loud complainer, and she tended to hold herself slightly apart. And there was something else on her mind. She'd spent the summer in a language program in Italy, where she'd lived with an Italian family and shared a room with an American woman who was divorced and had been in the air force. At first the roommate was a little hostile—she was a liberal, and she didn't know what to make of Elisa's daily Bible reading. When Elisa showed her a picture of some Patrick Henry friends, the roommate said they looked like "Ivy League school kids," which Elisa took to mean "preppy, snotty rich kids." Eventually the two became friends, although they remained very different. Like everyone else in the language program, the roommate went out drinking and partying most nights and "quite honestly, I ended up going along with her because I wanted to make sure she could get back home," Elisa recalled. It was a window into the pitfalls of a single life, and it made Elisa wonder about her own future.

Elisa had loved Italy since her family lived there, and on weekends she went out touring by herself. On one of those weekends she found herself thinking, "This could be me in a year. I could be on a business trip making it big. I could be doing a great job and really impressing people. But I would be alone. Is this really what I want my life to look like?"

"Part of it is obviously, 'Oh, my gosh, I'm a senior and I'm single.' But it's more. Being away from school gave her a new perspective on the previous year. She felt she'd fallen into a state of bitterness and self-righteousness. She felt that perhaps she'd been somewhat unfair to the last guy who'd courted her. She wasn't exactly yearning to be with him in Italy, but he was on her mind. "I went to the Palatine, and I thought he would really love this."

"He" is Aaron Carlson, a senior who'd courted Elisa the previous year and who had since become student-body president. Last year she'd dismissed him as too conservative. Now she thought maybe she'd been too quick to accept other people's opinions of him. At the very least, she thought she had to apologize and maybe even give him a second chance.

In June 2005 I had written an article for the *New Yorker* about Patrick Henry. In it, I quoted Elisa talking about her conflicted feelings about Christian women having to quit their jobs to raise children. After the article appeared, some *New Yorker* readers were apparently horrified enough to launch two Web sites— Elisamuench.com and Matthewdumee.com—headlined "America's Taliban: Republicans and Christian Fundamentalists: Hate is their currency. Ignorance is their sacrament. Racism is their communion." None of that bothered Elisa as much as the comments posted by fellow students doubting her maternal instincts, and even then, the only one of her peers she cared to defend herself to was Aaron.

"Which Elisa am I talking to? The feminist one who is coming out against motherhood?" he e-mailed her after the story came out.

"No! Motherhood is great. I never said I didn't want to be a mom. I just want to work," she wrote back.

"Well, I never said I would never want you to work," he wrote.

Her best friend insisted that Elisa had always misread Aaron, that he didn't want her to change. There were obvious problems, though, among them was Elisa's wanting to live in D.C.—"and he can't get away fast enough." Still, she wrote Aaron a long letter of apology, not quite saying she wanted to get back together, but not quite closing the door. "We broke up once and I don't want to fiddle with his emotions." Since then, they'd gone shopping together, been to dinner and a movie. They'd had long cell-phone conversations that got cut off and resumed cutely.

"Hey, you didn't wait for my permission to hang up," he said.

"Sorry, Mr. President."

"I'm really strong willed," she told me one afternoon in the cafeteria. "I need someone I can follow."

CHAPTER 4

America Is a Christian Nation, Capital "C," Capital "N"

One Monday morning I sat in on Patrick Henry's flagship course, "Freedom's Foundations," which all students are required to take. Twenty students arrived on time and took out their laptops to take notes. That day the students were talking about the Federalist papers. The professor, Robert Stacey, had assigned three nonconsecutive Federalist papers to emphasize certain themes. "I know. The Founders are sacred, and we can't read them out of order," he joked.

Stacey pushed the students to think about Madison's skepticism about human nature: "If men were angels, no government would be necessary," he said, reading the famous quote from Federalist 51.

"What about our beloved President Bush? Is he an angel? Don't tell me he needs to be controlled!"

The students, who had been fully engaged on the basic theory, were silent. Bush had been president since they were teenagers, and the school newspaper's editorials almost never deviated from the White House position. Finally one student said, "None of us are angels."

"Come on, there's no law in the student handbook yet against criticizing Bush. That comes next year."

"No," said another student. "I guess he's not."

"Government is made up of people who 'stink on ice,'" Stacey quoted from a Mel Brooks movie. "That's a cultural reference, for those of you who were homeschooled. Madison is saying you can't give any of them unfettered use of power. You have to use someone else, who is just as wicked and fallen as they are. One Ted Kennedy, one George Bush."

Every campus has its academic rock star, and at Patrick Henry, Stacey was it, only without the usual ego. Stacey is short, with a trim ginger-colored beard and infinite energy. Students waited hours outside his office to see him, and he nearly always obliged, even if that meant having a Pied Piper train trail him to his car. Most days after class, he ate in the cafeteria, often with a group of students who otherwise wouldn't talk to one another. For students who sought him out, he played the role of mentor, surrogate father, and sometimes matchmaker. Stacey, in turn, loved Patrick Henry, he told me, because the students "really want to be here, which is very satisfying for a professor. I say to them, 'Let me tell you about Plato,' and they suck it up. They want to know more."

Stacey became an evangelical Christian during his second year at the University of Virginia, where he got his Ph.D. in government. His born-again experience had crystallized for him around Acts 4:12. Peter is explaining to the rulers of Jerusalem how a cripple was healed: "Salvation is found in no one else, for there is no other name under heaven given to men by which we must be saved," a verse as unequivocal as anything in the statement of faith. Still, while Stacey was impressed with his students at Patrick Henry, he worried that they sometimes reverted to jargon they'd picked up from their parents, "that the nation's founders just fell out of Heaven, that America is a Christian Nation, capital C, capital N. I want them to understand that these are myths, that the claims they're making are superficial." When he asked his students to defend a position, " 'The Bible says so' is never the answer."

As portrayed by Stacey, the Founding Fathers would have been recognizable to any serious historian, evangelical or otherwise. George Washington was an enigma, neither entirely Christian in a traditional sense nor enamored of the Enlightenment. Thomas Jefferson was a cheerleader for the Enlightenment and dubious on the divinity of Christ. "Anyone who left my class thinking Jefferson was an evangelical Christian must have been asleep," Stacey said. Patrick Henry, who is beloved by modern conservative Christians for his open support of state-sponsored religion, suffered the most. Stacey never missed an opportunity to remind his students that their school's namesake did not want to ratify their beloved Constitution.

Sometimes Stacey hit a nerve, and you could feel the anxiety level rising in the class. Around the middle of the second semester, he spent some time on the tortured writings of Immanuel Kant, in a segment called "The Kantian Revolution." This was the first foray into modern philosophy, and it came as a shock to some of the students. The existence of God was suddenly cast not as a given but as a philosophical puzzle to be painfully worked out.

"After Kant, people became more consistent about saying there is no good, there is no evil," Stacey told the class. "Nietzsche referred to him as the 'catastrophic spider.' He destroyed morality and then tried to build it up again because he was too cowardly to live without it."

This was Stacey's end-of-class summary on that day. Students shut down their laptops and got ready to head out—all but one, a thin somber boy with intense blue eyes.

"Dr. Stacey? Just so you don't leave us with this notion. I mean, it's important to know because we're supposed to influence the world, so it's important that our worldview is clear," he said. "You would encourage us to reject this kind of worldview, right? Just so we're clear?" The student was a formerly mellow kayaking type who'd had his own recent born-yet-again experience. "Catastrophic spider" was not the image he wanted creeping around his newly whitewashed room of a brain.

"We have to know this because he is so influential," Stacey answered. "How do we know what we know? Kant is asking a very legitimate question. Let's end there, on a more pious note."

And then he added, somewhat nervously, "Was I not clear?"

Like many Christian colleges, Patrick Henry hadn't quite figured out what to do with the heretical liberal arts. If founder Michael Farris had been teaching Freedom's Foundations, for example, the class would have sounded very different. Farris viewed curriculum much as a general might view a battle plan. He wanted his students to study Kant in the same way the army wanted soldiers to study a map of Baghdad and learn a few words of Arabic. Knowing the enemy would make them better soldiers and ultimately win more converts to the American way. There was neither truth nor beauty to be found in Kant, Nietzsche, or most of the philosophers taught at Patrick Henry. They were the equivalent of bombed-out cities crawling with insurgents, or giant oil spills: messes left behind that had to be mopped up before they spread any farther.

"Yes, we can read Nietzsche," Farris told Patrick Henry parents. "But we have to constantly ask the question, 'How is this consistent or inconsistent with the word of God?' And we have to ask it openly, not leave it to inference."

Farris's original idea was to found not a liberal-arts institution but a two-year legal-training academy where students could develop the rhetorical tools to conquer the culture. He retained that single-minded focus in his obsession with making the school into a debate powerhouse. At Patrick Henry, debate played roughly the role that football does at Notre Dame. Farris traveled around the country recruiting debaters and devoted a disproportionate amount of resources to the activity. His teams swept nearly every tournament at every level they entered, from novice to varsity. When I asked Farris why, he said, "No one ever asked George Bush or John Kerry to arm-wrestle. They need these verbal-communications skills to defend their ideas. There's no training like arguing against the best minds and then beating them." Referring to Matthew du Mee, a star debater seated nearby, he said, "Maybe one day he'll be the one standing before the Supreme Court, arguing to overturn *Roe v. Wade*."

In debate you have to think on your feet. You have to learn both sides of an issue well enough to convince a judge. Unlike in class or when you're writing a paper, there's no time for your conscience to kick in. And there's no penalty for taking the wrong side. A debate round is the only place where a Patrick Henry student could plausibly defend using condoms or legalizing drugs or civil unions without running afoul of the dean of students, who doubles as the debate coach. In fact, in debate the students were encouraged to appeal to as broad an audience as possible.

"That word 'sodomy' sounds harsh to my ears," Farris told a student in a practice round one afternoon. "I think it's better to cast it as 'gay rights.'"

In class, however, professors had to walk a fine line, nudging their students to take some intellectual risks without scaring them, carefully stepping around the land mines. One year a professor ran into trouble for ordering a copy of Dante's *Inferno* that had charcoal sketches of nude women drowning in the River Styx. Another year, *Wheelock's Latin* was the offender, with a full-page male nude—*Playgirl* for the classics crowd. In both cases, the professors apologized and advised students to rip out the offending pages.

Every year Patrick Henry goes through a "modern novel" crisis, as the literature department tries to find a suitable post-nineteenth-century work. Jane Smiley's *A Thousand Acres* was the first candidate, but it had too many "fucks." Tom Wolfe's *A Man in Full* was on the curriculum, but that was doomed from the start—sex-crazed crack fiends, child abuse, what were they thinking? "Change of plan," the professor said one day. "These books are optional." *The Death of Ivan Ilyich, Siddhartha, Brave New World*— too depressing, too hedonistic, too much sex. The year I was on campus *As I Lay Dying* was auditioned, and despite the sex and a close call with abortion, it somehow slipped through.

To me, classes often felt like *The School of Rock,* with the professors playing the Jack Black role, pushing their students to let out their shirttails. Foreign-policy professor Paul Bonicelli left in 2006 to run the Bush administration's democracy programs out of US AID. In the press and the blogs, his hiring was depicted as yet another example of theocrats dominating Bush's foreign policy, but at Patrick Henry, Bonicelli had represented the radical view.

"Let's say you're working in the congressional office of some Christian evangelical and you love it," he'd tell his students. "He's someone you've always admired, and he lets you work on pro-life issues. Then one day, he decides to take on the oil pipeline, and asks you to help. For this bill he partners with a Democrat, the most liberal Democrat or, heaven forbid, a lesbian. If you're not prepared to work under those conditions, don't do this—don't get this degree."

Every once in a while a speaker showed up who was only dimly aware of the school's mission, and then the students got D.C. unplugged. Once I sat in on a core class for the Security Intelligence majors the day the guest speaker was Rich Haver, a high-level intelligence analyst who had briefed many presidents and, more recently, worked closely with Dick Cheney and Donald Rumsfeld. "There's something wrong with the way we do intelligence," he told them. "Which is why I came here. I'm deeply interested in recruiting a new generation of people."

Haver then proceeded to give them a glimpse of the kind of people they might meet in their chosen profession: a sheikh double agent with a penchant for blondes, a.k.a. the "date rape sheikh"; fifty-year-old colleagues "who try the kinky approach to solving their problems. With you young guys, it's direct. Let's go have some fun! But it's the old guys who go out and buy the porn." In concluding he left them with this piece of advice: "When people tell you that you have to win over hearts and minds, say, 'Me, I'll grab another part of their anatomy!'" No one laughed, but they did invite him to stay for the final prayer: "Lord, we thank You for bringing Mr. Haver to speak to us today. We hope You will guide him in his work."

Bonnie Libby, who was in her first year teaching freshman English at Patrick Henry, had taught at Brigham Young, a Mormon university, so she knew what to watch out for. There, parents complained about *Frankenstein* for its demonic sorcery, and students objected to a dramatic reading of *Mother Courage* because of an occasional "damn." Here she hoped to push the students a little further. "I want to teach them not to be afraid to engage with works like this from a position of knowledge. I want them to think not just about combating evil but about exploring these issues of existentialism and nihilism without getting lost."

In the class I visited, her students were discussing Aristophanes' *The Clouds*. You'd think with two and a half millennia of distance, you'd be safe, but not so. The bawdy humor would have made Chaucer blush. Here is Strepsiades, having what we might call a midlife crisis:

> When I married her and we both went to bed,
> I stunk of fresh wine, drying figs, sheep's wool—
> an abundance of good things. As for her,
> she smelled of perfume, saffron, long kisses,
> greed, extravagance, lots and lots of sex.
> Now, I'm not saying she was a lazybones.
> She used to weave, but used up too much wool.
> To make a point I'd show this cloak to her
> and say, "Woman, your weaving's far too thick."

[THE LAMP GOES OUT]

XANTHIAS: We've got no oil left in the lamp.
STREPSIADES: Damn it! Why'd you light such a thirsty
              lamp? Come here. I need to thump you

"Let me get you guys' thoughts," Libby began the class. "Why would we assign a book to you that has dirty jokes?"

"Maybe one reason is to learn good literature by the negative?" offered one student.

"Because it shows the human mind can justify anything?"

"Because it shows us that vice is ancient?"

Slowly, she led them through the idea that literature that depicts immoral behavior is not necessarily immoral, that good art has to portray sin as actually tempting to be any good. Three minutes before class was over, she got them to stop one-upping each other with piety and give her something close to the answer she wanted.

"Well, we have to know what goes on without necessarily imitating it or approving of it. It's the PHC motto, right? When we get out there in the world and hear people cussing, we can't just run away," said one freshman. "We can hear it and disapprove without being shocked or horrified, without saying, 'I can't believe what I just heard.'"

"Yes. Thank you."

The students liked to say that you went through the baby stuff freshman year to soften you up for Robert Stacey's class. "Stacey taught us how to think," was the refrain of students at every point on the Patrick Henry political spectrum. For those with inquisitive tendencies and flexible minds, Stacey acted as the pass to an open road, leading them to the most intellectually adventurous version of themselves. He taught them to read widely and critically, and to question all received wisdom. When they bragged to the outside world about the school's academic excellence, Stacey's class was what popped up in their minds.

But how much of Stacey's skepticism the average student absorbed was hard to say. They might love his jokes and do well on the tests, but "float away on the same bubble they rode in on," one of his fellow professors told me. By teaching about the nation's founding at a conservative evangelical college, Stacey was fighting an uphill battle against "Christian revisionism," as he called it in class, or sometimes "kooky Christian revisionism." At home, in their homeschool textbooks, and from visiting lecturers, the students were hearing some version of the view dominating conservative Christian circles these days: that the nation's great leaders were openly Christian and intended the nation to be the same, and that a hostile secular culture had colluded to obscure that truth.

Among the revisionists, every possible utterance of faith by the Founders is seized upon as proof that they had more in common with modern-day evangelicals than with today's secular elite. By now the details are familiar to anyone who's waded into this propaganda corner of the culture war: that George Washington improvised "so help me God" at the conclusion of the first presidential oath, that Lincoln quoted the Bible endlessly, that even Thomas Jefferson, author of "separation of church and state," was comforted on his deathbed by a passage from the Gospel of Luke.

Even as you walked out of Stacey's class, the iconography of Christian revisionism was evident everywhere in Founders Hall: replicas of famous portraits of Washington, James Madison, and Daniel Webster; a painting of Patrick Henry with a divine shaft of light guiding his famous call to arms—a set of symbols designed to convey that God, not John Locke, inspired our nation's founders.

The indoctrination started early; in freshman Derek Archer's case, his third-grade textbook painted America as the New Israel founded by godly men. The chapter titled "Freedom for a New

Nation" opened with Patrick Henry. George Washington famously refused to kneel, take communion, or have any prayers said by his deathbed; in thousands of letters he never mentions Jesus Christ; his biographer, Joseph Ellis, called him a "lukewarm Episcopalian" and a "quasi-deist." Nonetheless the textbook calls him a "godly leader" who "encouraged the American people to pray and follow the Holy Bible," which is accurate, but tells only half the story. Jefferson is the only one beyond rescue, meriting only mild scorn: "Not everyone in America that helped to start the United States believed in Christ," the section on him begins.

By high school, Derek's textbook, *God and Government*, filled in the backstory; "For generations the true story of America's faith has been obscured by those who deny the providential work of God in history," begins the chapter called "The Christian History of the United States." "Some historians even deny the Christian commitment of those who made this nation great . . . A deliberate attempt has been made to distort the facts of the past in order to manipulate the future." The chapter continues to promise "a staggering amount of religious source material that shows the United States of America was founded as a Christian nation."

A couple of times I encountered Patrick Henry students flushed from having just tagged along on one of David Barton's "spiritual heritage tours" of the United States Capitol Building, and eager to show off their newly acquired facts: that the Capitol building once served as a church, that nearly half of the signers of the Declaration of Independence held seminary degrees. "Even Jefferson signed letters 'in the year of our Lord Christ,'" Barton was quoted in the *New York Times* as telling one group. "What would happen if George Bush did that? They'd rip his head off!"

Barton, the point man for Christian revisionists, was the vice chairman of the Texas Republican party. Through his organization, WallBuilders, Barton dedicates himself to "educating the nation concerning the Godly foundation of our country." He's consulted with California and Texas public school systems on "Revisionism: How to Identify It in Your Child's Textbooks" and has convinced a dozen states to pass "American Heritage Education Acts" allowing teachers to discuss the role of religion in American history.

Barton's particular method is to quote the founders selectively, or to use contemporary sources who, like him, had a vested interest in religious hagiography. (The era's version of religious kitsch was paintings of the Founders, particularly George Washington, floating up to Heaven on cloud puffs and angel wings.) In "Was George Washington a Christian?" Barton relies heavily on the account of Washington's granddaughter, Nelly Custis Lewis, who described him in a letter as "praying fervently." But Custis Lewis herself was a devout Christian who feared for her grandfather's soul, and the passage was clearly designed to secure him a proper godly legacy. For every example there is a counterexample: In another contemporaneous account, one of Washington's slaves said she never saw him pray and witnessed mostly "card-playing and wine-drinking" on Sundays.

It takes only an amateur historian to realize that the Founders are not definable in modern terms: as either evangelical Christian or secular elite. They were each in their way devout and struggled, with varying degrees of intensity, to reconcile their faith with their notions of freedom. Barton was no doubt right that the Founders could not have imagined a country as secular as the contemporary United States. But he failed to mention how dim a view they took of religious fervor of the type practiced in chapel every morning at Patrick Henry. Jefferson referred to Christianity as "our particular superstition." He took a razor and literally sliced out every portion of the Bible that referred to Jesus' miraculous doings, as opposed to his philosophical writings, the difference "as easily distinguishable as diamonds in a dunghill," he wrote. "Question with boldness even the existence of God," he wrote to his nephew; "because, if there be one, he must approve more of the homage of reason than that of blindfolded fear."

Washington mentioned Jesus in his writing even less often than Jefferson did and refused to address the public about whether or not he was a Christian. In his writings, he tried as often as possible to call "God" by other names: "Great Ruler of Events" or "Higher Cause" or, more often, "Providence." Like his fellow Founders, he was influenced by deism, an Enlightenment version of religion that turned up its nose at the supernatural and located its faith in the observable natural world. If they were alive today, neither Jefferson nor Franklin, and possibly not Washington, could in good conscience sign the Patrick Henry statement of faith.

"It cannot be emphasized too strongly or too often that this great nation was founded, not by religionists, but by Christians; not on religions, but on the gospel of Jesus Christ!" For a long time this quote, attributed to Patrick Henry, was one of Barton's favorite lines, picked up and repeated on innumerable Christian Web sites. Recently, however, he had to concede that it could not, in fact, be located anywhere among Patrick Henry's recorded writings or speeches.

Not long ago, sociologist Christian Smith set out to define what American evangelicals mean when they say that they believe in a "Christian America." The most frequent explanation he came across was that America was founded by people who sought religious liberty and worked to establish religious freedom. Any grade-school textbook would agree with that. The second-most-frequent explanation offered was that a majority of Americans of earlier generations were sincere Christians. This, too, is empirically true, although in the case of the Founders often exaggerated.

Another sizable group said that what they meant by a Christian nation was that the basic laws of American government reflect Christian principles. This sounds something like the basis for a theocracy. When Smith asked a follow-up question, however, the picture muddied a bit; respondents said that by basic laws they meant representative government and the balance of powers, both democratic concepts inconsistent with a real theocracy. From these answers Smith drew the comforting conclusion that many evangelicals think of "Christian nation" as a simple historical fact and make no connection to present events.

This, of course, was not true of Farris. "Shape the culture and take back the nation" made his intentions clear. Farris made it easy for critics to place him at the center of a right-wing conspiracy to impose a theocracy on America. He always wriggled out of it, but just barely. During his run for lieutenant governor, the *Washington Post* editorial board asked him if he thought America was founded as a Christian nation. "I said, well, there's a difference between government and culture. As a culture, yes!" In class, Farris taught his students that "our rights derive from the hand of God," or "Biblical principles, correctly construed, are what led to freedom." But this is not much more radical than what Bush said in a State of the Union speech about Iraq: "The liberty we prize is not America's gift to the world, it is God's gift to humanity."

Once Farris's name surfaced on a roster of the shady group called Coalition on Revival, whose manifesto reads, "We believe America can be turned around and once again function as a Christian nation as it did in its earlier years." Farris acknowledged having briefly belonged to the group, he said he had left over differences and that he did not know how his name remained on the roster.

One afternoon I stopped by Farris's office to talk to him about his views on a Christian nation. While I waited, I looked closely at a framed print hanging outside—*First Prayer in Congress,* from 1774 in Carpenters' Hall, Philadelphia—a favorite of Barton's. In it, the congressmen do not sit primly in their chairs with their heads slightly bowed, the way the Patrick Henry kids do when they say grace in the cafeteria. They're down on their knees, or draped over their chairs, clustered in groups of two or three. They stare up at the sky or down at their feet with wide eyes and open mouths, like men possessed. From their expressions, you'd think Leviathan had just tromped through the Senate floor. It does not seem an efficient stance from which to conduct the nation's business. The center does not seem to be holding.

As a constitutional lawyer, Farris was what's known as an originalist. He believed that the Supreme Court "has twisted the Constitution and made it an instrument of tyranny," as he stated in the constitutional-law textbook he'd written for homeschoolers. In order to divine the original intent of the Constitution, Farris had turned himself into an amateur historian.

Farris was dressed casually that day, in a white polo shirt and khakis. On his computer screen was part of the introduction to his latest book, *From Tyndale to Madison: How the Death of an English Martyr Led to the American Bill of Rights.*

Farris traveled in the same circle as Barton, but would not publicly endorse views quite as crude as his. "To say the Founding Fathers have one theological bent is crazy," he said. "Most of them had their good days and their bad days. There's nothing that an honest evangelical has to fear from a sophisticated look at the founding."

At the same time, Farris didn't see his role as debunking the prevailing conservative Christian view. "Benjamin Franklin was a deist, but he still thought public prayer was a good idea," he said, and mentioned a famous incident during the Constitutional Convention when Franklin asked, "Why aren't we praying?"

Farris had been polishing his public position on this question for thirty years and did not seem much interested in discussing it further. He was much more interested in discussing the publication of his book, which he saw as dropping a bomb that would blow open a new front in the ongoing war over the nation's founding. John Locke and Thomas Paine were not enemies worthy of his attention. Instead, Farris wanted to refight the sectarian wars of their age and take on the Puritans, especially the Calvinists and the Anglicans, "supposed friends of religious liberty who are actually enemies."

As far as I know, no one denies the Puritans their role in helping to set up representative government. And no one denies their dark side, either. They landed at Plymouth Rock; they set up their "civil body Politick"; they burned witches. That's what my third-grade history book said. But Farris took on the subject with fresh rage. Calvin was in league with Christian persecutors. He sanctioned burning people at the stake. He and his henchmen—mostly "philosophers and worldly-wise men"—aimed to set up a "coercive utopia," where religious dissenters would be silenced.

The real heroes of religious freedom were the uneducated Baptists and Quakers, who wanted to engage with their Bible in their own way, unmediated. "Me and God, that's where liberty comes from," said Farris. Their advocate was William Tyndale, a tutor who translated the Bible so it could be available to anyone, "even the uneducated ploughboys."

Now it happened that most of the professors on Farris's staff were Calvinists, and philosophers to boot. It also happened that Tyndale, as described by Farris, sounded a lot like Farris, or at least like Farris as he liked to see himself: an educator, a Baptist, a scholar, a crusader for the rights of Anyman to speak to his God directly. If Farris's version of historical events was likely to either embarrass or infuriate half the professors on his staff, so be it: "I'm just trying to tell the truth."

Political theory is not like scientific creationism; the Bible says nothing about whether George Washington did or didn't kneel or what Benjamin Franklin thought about prayer. These ideas exist on a continuum, and in a moment of mutual interest and good-will, it's possible to believe that there is ample common ground. So it's easy to see how, when Stacey first met Farris, he thought of them as men who could see "eye to eye."

At the time, Stacey was in a tenure-track job at Lee University, a mostly Pentecostal college in the foothills of the Appalachian Mountains in Cleveland, Tennessee. The college was climbing in the rankings but still had some vestiges of Pentecostal anti-intellectualism; as recently as the seventies, Ph.D.s were seen as suspect, and an open-enrollment policy placed serious students alongside functionally illiterate ones.

Stacey saw Farris's ad in *World* magazine that was looking for a professor who could take the concept of freedom and explain it through intellectual history and political theory from a Christian point of view. It sounded like Stacey's dream class.

Stacey called and was invited in for an interview. Farris struck him as "results oriented," like "someone who really wants to advance an agenda," but his project seemed nonetheless intellectually exciting, not just another job but a grand experiment. The college was just about to open. Dorms were not even built yet; the first class of students would have to live with host families in Purcellville. Only students with reasonably high SATs would be accepted; together, the professors and students would be modern pioneers, forging God's Harvard.

Farris told Stacey that he and everyone else would be required to sign a statement of faith, but this didn't bother Stacey in the least. He flew home excited. "This is something I can get behind," he told his wife. A few months later he was hired.

From Farris's basic premise, Stacey set about designing the course. It would start with ancient views of freedom, first in Israel, as described in the Bible, then in Greece. They would move on to Augustine, Thomas Aquinas and Martin Luther before they came to the Puritans and the American Founding. The second semester would move through Tocqueville, Kant, and Nietzsche, and end with the American Culture War. The aim of the class was to "apply a Biblical worldview to the study of government and political philosophy," but Stacey did not accomplish that in the way students might be accustomed to.

On nearly every topic of discussion, he pushed them out of their comfort zone. He was witty, though not unkind, on the subject of homeschool culture. He called on people indiscriminately to explain the reading assignments, and offered them more coffee if they floundered. It took their intense concentration just to keep up with his low-grade sarcasm, and fifty minutes of his Socratic spitfire always passed quickly.

"Kelsey, what did you think of Robespierre?"

"He's pretty charismatic."

"Charismatic? You mean like a Pentecostal? That's a good point. He does talk about public virtue being necessary. That sure sounds Founderesque. Listen to this: 'ambition to serve glory and country.' That could be Madison."

Robespierre? The French guy? The Reign of Terror guy? The one who tried to kill himself? Founderesque? For a moment, he let them stew in their discomfort.

"Well, the Founders had this thing about passion. They didn't like it," someone offered.

"Good point," Stacey answered. "Their assumption was that even good passions could have a negative impact, that passion corrupts reason. Have you ever known people who have fallen in love with someone of the opposite sex? Not that any of you would ever do such a thing. Well, their reason overcomes passion, and they do dumb things."

"Do not be frightened from this inquiry by any fear of its consequences," Jefferson wrote to his nephew. To the more impressionable or possibly reckless students, this seemed like the secret code they were picking up in Stacey's class. They transferred their allegiances to the cult of Stacey, and how could they not? He seemed smarter, kinder, and cooler than any other adult they knew; if he was the catastrophic spider, they wanted the poison. But there was a price to pay. For the tender, sheltered home-schooled mind, the first steps toward intellectual exploration could lead to severe cognitive dissonance.

"Knowledge leads to God," was what they heard in chapel, but it didn't always work that way. "The more you know, the more you question," one especially astute sophomore told me. If everything your homeschool textbook taught you wasn't true, then everything the esteemed Dr. Farris said wasn't necessarily true, and what your parents said might not be true, either. The hierarchy was starting to unravel.

This student had found herself sitting in a biology class, listening to an explanation about the age of the Earth and why God could have tricked us by leaving fossils behind, and thinking, "Give me an answer. Why? Why does it have to be so literal?" Pretty soon she was right back in Creation, taking a bite out of that apple: "Why should I deprive myself of sex? Because 'God is the answer'? Well, that's not good enough."

When they were younger, they had the impression that the culture was not worth saving or knowing. Their kitchen, with their mom and their siblings and worship music playing, was like Augustine's City of God, with the fallen men living out there, somewhere far away. But when you are forced to engage with the culture, "you lose an element of critique," this sophomore said. Was all this music really immoral? Was Nietzsche really beneath contempt? It was easy to feel trapped between two miserable choices: "the Farris choice where the culture is twisted and sick they're all going straight to Hell versus, 'Oh, I'm not going to judge. It's all okay. Just get to know the culture and accept it.'"

I'd seen kids in this phase go on the intellectual equivalent of a cocaine binge: They inhaled all the punk and bad TV they could get their hands on; they cut up the rule book; they took out their old copies of Farris's *Joshua Generation* that they used to read like a second Bible and underlined in angry red, scribbling in the margins

Ridiculous! Hypocrite! Sadist! For a while they were left dangling, betrayed to a preadolescent rage of rebellion that gripped them five years too late.

But only for a while. In all my time at Patrick Henry, I never met a student, even among the enraged and disillusioned, who declared that he or she no longer believed in God. Eventually, all of them found their way to safe ground, even if it wasn't the same ground they walked in on. They'd go back to the Bible and find verses that felt more refined and obscure, like 1 Peter 3:15: "Always be prepared to give an answer to everyone who asks you to give the reason for the hope that you have." They'd join an Anglican church where they didn't have to raise up their hands and sing those goofy love songs to Jesus. They'd turn to Stacey for spiritual as well as intellectual guidance. Slowly, they'd start to walk themselves back.

"Stacey is my beginning and end of PHC," said sophomore Farahn Morgan. "Something clicked with me in that class. I really got to know myself." Being Christian, she learned, "doesn't have to be just, 'Jesus Saves, Hallelujah,' all the time! It's just a set of transcendent principles. And wow, that really helped my relationship with God."

CHAPTER 5

Farahn's Attempt
to Hide Her Midriff

Sophomore Farahn Morgan missed the first e-mail, and the second, but she had a good excuse. She had rented a room in a townhouse off campus, and for a few weeks—unimaginable though this might be to her fellow students—had no Internet access. "I noticed your bra strap was showing. You are in dress code violation." That was the first message. "You must contest the violation within twenty-four hours or you will have to make an appointment with Dean Wilson." That was the second, and twenty-four hours passed before she saw either. Now she had no choice but to visit the dreaded dean of student life.

I met Farahn in the college cafeteria during her freshman year in the first week I visited Patrick Henry. She was getting her lunch, and she looked as if she'd walked onto the wrong movie set. In a crowd of vests and tweed and taupe suits, Farahn was wearing her candy-pink coat and red rhinestone earrings; her "lunch" was a bowl of Goldfish crackers and a can of Minute Maid Light she'd brought with her. One of the first things I'd noticed about the Patrick Henry students was how they talked: They sounded not just polite, but *rehearsed,* as if they'd spent years preparing for me to take out my notebook and ask them about their ambitions, as if they'd grown up with TV cameras trained on the kitchen table.

But Farahn was different.

"So why did you come to Patrick Henry?" I asked her.

The real reason I found out much later from her mom. Farahn was supposed to go to Virginia Tech but when she showed up on the first day her roommate had a buzz cut and was wearing men's clothes. This was not the "best girlfriend" experience she'd hoped for. She complained to the guidance counselor that her roommate was a lesbian, and the counselor told her to suck it up; this was part of the college experience. So she and her mom called Patrick Henry.

Another student would have trotted out that story instinctively, as an artifact of the culture war that justified Patrick Henry's existence. But Farahn said only, "I have no idea what I'm doing here," and shifted, as if even the hard cafeteria chairs made her uncomfortable.

Farahn was born in West Virginia and she is a misfit, so her Southern charm shares space with a need to say inappropriate things. When she lived in the dorms freshmen year she liked to provoke her roommates by saying she was going to Victoria's Secret. ("People, *everyone* wears a bra!") On the Monday after Thanksgiving break, Dr. Stacey asked her in front of the class how it felt to be back at school: "Well, it's like you were once in Hell and then God let you go back to earth for a while and then He decided, 'Sorry, you have to go back to Hell now.'"

Every year, the student body settles on a reverse mascot who represents the antispirit of the school. There is no actual election or competition, and the issue is never spoken of. Nonetheless, by some mysterious process, a consensus emerges. The girl—it is usually a girl—can vary from recklessly defiant to bold to somewhat mysterious. She is often at least pretty and may be beautiful. She must be in some way vulnerable, meaning that she has no obvious campus base of support, especially among the female students. On her brazen chest the feminine forces of Patrick Henry look to pin the Scarlet Letter.

Farahn started the year as the front-runner, and in many ways she was a promising target. Although she had all the ingredients for popularity, Farahn spent much of her time alone—a lethal combination that left her susceptible to rumors. She looked like a Slavic runway model, nearly six feet tall and always put together like she had just walked out of a fashion shoot; one day a pencil skirt and Audrey Hepburn sunglasses, the next day a bohemian skirt and fuzzy mukluks. The heavy charcoal eyeliner and glitter she put on most days made her cocoa eyes look even more enormous, and her hair was most often pulled into a tight bun reminiscent of the ballet dancer she'd been for most of her life.

Ballet, she thought, had schooled her in a distinctly female form of politics. In her mind, women were people who elbowed you out of the way so they could get to the top; her friendships with other girls seemed fleeting, and in public she was most often seen in the company of men. But mostly she was not seen much at all. She rejected all offers of roommates her own age and instead had rented a room from a fifty-four-year-old woman who lived in a development less than a mile from campus (hence, no Internet).

Farahn seemed too hyperaware to speak in sound bites, a habit that was close to heretical in this cocoon of certainty. When fellow students put that comforting hand on her shoulder and told her they knew God's plan for her, she would answer, "If He talks to you again, can you let me know?" or "Is God talking behind my back again?"

Absence breeds mystery, and mystery breeds gossip. If there was one sin of which nearly all the students at Patrick Henry had to repent, it was spelled out in honor code number six: "I will not spread slander or gossip." The campus dorms were set up in an arc around a lake. Some called this arrangement a "fishbowl" because it facilitated easy spying. Walk with a girl to chapel a couple of times, and within forty-eight hours you'd pick up on rumors that you were courting. With three hundred students, the school was not quite small enough for a feeling of casual family intimacy, and not quite big enough for anonymity. The result could be lethal: Everyone thought they knew you, but they didn't.

Over two years, all manner of rumors stuck to Farahn: that she was rich, that her father owned half of NASCAR, that she had kissed two boys in one weekend, that she was dating a Marine and a local reporter. None of these was true, or at least none was entirely true. What was true was that Farahn was elusive, as many hopeful suitors had realized when they tried to pin her down. What was true most of the time was that she was sitting home alone, reading Harvey Mansfield, writing her papers, watching *Arrested Development*. When she went out it was usually to the Sweetwater Tavern, where she'd order a smoked-salmon appetizer—hold the sourdough crackers—and explain once again to the waiter that, yes, this pretty girl was spending her Saturday night alone, "detoxing," as she puts it, from another frustrating week.

"I don't know why they target me," she said. "It's not like I'm out late partying with the rock stars." Or, as she once put it in a late-night IM to a friend:

I know what people think about me.

and I'm sick of it

who the hell are they to judge me about something?

There are times when the self-restraint of the True Love Waits generation produces an atmosphere that feels wholesome and sweet. As the parent of a young daughter, I sympathize greatly with the instinct to preserve girlish innocence as long as possible. Couples at Patrick Henry could spend hours on a couch, talking and holding hands and nothing more (a "sweaty-palm night"). Girls might shun boys altogether and spend a Saturday night sitting back to back in a circle, reading *Alice in Wonderland* to one another.

During the year I spent at Patrick Henry, a cover story came out in *New York* magazine about my old high school, Stuyvesant, in downtown Manhattan. The cover line was "Love and the Ambisexual, Heteroflexible Teen." It featured Alair and her "bi-queer, metroflexible" friends who liked diving into "cuddle puddles" during tenth period (don't ask). The cover showed Alair resting her lightly acned cheek on the chest of an obviously naked boy. Apparently, her mother let her pose for that cover. Given a choice for my daughter, I'd take all-girl reading circles over that any day.

But at other times, the atmosphere at Patrick Henry edged too close to the Cultural Revolution, or to the Harvard Square of

The Handmaid's Tale. Students did spy on their comrades, and they seemed to take a certain pleasure in it, or at least a certain satisfaction. Rewards accrued for the person who with brutal efficiency rose to the top by informally policing his own. Those who resisted the constant scrutiny suffered, and their punishment was assumed to be divinely ordained. In the school's first year, a student who was sneaking off campus to sleep with his nonstudent girlfriend got her pregnant. The community pressured him to marry her, and he did, but the baby died, tragically. One of the professors later told me a group of students in his class had concluded that "God was teaching them a lesson."

"For Christ & for Liberty," reads the campus motto. As political philosophy, the view is at least arguable. But in the day-to-day life of the hunted student, the pair can seem comically mismatched.

The facts are these: It was not Farahn's bra strap that was showing, it was an undershirt she was wearing under her sweater to make sure her midriff wouldn't show. The women of Patrick Henry got dressed in the morning with military precision. Some did the "triple test"—raise your arms over your head, then bend down to touch your toes, then twist your arms sideways—all to make sure their shirts didn't ride up from any position. When she lived on campus during her freshman year, Farahn had a roommate who told her when she was going overboard. But this year she was on her own, and the undershirt she'd meant as an extra measure of precaution had backfired.

She walked the few hundred yards from the parking lot to the dean's office, which was in the basement of one of the dorms. The bra strap she could explain easily, but she had an agenda of her own, namely a list of grievances she'd typed up and printed out

130

and was carrying in her ever-present pink backpack. For the meeting, she'd chosen a slightly more conservative ensemble than usual: a cream-colored cardigan and a brown skirt.

Farahn walked from the parking lot to the dean's office in a state of high irritation, about the bra strap and everything it represented. "I'm nineteen years old and I should be able to make a decision about what movie I want to watch, even if it doesn't present its message in a neat little Christian package," she said. "If you want to produce 'great leaders to influence the culture,'" she added, in a mock-lecturing voice, "you can't keep them cloistered like a bunch of monks." She went on fuming about Stalin, Saddam, and Caligula, who hung arbitrary rules up high on a pole where no one could see them.

"The system," she said, "promotes a binge/purge approach to sin. You can't say, 'If I disagree with the drinking rule, I'll have a couple of beers.' Instead, it's 'Let me drink until I black out and come back to my room escorted by the police.'"

Before going down the steps, she looked into the ground-level window to see what the dean was up to. At any time of day, a student or a group of students could generally be found sitting in the seats facing Dean Wilson's desk, talking or praying with their heads bowed. Students came to him to unload their guilt, to share news they know he would applaud—a mission trip, an engagement—and to "hold their brothers in Christ accountable." If evangelicals went to confession, Wilson's office would be the booth. This particular day, a couple of students were already waiting outside.

In Christian conservative culture, the counterpart to the updated happy homemaker is the newly sensitive Christian man—the "soft patriarch," in Wilcox's phrase. This type found his outlet in the Promise Keepers movement of the nineties, in which, in the interest of accountability, "real men" were encouraged to share their feelings. Of this era, Wilson was the archetype. A former wrestling coach and math teacher from California, he looked fit and tan, with a tight energy that seemed always about to erupt. At the same time, he cried occasionally, and sometimes ended sessions with a hug or an "I love you." Some kids treated him as a father figure and spiritual mentor. Some dismissed him as a meathead unworthy of his high-minded surroundings. But the truth was, he unnerved even the intellectual snobs. He took everything they did seriously, and personally. In his office, every day was Judgment Day, and what the students considered teenage pranks he would elevate to the rank of sin.

If there were a remake of the eighties movie *Porky's*, Wilson would be an easy target, the guidance counselor intent on fixing the sexual habits of teenagers. In the twenties, he would have been a Prohibitionist, hunting down the brothels and gin mills. In his world, girls were prey and men were predators, and it was his job to keep them apart. "The girls in the homeschool world have an ignorance of the way guys are and I think if they knew they would disassociate themselves," he told me. "Our guys are capable of doing some pretty bad things." To the girls he would whisper, "I'm your daddy on campus." He warned the boys about an "addiction to porn." (At Patrick Henry one peek at Playboy.com would land you on the campus equivalent of Amber Alert.)

"Come in," he said, and Farahn sat down. She explained about the bra strap and they moved past it quickly. She said she didn't have a problem with the dress code. But then she took out her list. She talked about forced church attendance ("I don't think anyone needs to know where I worship"). She talked about the movie rule. A Southerner to the core, she kept her rage invisible. "I think Dr. Farris's overall mission is a beautiful idea, but the way he's going about it is not so productive."

Wilson heard her out and answered mildly, explaining how the rules came about and why they were important. Wilson had started the year optimistic about good morale, pleased that a group of agitators from the previous year had graduated. He had called this year's class "a new start" and "pure." The freshmen had taken the compliments to heart and thought of themselves as a collective exorcism, casting out the old demons. Farahn's list of complaints was the first clue that the spirit of rebellion hadn't been completely snuffed out. As many a disappointed fundamentalist has discovered, the age of purity is always just out of reach; the demons still lurking among the ivy.

The meeting was conducted without much overt drama, and it lasted all of fifteen minutes. But when she stepped out, Farahn looked defeated, and her shiny dangly earrings seemed suddenly all wrong. "I have to leave this place," she said. "It's hard to come in every day and know I'm being judged. I've been to many places and felt different but I've never felt put down. Now, it's like I'm just lumped in with all the bad Christians."

If you want to understand how conservative American Protestants separate a "good" Christian from a "bad" one, it makes more sense to ask Dean Wilson than to look in your Bible. The Bible does not say you can't drink, dance, smoke, watch *Braveheart,* or wear cargo pants with stitching on the pockets. Quite the opposite: Miriam dances, Jesus turns water to wine. "Does the Bible prohibit these things?" Aaron Carlson, student-body president, asked on the day he introduced the new honor code. "No, but we want to be above reproach."

In conservative Christian culture, the prohibition against certain vices is known as "prudential," as opposed to scriptural. In addition to reading the Bible literally, some Christians subject themselves to what we would now call lifestyle rules as a measure of extra precaution. The idea is that after the Fall, we humans were left with a powerful sin nature that will overtake us unless we are very careful at all times. A prudent Christian will not let himself drift, step by step, into perdition. He avoids that road entirely, like a meat-lover turned vegan who moves to the countryside to stay out of the path of McDonald's. In this view, all that stands between the saint and the sinner is a few hard drinks. "A man can slip into Hell with his hand on the doorknob of heaven," warned Billy Sunday, the famous temperance-era preacher.

Prudence makes fundamentalists seem almost Talmudic in their obsession with rules. Prudence is what's kept alive the stereotype of the fundamentalist. Patrick Henry students made fun of Bob Jones University, the Christian college that's the gold standard of vice patrol, but by most people's standards, they were not far behind. Never would you find a group of better-behaved teenagers than on the campus of Patrick Henry. As far as I'd been able to tell, these were the worst things that had happened in six years of Patrick Henry's existence: A few students had had sex, some on campus. One student was reportedly involved in dealing drugs, although no one could prove that. Once a student had stolen his roommate's credit card and ordered some gay porn. He was labeled disturbed and sent home. Otherwise, the vices that showed up in Wilson's office were a night of drinking, a broken curfew, an errant bra strap, an overheard curse.

The few serious transgressions haunted the campus the same way they would a great Victorian family: deep, shameful secrets no one must ever mention lest they imperil the school's name. Meanwhile, the possibility of sin kept the students in a state of fear, as if a plague raged a house away. To avoid it, students spent much of their time policing themselves and each other. They struggled over whether to wear tight jeans, go to a rap concert, play drums in chapel, watch *Curb Your Enthusiasm,* read Bret Easton Ellis, or see movies in the theater—where you couldn't skip over the naughty bits. Nearly every week mini–culture wars broke out in class, on the campus online network, in the newspaper, at a lunch table, or in the gym. Through these arguments a more enlightened evangelical view emerged and was immediately quashed. One student wrote an article titled "Why Bono May Be a Better Christian Than You" citing the star's "musical brilliance," and also his "open faith and charitable works that have given hope to millions." Another wrote back outraged, pointing out that the band members "drink, smoke, and curse at their concerts." One student put on AC/DC while lifting weights in the communal gym (*"She was a fast machine . . ."*). A girl came in and priggishly turned it off. One student ordered a CD by the band TV on the Radio with liner notes that included the F word. For that, he lost his interlibrary-loan privileges.

Christians like to say that vice is eternal, but the particular prohibitions shift over time. Lately, as evangelicals try to break into the mainstream, the rules are relaxing. These days refusing to drink at all puts you at the far right of the conservative spectrum. Many Christian colleges prohibited movie watching until the sixties, when the "Jesus film" uncovered the medium's potential as an evangelizing tool.

For much of the century, dance was considered a godly woman's ticket to ruin. "Young men can drink and gamble and frequent houses of ill fame, but the only way a girl can get recreation is in a narrow-gauge buggy ride on a moonlight night or at a dance. If you can't see any harm in this kind of thing, why I guess the Lord will let you out as an idiot." That's from the famous 1915 Billy Sunday sermon, "Theater, Cards and Dance." At conservative Protestant colleges that view hung on until recently.

In 2003 Wheaton College, Billy Graham's alma mater, lifted its 143-year ban on dancing. In the years since, smaller colleges such as John Brown University of the Ozarks followed suit. The change reflected an accommodation to the culture as much as a change in evangelical tastes. Conservative Christian parents began to reevaluate dance as something desirable, even wholesome. Homeschooled kids took classes in the art of the nineteenth-century line dance or "thunder clogging," a sort of tap dancing with clunkier shoes. When their parents were growing up, conservative churches considered swing dancing akin to sex with clothes on; then it became the latest rage in homeschooling circles, a relic from an innocent age before grinding took over the high school prom.

Like many prudential restrictions, Patrick Henry's dancing rules were fairly arbitrary. To accommodate the fundamentalist faction, the rule book forbids "dancing (guy-girl, with music) on campus." But the college "does not take a position on what types of dancing students take part in away from the campus." The result was that during the week the girls kept their headphones on, and on weekends the more adventurous ones went clubbing in downtown D.C.

Every year Patrick Henry held two official dances—both off-campus, to maintain the rules. For the fall Hoedown, students wore jeans and cowboy hats and square-danced around bales of hay. Spring brought the Liberty Ball, a highlight of the year. The students wore gowns ranging from low-cut prom dresses they got at the mall to Jane Austen costumes they'd sewn themselves. For one night, a true spirit of courtship prevailed. Boys who'd been too shy to ask all year finally did. The students danced for hours in line formation; some couples snuck away for long walks through a garden of spring flowers. Still, Farahn was not impressed. "I mean, to get all dressed up like that to go contra dancing? It's just wrong."

As an alternative to the formals, some students organized the Valentine's Day Dance, which was held at a nearby Anglican church in Purcellville. A committee of students raised the money, issued the invitations, decorated and hired the DJ. Farris and his wife stopped by once, the first year. When he failed to show the second year, the students turned up the heat with 50 Cent's "In da Club" (*I'm into having sex, I ain't into making love*"), but even so, everyone made it back by curfew.

This year the event's treasurer felt that the raunchy playlist excluded the more conservative students. A long stalemate ensued. Finally, the organizers held a somber evening meeting and came up with a compromise. They would intersperse "normal" dancing with swing dancing, slip a Sinatra number between Beyoncé and Snoop Dog.

In the end, the dance transpired blissfully. The dance's organizers strung lights all over the church rec room. Students brought pretzels and home-made brownies and cans of soda. The crowd included some surprisingly conservative kids along with the campus rebels; the two sides ribbed each other playfully. Along with prizes for best male and best female dancer, there were awards for "most disgusting PDA" and "most likely to recommit himself to

Jesus after this dance." The girls' dresses could be described as ranging from elegant to tastefully sexy. Even engaged couples maintained distance between their bodies.

Still, one of the students wrote a blog entry about the experience called "On Orgies":

> When possible names for dance moves are "cat scratching back on pole" and "ripple and intertwine," something inside me screams like a Looney Tune and runs out the back entrance. This is not based on some hyperpuritanical distaste for seeing more of a human body. But when women are wearing as much material as could make up a rubber band and are actively wiggling themselves out of it—and when men are actively wiggling right along with them—something is wrong.
>
> It struck me this morning after talking with my roommates that we would have seemed a pretty sorry picture had Jesus come back during the dance. Would we have invited Him in for a number?

In the house where Farahn grew up, many of the walls and tabletops were given over to formal portraits of her dancing in various ballets. Farahn saw her first production *Snow White* when she was three. She remembered being scared out of her wits that the trees were moving. Her bedroom was still a museum from that era, and it was a source of embarrassment to her. It looked like the room of a little girl, with a satiny pink-and-white ballet quilt on the bed and nearly every available hook and surface covered with ballerina angels and toe shoes stuffed with dried flowers and dolls in Victorian dress. When she was at home, she usually escaped to an adjacent oversized powder room done up in plain white, to relax or read and "not feel like I'm six years old."

If there was a grim realism at the edge of Farahn's convictions, she came by it honestly. Farahn grew up in West Virginia on the border of Kentucky, where her neighbors still butchered deer in their front yard. It is territory hostile to the slick, updated megachurch; the signs you pass as you climb the endless mountain roads look much as they probably did thirty years ago: CAN'T GET NO SATISFACTION?: TRY JESUS! and REVIVAL—wood planks pointing the way down a dirt road. Even the hair salon was called Genesis, and at the Chevy dealership owned by her father, Timothy, the Ten Commandments hung by the water fountain, right by the sign that said, NO SKOAL OR TOBACCO PRODUCTS.

Her family was well off only by comparison to their neighbors. The dealership was successful enough that Farahn's father was able to build a spacious house overlooking the mountains at the end of a street lined mostly with trailers. It was true that he loved NASCAR and he owned a team, but his car wasn't doing too well. "Meth capital of the world," Farahn sometimes said when asked where she was from. The extended Morgan clan did include some characters in unfortunate circumstances. Her parents lived very comfortably, but they were only a generation away from coal miners living in hollers, from "poke and eggs" being a commodity so rare you had it only at Christmas. "We were all poor, but we were too proud to get handouts," her dad recalled.

On the day I visited, Farahn's mom, Donna, was in their enormous kitchen cooking a breakfast of eggs, bacon, and biscuits. The kitchen, like the rest of the house, was decorated in formal Southern style, with marble counters, brocade curtains, lots of antiques, and large windows. Apart from a slight accent, Donna did not give off an air of Southern housewife; she was trim and wearing jeans and a stylish, long-sleeved shirt; Farahn was dressed festively, in a peasant skirt and a jeans jacket, but she looked subdued, as if her mind were elsewhere. They had just seen the Narnia movie, and they were discussing the costumes. Farahn thought they were amazing, especially the one for the White Witch. "But I was always surprised the book used women to portray such evil. When I think of women, I think of purity."

"Well, Satan is cunning in the way he presents to us," said her mother as she doled out the sausages. "He can put evil in a package that looks appealing."

Farahn was homeschooled partly because of the quality of the local schools and partly because of her dancing. For a few years her mother drove her to a ballet school an hour away. When she became really serious about dancing, at age fifteen, her family moved to North Carolina, where her father had inherited a house from his family and where she joined the North Carolina Dance Theater. "How you feel when all the emotions inside you are about to explode, that's how I feel about dance," she once told me. As she got older, she got used to being the only serious Christian ("meaning the prude") in any production, and the other dancers got used to her; when they went partying after rehearsal they knew not to invite her along.

In her senior year of high school, Farahn's best friend at NCDT was another dancer, a boy named Kevin. He invited her to his senior prom. When she went to his house to take their prom pictures, another boy was there, also dressed in a tux. "Oh, he's my other date," Kevin explained. When they got to the prom, the guy continued to hang around them, and then he and Kevin "started power-grinding." Farahn got really upset and decided to go to another party she knew about, but that scene was barely better. "People were drinking too much and playing truth or dare and spin the bottle and making out in front of everyone."

She met up with Kevin again after midnight, and they drove to a Waffle House together.

"Did you have sex with that guy?"

No answer.

"Do you think I'm a bad person if I did?" he asked finally.

"That's not up to me. I think you need to ask yourself that question. You profess to be a Christian, so what do you think?"

At 3 A.M., she called her mother, sobbing, "Mom, I want to come home."

Later Farahn wrote Kevin a letter: "I'll always be your friend and I'll always support you if that's the lifestyle you choose to live. I think you're a believer but I think you're mixed up." Kevin lived with his grandmother, and Farahn wrote to tell her that Kevin was using girls as a cover. The grandmother wrote back, saying that Farahn was Kevin's only true friend, which "really broke my heart," said Farahn. "I'll always love him." A few years later, she ran into him in Miami, where he was dancing with the city's ballet company. "I don't think I'm gay," he told her, and said he'd been to Genesis, an evangelical group that "cures" homosexuals.

Farahn told me this story as we were finishing up breakfast. "You remember him, don't you?" she asked Donna.

"Sure. You did the right thing, Farahn," Donna said. "If you love somebody, would you encourage them to destroy themselves? It's an abomination to God, and as Christians, we can't accept it."

Dance has always been Farahn's passport to exotic and (her mother would add) sketchy locales. For the last couple of summers, the two of them had decamped to New York so that Farahn could take dance classes and audition for shows. In the semiprofessional studios of New York you could run into anyone:

young men in lipstick, aging transvestites, middle-aged women too old for their glittery bodysuits. While Farahn took classes at Alvin Ailey, Radio City, and Steps, her mom trekked around the city in her jeans and sneakers, shopping and sightseeing. Once she came early to pick up Farahn and watched as a teacher led a group of twelve-year-olds from a North Carolina dance troupe in a hip-hop class. "Pump your cherry! Fuck Fuck Fuck!" he yelled as they gyrated their hips. "They were just the sweetest, most innocent things," she recalled with horror.

For two months they lived in Parkside Evangeline Residence for Young Women, a kind of upscale flophouse owned by the Salvation Army across the street from Gramercy Park. ("My back-yard is almost as big as that park," said Donna.) The building housed misfits and oddballs, older women forgotten by their families, Midwestern girls who wouldn't accept that their modeling careers were never going to take off. For the summer, Farahn's mom was the resident faith healer, bringing the lost and wounded to Christ: the forty-two-year-old having an affair with a married man in her office, the plus-size model with the cruel stepmom and even crueler friends, who wound up "hugging me with big fat tears rolling down her cheeks holding on to me like I was a family member or a dearest friend," Donna recalled.

Farahn went on auditions, but found them always a minefield. One summer she was called back to do an audition for the movie version of *The Producers*. She and her mother didn't know much about it, so they went to see a production. "It was horrible," Donna recalled. "We had to leave midway through. There was one song, 'Keep It Gay.' That's just so inappropriate. Absolutely no class. No taste. No value. There were guys there dancing around with huge prosthetics. Just huge. It was offensive."

"There are very few jobs for a Christian person," Farahn

142

added. She'd worked a lot with the Rockettes in hopes of landing a part in the Christmas show, because the "costumes are not horribly risqué. In lots of shows—*Cabaret, Chicago, Sweet Charity*—"you're basically just wearing underwear," her mom added.

"I don't really care how other Christian people look at me," Farahn said.

"Yes, honey, but some of these shows are so suggestive they look . . . well, like pole dancing. It's like they're saying, 'Let's see how vulgar we can get.' Ballet is beautiful."

"I don't like ballet," Farahn answered. "I like contemporary choreography. Alvin Ailey and Paul Taylor and William Forsythe and Dwight Rhoden."

"Yes, but in classical the hips are going to be rigid. Right there in their place—*zip!* In contemporary, the hips move and gyrate. It can be tawdry."

"Mom, that's not necessarily true. Ballet can take a story and make it tawdry."

"Well, that's very rare. Jesus said don't walk among the ungodly. So you try and avoid it. You don't just join arms and go on a big weekend outing together."

I'd seen Farahn in contemporary-dance classes and it was true, that the routines invariably included a lot of hip gyrating and come-hither moves. Still, the argument had seemed sharper than necessary. Usually Farahn and Donna were as close as best friends. They could live together for weeks without the usual buildup of mother-daughter tension; they talked on the phone several times a day. It took me a while to figure out that something wasn't quite right, that this conversation was a proxy for a deeper rift between them. Only later, when we took a drive, did it all come out. Her mom took us to the border to see the coal mines near where she'd grown up. Farahn was pretty quiet for most of the ride; she popped in an Interpol CD that a friend had sent her and tuned us out.

On the way home we stopped at Robo's, Farahn's favorite place for a cherry nut ice-cream sundae. I got out to help her carry our order back to the car. As soon as she shut the car door, she exploded. "I can't even look at her. I can't wait to get away." As soon as it came out, her anger was gone, a knife chucked in the lake.

Farahn had a boyfriend. And he wasn't a Christian, at least not a Christian in the way her mother understood. When Farahn got out of the car again to throw away the garbage, I heard the other half of the story.

"Choosing someone to marry is not like choosing a pan or what outfit to wear," Donna said, appealing to me as a fellow mother. "God tells us in choosing a mate they can't be unequally yoked. She needs a person of faith. She says she wants to bring him to salvation, but we can't offer salvation. Only God can offer salvation. Some seeds can fall on fallow ground."

His name was Jared. Farahn had met him in New York the previous summer. New York is full of beautiful women, but Farahn, in her white sundress and Southern innocence, stood apart like an angel floating above the grime. Wherever she went—the subway, Starbucks, Gramercy Park—men from twenty to sixty-five tried their luck. This one followed her out of the subway. He was an investment banker and older, although she wouldn't tell his age. He got her number and took her to the Union Square Café. On their second date she asked how many girls he'd slept with, and he gave a number that was well above zero.

"Well, *I'm* not sleeping with you," she told him. "God doesn't want you to sleep around."

"But if you love someone it's only natural," he told her. "God put that desire in people, so if you're really close to a person physically and emotionally, it's only natural."

Still, they lasted through the summer. Jared came to visit her, in school and at home over Thanksgiving break. She told her mother about him, of course, but the more Donna learned, the less she liked. Jared had already lived with a woman, and to Farahn's parents, that was as bad as if he'd been married and broken his vows. A few months earlier one of Farahn's old friends, a Christian girl, had been pressured by a boyfriend to sleep with him, and she'd succumbed. They were not going to let that happen to Farahn. They took away her cell phone and gave her a new one and warned her not to give Jared the number.

Donna tried a feminist tack, too. She told Farahn that while she loved Farahn's dad, she sometimes regretted not waiting until she was older than eighteen to marry. "He's taking up all your time," she said. "You're nineteen. He's so controlling. I want you to focus on your studies at this point in your life."

But Farahn liked Jared. "He's sweet," she said. She might even love him. He was smart and aggressive and just a little bit lost. He'd given her a skirt from Anthropologie and pajamas with ice-cream cones on them.

Later that day, we visited her dad at the car dealership. In a garage next door, he showed off his pride—a virtual Chevy museum—fifty cars dating from the thirties to the seventies, all in impeccable shape. He let us try out his newest model: a 2006 Corvette he had just sold. He loved Chevys, he said, because Chevys were made in America. If you gave him a present that was not made in America, he'd return it. Once Nikon offered to sponsor one of his best NASCAR drivers. He considered it, but only for a few seconds.

Later we went back to his office to talk. Farahn's dad was

a man of theories; in half an hour he ran through all the old Christian-right standbys—welfare ruined the poor, Democrats are socialists, gay rights are ludicrous, the Civil War was not about slavery, the Bible used to be a standard school textbook, God blessed this nation above all others, Rush Limbaugh might not be a Christian, but he was a pretty smart guy.

Farahn once gave him St. Augustine's *The City of God* as a present, but he didn't read it. "That hurt my feelings," she said. These days, when she went to NASCAR races, "I'm bored out of my mind." She sat at his desk sandwiched between him and her mom as we talked, writing notes to herself on a little blue legal pad, scribbling one on each page.

> *Please God help me.*
> *How will I know?*
> *By faith alone*
> *Go to Nineveh*

Farahn felt like stubborn, resistant, desperate-to-run-away Jonah. A stronger power was making her do something she really did not want to do.

On the drive home, she said, "Mom? Do you think I am what you wanted me to be?"

WHAT DOES GOD want me to be? What does He want me to do? God, give me a clue here!!!! These sentences showed up in the Patrick Henry kids' personal diaries, on their Facebook entries, in their Xanga posts. Should I apologize to my roommate? Should I study or go see a movie? Should I date this guy or not? Farahn was growing up in an age when a "personal relationship with Christ" meant exactly that—Jesus was held as close as a mother, a best friend, a girlfriend or boyfriend and, ultimately, a husband or a wife. No shift in routine or daily decision was beneath His attention.

The intimacy gave Patrick Henry kids a feeling of being guided, of things always being just as they should be. "Everything happens for the good, in a local and geopolitical sense," one freshman told me. But it also made them panic about losing the thread. The predominant view among Patrick Henry students was that "you choose your life path, not that things happen to you," Farahn once explained to me. "A lot of people here, if they lose control—even for a second—they have a breakdown." Sometimes among these type A overachievers faith felt like yet another tool for maintaining discipline and control, part of the daily checklist of obligations ("take vitamins, do sit-ups, study, read Bible," read one student's Post-it above her bed).

"No excitement, no element of surprise. God is the God of order. And so they are psycho every minute of the day," Farahn said.

Farahn believed what her mom told her, "that you are created by God for a reason and that reason will be revealed in God's time." But there were degrees of humility in how a believer approached that question. For Farahn, life was less a bright yellow brick road with a few distractions along the way than a minefield to be braved. "People say, 'With God's strength we will overcome,'" she said. "But in my view God puts those obstacles in your way to help you be who you are." We are all Jonah vomited out in good time.

The Patrick Henry kids came of age when Bush was elected president. For most of their conscious lives, he served as the most prominent Christian in America. During his presidency, the same kind of doubt-free faith common at Patrick Henry prevailed at the White House. Every morning Bush was supposed to have read a book that showed up on many Patrick Henry reading lists: *My Utmost for His Highest,* a calendar of Bible thoughts by turn-of-the-century Scottish minister Oswald Chambers.

Chambers discourages second thoughts or critical reevaluation. He argues against layered readings of the Scripture or consorting with the "wise and prudent" to find hidden meaning. If you experience setbacks or disagreements, you should consider them part of the ultimate scheme set up to test your faith. ("Stay the course," Bush's war plan in Iraq, could serve as a summary of Chambers's philosophy.) His formula is simple: Once you have a personal relationship with Jesus Christ, knowing God's will becomes a sixth sense: "If you obey God in the first thing He shows you, then He instantly opens up the next truth to you," Chambers wrote. "But if we turn away from obedience for even one second, darkness and death are immediately at work again."

Patrick Henry students spent little time divining what exactly God's will was in their own lives, and even less on thinking about what it might be in the affairs of the nation. God's goals were mostly fixed, and the only question was whether the students were sufficiently loyal soldiers to carry them out. As with Bush, this focus was at the root of their optimism about the ultimate outcome of things, about their own ability to effect change. In Bush's case, it led to a lot of arrogance, as when, in a 2004 press conference, Bush couldn't name a single mistake he'd made. On the part of his loyal young followers, it produced something more like a reckless naiveté, a willingness to believe in someone merely because he was a "professing Christian," to believe that things were exactly as they should be when they so obviously weren't.

There's another way of thinking about God's will. You pray, you try your best, but you often fall short of the standard. This is a humbler way, and it's been in the shadows throughout Bush's presidency. Senator Barack Obama summarized it once in a speech about religion and politics: "Faith doesn't mean that you don't have doubts. You need to come to church in the first place because you are first of this world, not apart from it." Farahn thought this way, too, not because of some coherent politics or theology but because of her innate fatalism.

"I've come to the conclusion that people aren't really bad, after all. I think people are most essentially desperate . . . pathetic in the sense that life really is a tragedy, and even the most harsh people deserve a degree of sympathy. I still see being and humanity as a sort of tragedy, though. If the term Christian nihilist isn't contradictory, I guess that's what I am."

Farahn seemed especially drawn to people who'd missed their destiny, or had come to it through a perverse path. She was deeply interested in Richard Nixon, for example. "I have a thing for people who try to do the right thing and then really mess up." Also Jesse James, for a slightly different reason: "because society looked down on him and he ended up being right." Her favorite book was *The Education of Little Tree,* a sad, sweet coming-of-age story about an orphan boy adopted by Cherokee grandparents. (Farahn is part Cherokee.) Little Tree learns how to trust nature and "granma" and "granpa" and nothing else—not the glib politicians or the gruff soldiers or the dumb hollering preachers who yell that everyone's going to hell. In his dreams he sees a Christian version of a used-car salesman. The man holds out a box of candy and says Little Tree can have it for fifty cents, although it's worth a whole lot more. But Little Tree doesn't have fifty cents, so he can't buy the candy.

"It's part of my darker side. I don't hate people. I just see the reality of things. People work really hard to be one way but it's obvious they're not really that way."

What put Farahn in a really bad mood was sitting next to one of the kids in morning chapel who smiled stupidly and loudly groaned, "*Mmmmmm*" throughout the sermon, no matter how banal. "Nowhere in the scriptures does it say you have to plaster a fake smile on your face and be happy, happy all the time," she said. She had tried out some of the megachurches near Patrick Henry, but "they would just alienate me. 'Oh, come join us, the joy of the Lord is in the air!'" Some Sundays, instead of going to church, Farahn would pull over, sit in the car alone, and listen to sermons on the radio.

Unlike many Patrick Henry students, Farahn seemed highly conscious that she was blooming in a very tight space. She and the other misfits kept banging their heads against the close-in walls, craning their necks to see if they'd missed an open window somewhere, and giving themselves headaches in the process.

"*Life is pain*," Farahn's friend wrote to her at one in the morning in an epic IM session. "*i believe that, farahn. I wasn't lying when i told you that. i believe it. i think it's a biblically, emotionally, and intellectually defensible position.*"

CHAPTER 6

"This Is It! Go for Smiles! Go for Christ!"

Derek was squeezed into the backseat with another fresh-man, his online Bible out on his lap. He was heading down to Virginia Beach to be a foot soldier for Jerry Kilgore, the Re-publican candidate for governor in 2005. The roads were clear, so it was not the traffic that was annoying the driver, junior Shant Boyajian. The former head of Patrick Henry's College Republi-cans, Shant was trying to pump up the freshmen: Timothy Kaine had caught up to Kilgore over the summer, and now polls showed them even. The team's efforts could make or break this race.

"I read that President Bush is coming to speak for Kilgore."

"Yes, well, that can be a sign that the campaign is in trouble," Shant pointed out. "And last time Bush came, Kilgore did not even want to be seen with him."

This did not compute with the freshmen. Not want to be seen with Bush? Who would not want to be seen with Bush?

"The Lord will provide," Derek said. "The Lord will provide."

Shant answered with a resigned "yes." Later, when he was out of the car where the others couldn't hear him, he seethed. "I wish they would stop with that crap: They're all like, 'God is on our side, God is on our side. We can do everything.' I mean, I know it's terrible, but I'm just trying to be more realistic. I mean, maybe I'm being cynical or something, but I don't want to lie."

At Patrick Henry, campaigns serve as a rite of passage, much like fraternity hazing or basic training. Every campaign gives you more hair on your chest and bragging rights, pushes you from tender young thing into impatient veteran. The kids start at home, working on races for school board or state legislatures, and eventually graduate to senate or presidential campaigns. By the time they get to Patrick Henry, they can compare histories in shorthand: "I did a bunch of lit drops in '04," or "I was on GOTV in Ohio." By junior year, the political junkies of PHC have picked up the habits of Washington insiders, including their irritability.

Shant sported the trademark of a Patrick Henry rebel: the trim goatee, a gentle nod to the demonic. He talked about Derek and the other freshmen the way one imagines George Bush's advisers talk about James Dobson and the other titans of the Christian right once the microphones are turned off: ("nuts" and "goofy," David Kuo, second-in-command of Bush's Office of Faith-Based and Community Initiatives, wrote in his tell-all book). It's not that Shant and Derek disagreed about candidates or policy positions or even matters of faith—they didn't. It's just that Shant had a checklist to get through and state party professionals to answer to, and only three days to get everything done, so he didn't have time for the happy-happy praise-the-Lord talk. "I don't have a problem manipulating them to get them to do what I need them to do for this campaign," Shant said. "Maybe, eventually, they'll learn something."

They arrived in the evening at a Comfort Inn, at the end of a strip mall. Inside, a cheerless forest-green-and-maroon two-room lobby had been transformed into an impromptu war room crowded with about two hundred high school and middle school kids from Generation Joshua, a group founded to involve home-schoolers in politics. For the next three days they would serve as the flunkies' flunkies, doing the bidding of their Patrick Henry elders. For the high schoolers, it was a civic-education field trip. For the Patrick Henry students it was a test run at leadership—the local party officials were actually counting on them to get out the vote. They divided the group into teams and handed out stacks of campaign literature and maps. Then they plotted out driving routes that would lead them to Republican houses where they would drop off flyers and remind people to vote. At 11 P.M., in this distant corner of Karl Rove's empire, no one showed any signs of flagging.

In a speech at the American Enterprise Institute after the 2000 election, Rove said that the president had lost the popular vote because fewer-than-expected "white, evangelical Protestants" had come to the polls. During the off-year in 2001, a handful of races did a test run of the "72-hour task force," an organized grassroots get-out-the-vote campaign. One of Rove's principal strategies for victory in 2004 was to combine these two election strategies. He mobilized evangelicals, and he put them to work in 72-hour task forces. On election day, four million more evangelicals voted than in 2000, a margin Rove often credited for Bush's victory.

From their inception, both Generation Joshua and Patrick Henry College served as satellites of this Republican get-out-the-vote operation. Gen J, as it's known, was launched officially in 2004, although it existed in other forms for several years before that. In 2001 Patrick Henry students participated in Rove's Virginia experiment. They worked on Mark Earley's race for governor. Earley lost, but the strategy worked in the lower-profile races.

In 2004 Gen J paid around $60,000 for hundreds of home-school kids to work on campaigns of mostly conservative Christian candidates, coordinating closely with the Republican party hierarchy. The group is run by Ned Ryun, a former presidential writer for Bush and son of former Kansas Representative Jim Ryun. Its offices are on the campus of Patrick Henry and their philosophies are identical: "to ignite a vision in young people to help America return to her Judeo-Christian foundations," as Gen J's mission statement reads. The Gen Jers are the evangelical version of child soldiers, armed with clipboards instead of guns.

Inside the hotel lobby, a group of ten year olds crowded onto the rose-colored velour couch to watch the Fox News update with the frozen faces most boys their age reserve for favorite cartoons. ("Next up: We'll talk about ethics violations in the White House.") Behind them an eight-year-old girl carried her baby sister on one hip and a bundle of precinct maps on another. Another girl who looked about four trudged by wearing an over-sized Bush/Cheney T-shirt and a way-too-huge backpack; she was yawning and slumping under the weight. "Aww, I guess she'll be a great campaigner when she's six," said her mother, nothing in her expression indicating a joke. Groups of boys who looked to be around fourteen or fifteen, the major contingent, sat around tables, drinking Pepsi and reminiscing about the good old days on the Bush campaign.

"These Kerry kids were saying Bush was bad because he violated the separation of church and state, and we were like, 'That's not in the Constitution,' and they just said, '*uhhh, uhhhm.*' And we said, 'You should read the Constitution. It's a pretty good document.'"

They chuckled and high-fived.

In 2004 Derek had been right down there with them, a Gen J kid working the Bush campaign in Ohio, having his mom drive him around and being told by some college kid what to do. This time he was on the other side, a team leader with his own group of high school students to manage. Right now Derek had to find his kids and get them to the van. He had to find a driver and then navigate. He had to motivate them to knock on strangers' doors and say the right thing. He had to appease their anxious parents.

He woke up on Sunday, Day One, and ate a healthy portion of the only available breakfast: French toast and corn muffins. It was time to take charge, but he wasn't feeling it.

"I mean, I've babysat before, but . . ."

"It's like a whole paradigm shift, from being told what to do to taking charge. I don't really feel older, but my responsibilities are a whole lot different. I've been given a position of authority, but it hasn't really sunk in yet. I still kinda feel like a kid."

The van ride was rocky at first. The maps were faded, and they didn't seem to track the streets perfectly. Everyone was wishing they had access to MapQuest. At some point Derek called his mom and she said, "I'm praying for you." Eventually they got through all the neighborhoods; Derek seemed greatly relieved at lunchtime. No one had gotten lost and everyone had food, and he could sit and just be one of the kids eating tacos and sucking on strawberry Blizzards.

When they got back to the hotel in the late afternoon, the other team leaders from Patrick Henry were buzzing around the war room. Kyle, Shant, and Amber, a blond, blue-eyed Republican press-secretary-in-the-making, seemed as if they had been born with clipboards in their hands. "Listen up," they said, and their tired team members sat up straight. Young as they were, they'd already participated in the making of history, helping usher in a right-wing revolution in American politics. Their stripes were their T-shirts, mementos from the campaigns they'd worked on: THUNE '04 and COBURN FOR OKLAHOMA and WOMEN FOR BUSH! Some had worked on successful races in 2004, when a critical mass of outspoken, ambitious Christian conservatives won seats in Congress: Jim DeMint and Bobby Jindal and John Thune and John Hostetler and Tom Coburn. Between them they'd worked rural, suburban, and urban precincts and had improvised their way through many a mishap, so they could tell a good operation from a shoddy one.

That afternoon after church the PHC students drove to church parking lots to put flyers in car windows. Derek was pleased to see the flyers. Earlier that week he'd seen Kilgore at a campaign rally. The candidate had given his standard stump speech, calling himself a "pro–gun owner, anti-tax, limited government, anti–illegal immigration, pro–public safety, trust-the-people conservative," and labeling Kaine a "typical liberal" who couldn't be trusted with the state's death-penalty laws.

But Derek felt something was missing. "He mentioned the culture of life briefly, but I wished he would talk about his pro-life stance more," he said. "Kilgore is very pro-life. Kaine is not whatsoever." Kaine had made his faith a central part of his campaign strategy. He had talked about growing up a devout Catholic, and how a mission trip changed his life. In a pro–death-penalty state, he rejected the practice because his faith demanded it. But Derek didn't take this into account. He called him "very very very liberal," and the church flyers echoed his thoughts: "LIBERAL TIM

KAINE: Supports abortion without restriction. Opposes a constitutional amendment banning gay marriage. Supports gay adoption. Believes the effort to place the motto 'In God We Trust' in schools is ridiculous."

Kyle, the professional in the bunch, found this piece of lit "crude." The quotes were old culture-war standbys and sounded made up. The tone was a little too vicious. The picture of Kaine made him look like an overstuffed turkey flapping his wings. It was so extreme, it could have just as easily come from the Kaine campaign. "There's a right and a wrong way to do church lit drops," he said. The operation was a sensitive one because churches were "nervous about the law." They didn't understand that a flyer comparing two candidates—no matter how unfairly—was perfectly legal.

The first stop went without a hitch. Derek and the others rushed out and placed the flyers under windshield wipers. At the second stop, they ran into trouble. One of the deacons saw them drive up and came out a side door. "We'd really rather you didn't do this on a Sunday. We're worshipping in there. We'd like a break from all this."

The kids apologized, removed all the flyers, and got back in the car. Kyle was a little annoyed. In a good operation, the campaign would have called the pastor or the assistant pastor to let them know they were coming "but the RNC must have called the secretary or something." Derek was more puzzled. It had never really occurred to him that a church would consider campaigning and worship to be at odds with each other; in his mind, they served the same purpose. Now he could see, "it's rather controversial."

On the morning of Day Two, the high school kids were giddy. There was a rumor going around that someone had been caught playing spin the bottle in the stairwell during the night. Alfred the Elephant, a blow-up mascot they were passing around, kept landing in the lap of a pretty fifteen-year-old girl in tight jeans, making everyone giggle. Ben Mills, a Patrick Henry junior, quieted them down for that day's pep talk. He read from Matthew 5, about the meek inheriting the earth, and the children of right-eousness. "You are the salt and light of the earth," he said. "These next couple of days will be tough, but what you do here will make all the difference in the world. You will be out there talking to people. Make sure they see Christ when they see you. Now, go out there for Kilgore, one hundred percent for Kilgore, and give it your all. "

"Go, Kilgore!" they yelled, and gathered their bags.

After a day in charge, Derek had cemented his role, and now his team was lost without him. "I need to talk to Derek. Where is he?" one fifteen-year-old boy asked, roaming the lobby. At that moment, Derek walked out of the elevator, in a flannel shirt and jeans, still with his gangly Jim Carrey walk, but in control. "Yes, I'm the team captain. I have the maps." Kyle and Amber and Shant had been up all night strategizing. Kyle, who looked like a pinup boy on a good day, was looking pale and ragged, with a three-day growth and flip-flops. Amber was sick, too sick to drive. The rental-car agreement stipulated that a driver must be at least twenty-one, and there was only one such person available: me. Amber handed over the keys.

Mothers of older kids have always told me that driving your kids around affords a unique opportunity for spying because they talk to their friends and forget that you're there. This piece of wisdom turned out to be true. Six hours of uncensored backseat talk (no radio, because you never know what might come on)

158

gave me a window into the mind of the homeschool child. Here is the secret file: They love George Bush so much, they sometimes dream about him. They also love *The Princess Bride* and *The Incredibles,* a Pixar movie about a race of domesticated freaks trying to pass as normal who save the planet. On public schools: "Don't get me started. They teach you that kids are descended from monkeys and a godless view of history. No wonder they live such a degraded lifestyle. That's really not something I want to be exposed to right now." On extracurricular activities: "I socialize with the heathens on my swim team." On college: "I want to go to Cornell. Have you heard of it?"

"Yeah," answered one boy. "I heard football players get really drunk and they almost, like, rape the girls."

During the long stretches of driving, they got a little naughty. One girl suggested ripping down some Kaine signs that were stuck near a highway overpass. ("Let's not and say we did.") They gossiped, but the news was slightly out of date: Britney is "pretty much a slut" and "Jennifer doesn't want a baby." And "that girl with Tom Cruise, she's pregnant." When we got to McDonald's, they perked up because they got to watch CNN. (Gen-J rules allow Fox News only.) One time I looked in the rearview mirror and was shocked to see a girl leaning her head against the boy seated next to her. What should I do? Pry them apart? Tell their moms? And then I put the clues together: They were brother and sister, and four of the others were siblings, too. When the girl lifted her head, she asked, "Is playing spin the bottle, like, illegal?"

When we got to a designated neighborhood, they launched with Von Trapp efficiency. Someone would open the van door, and then Derek or another team leader in the car yelled, "This is it! Go for smiles! Go for Christ!" and the blitz was on. They ran out—yes, ran—to their assigned houses. From a distance, the scene must have looked like a heist. We did upscale gated communities and trailer parks, houses with flags and neat rows of pansies, and others with laundry bags full of rusted tools on rotting wood stairs.

At one door, a girl who looked about twenty answered the door in cutoffs and a tight T-shirt; Derek handed her the flyer and ran away, for which he was much teased. ("You meet a pretty girl and you run!") One of the Gen Jers emitted an *All About Eve* vibe; he stalked Derek, reading the maps for him and pestering him about constitutional-law camp. He bragged about the briefs he'd already written and the debates he'd already won. He talked constantly on his cell phone. (Derek didn't have one.) But Derek wasn't bothered. "It's such wonderful campaign weather," he said. "The Lord has really blessed us."

It was the kind of fall day that can leave you light-headed—warm enough for short sleeves, a bright sun floodlighting the red and gold trees. At three we were on a suburban street, and the neighborhood kids were starting to come home from school. A couple of guys shot hoops outside the garage in Bermuda shorts and high tops; two more popped wheelies off the curb, and a skateboarder rode around the cul de sac, tugging at his Billy Idol shirt. This was what most of America's teenagers would do on this gift of a fall day—or wish to do—but Derek and the others didn't notice. They had three more precincts to cover before sundown.

By nightfall Derek was exhausted, but he worked himself up for one more round of phone banking. He and five other Patrick Henry kids were driven to a site set up by the Republican party, a tiny room with phones on three long tables. They were given a list of likely voters to call and access to a supply of Sun Chips, Snickers, Coke, and Mountain Dew.

"Hello? My name is Derek Archer and I'm a volunteer with the Republican party of Virginia here to remind you to vote tomorrow for Jerry Kilgore for governor." He talked in the slow, even tones of someone used to talking to the elderly. He was reading from a script, but he liked to add a personal touch.

"Hello? Mrs. Letzelder?"

Someone by the snack table just behind him sniggered.

"Letzelder?"

He was a tall kid with a mop of black hair and chip crumbs by his lip. He was wearing a T-shirt that said: I'M NOT UNMOTIVATED, I'M JUST LAZY. He had the sly expression of your average teenager, but Derek looked at him as if he was a talking quetzal, an exotic bird that had escaped from the jungle.

"We're with Generation Joshua," explained Derek. "We like to mobilize young people to help elect candidates who share our conservative Christian values."

"Oh, I'm pretty much too lazy," said the quetzal, true to his T-shirt. "I just like to chill with my friends." He stretched and checked his watch. "Four more hours and I'm done."

Apparently, he'd been assigned to make campaign calls as part of a school project. He explained this to Derek and then launched into a story about how last night he and some friends had gone to Newport News and decided to walk on top of some cars parked down by the beach. "And then some lady hit us. *Wham.* On purpose!"

"Praise the Lord! Were you okay?"

This got no response, so Derek tried again.

"You mean they hit you on purpose? That's insane. Why would someone actually intend to hit you with a car?"

"I don't know. But it was fun, man."

Derek made it a point to connect with everyone: bus drivers and lunch ladies and clerks at the Subway. But he had no way of connecting with a kid his age who was drifting through life and was psyched about it. He turned back to his phone and his script. "Hello, ma'am? My name is Derek Archer and I'm a volunteer with . . ."

In the evening, he tried his own version of letting off steam. He was about to go up to bed when he spotted a group of the younger kids having a "crab race"—on all fours, but belly up. It looked like an old person's idea of young people having fun.

At about 10 P.M., I left the campaign team in the lobby, where they were hashing out the next day's plan, and retreated to my room. Flipping through channels, I came across *Laguna Beach,* the MTV reality show about rich teens in the "real Orange County." I'd never seen the show, but I'd read about it. Critics loved it for perfectly rendering routine teenage magic—the poignant drama of missed cues, longing, euphoria and desire. Nothing much happens. Stephen comes back from college, LC still likes him, he likes Kristin. That night was the very last episode of the season; LC and her friends were sitting in a kitchen eating popcorn and planning a good-bye party. Their mundane interactions—putting their feet up on the table, digging for kernels—did not seem familiar to me. I must have been trapped in that van a long time because I was finding this fascinating—and somewhat illicit.

DIETER: You know what my dream of the night would be?

LC: (*Throws popcorn to Jen*) What?

DIETER: I want everyone here and we'll get like a bunch of cool food and like . . .

They spent a long time debating whether Jessica seriously kissed Jason, whether the party should be dressy or just "summer dressy," and whether Kristin needed new shoes ("I always need new shoes"). Derek might find it intensely pointless, and on some days I might agree. But that night, Reader, I was riveted, and did not even take off my own shoes until after the very last blood-orange sunset.

On election day, it was Derek's turn to give the troops a pep talk. He was wearing a flannel shirt and khakis, and before he talked he jumped up and down like a pogo stick to shake out his excess energy. He began with a parable from Luke that Jesus told to a restless crowd. A king wants to test the loyalty of his subjects by asking them to invest his money. Those who fail to invest he punishes. The one who invests wisely he rewards with rule over ten cities.

The day before, the kids had knocked on 5,337 doors and made 1,400 phone calls. "What we're doing here is grassroots work, knocking on doors and the like, and it might not seem significant, and it might seem boring. But God wants you to be trustworthy, to be faithful in the small things. If you're not faithful in the small things, God won't trust you with the big things. If you're not faithful in the small things, when it comes time to say, 'Hey, I want to be president of the U.S., God will not give you those things.'"

"So let's knock on those doors and make those calls, okay? Now let's pray . . ."

Because the kids didn't listen to the radio, they didn't know anything about the polls, and missing a few hours of sleep had made them light-headed. They stood by the side of the main road holding campaign signs, singing, doing the wave, yelling, "Vote Jerry Kilgore! Have a Blessed Day!" and hoping the truckers honked.

In the afternoon, they did one last stretch of calling: "Only a few hours left," Derek said. "Give it all you got." By 6:30 the lady in charge told them to quit because the polls were about to close. "I'm almost done with this page, ma'am. May I finish it up?" Derek went for about fifteen more minutes. "Now we go to the victory party. And it will be a victory party, God willing."

Derek drove the hour to Richmond in Ben Mills's old Dodge; fortunately the radio was broken, so they couldn't be tempted to listen to exit polls. As they climbed the stairs to the main hall, the kids trailed him like a pack of puppies.

"I hope we win," one boy said.

"Absolutely," Derek answered.

"Amen."

"If God wills it."

"It's all up to Him."

Upstairs the trappings of a Republican frat-style victory party had been laid out: orange balloons, beer, wine, martinis, no food. People were drinking but they were doing it grimly, huddled in corners. Many were sitting down and talking on cell phones. One little kid was already asleep under a Kilgore sign. The Gen J kids didn't notice the subdued atmosphere. They charged in from a side door, yelling, "Kil-*gore*! Kil-*gore*!"

Derek did not join in, but he didn't stay outside with Kyle and Shant, either. He stayed at the edge of the group chatting with some old Gen J friends. I asked him about the race but he didn't want to talk. "Do you mind asking me when it's more concrete?"

At 10 P.M. Fox called the race; with 88 percent of the vote counted, Kilgore had lost, 46 to 51.6 percent.

"Yes, ma'am."

"We lost, ma'am."

On the three huge TV screens at the front of the room, the Fox analysts had launched a postmortem designed to break Derek's heart. They were saying that the race was the most closely watched of the election season, that it meant "the Bush magic is over," and that "Bush is at the lowest point of his presidency." They were already predicting that "the Republicans can see their own doom," and they would probably lose control of Congress in 2006. They were saying that Bush's favored strategy of "mobilizing conservative voters by dividing the electorate on hot-button cultural issues failed." They were saying that Kaine proved a "Democrat can talk about his faith and make an enormous difference," and that in the future other Democrats could "win back the faith vote." They were saying that Derek's formula for understanding the world was no longer making sense.

But Derek was not listening. He had been swept away on one of those oceans of prayer that sometimes overtake Christians in hours of desperation, confusion, and need. They stood close, in circles of twenty or more, eyes closed and bodies pressed against bodies, nobody worried or noticing. They held each other up as if they were in a mosh pit. There was no leader or obvious direction, but the words flowed smoothly, coming from here, now from over there, like waves of light:

"Dear Lord. Please help us to understand. We campaigned with all of our hearts for Kilgore. Please help us to get over this."

"Lord, please help us to learn from this, to understand."

"Lord, regardless of who wins, You are in control."

"Yes, Lord, it's not about Democrat or Republican. We are working for You. Whoever You put in office, that's in Your control."

"Lord, You have Your reasons. I just pray You help us accept that."

Later, much later, when he had opened his eyes again, Derek began to work through it. "I don't think I approached this race with quite the same sincerity as I did last year. Last year I took it more seriously. I prayed a lot more.

"If I look at it through my eyes, I say, 'Oh no, oh dear.' But God has His own plan," he said, and quoted an eighteenth-century Lutheran hymn:

> Blind unbelief is sure to err
> And scan His work in vain;
> God is His own Interpreter,
> And He will make it plain.

Outside the ballroom, Kyle had already moved on and was outlining a paper on Aristotle. Shant was pacing, wishing he went to a different school so that he could drink. Derek stayed inside with the kids; one of them had turned sixteen that day, and he wanted them all to sing "Happy Birthday." He didn't tell them yet that a wicked storm had just broken outside and they didn't have any umbrellas.

CHAPTER 7

The Den of Sin

Farahn walked into the cafeteria with bits of mud and grass on her pointy flats. Her eyes were nearly as red as her rhinestone earrings, and her legendary eyeliner was starting to smudge. She'd been tramping around the soggy shores of Lake Bob behind the dorms, an activity favored by Gothard girls for its romantic tableau possibilities, and by chaste couples wishing to remain always in view. Farahn had been in search of a soft, dry spot to dig a grave. For her fish.

"Your *fish?*" asked an incredulous sophomore who barely knew her.

"Yes," Farahn said. "His name was Winston. Winston Spencer." Winston was a midnight blue betta, and Farahn swore that he could dance if you turned on the right music. When she came home from school, she would talk to him, and he seemed to be listening. Often, she said to the sophomore, she'd thought he might be her only true friend. She wasn't joking. She continued earnestly with the story. When she woke up that morning and found him floating, she said a prayer. Then she wrote it down and put Winston and the prayer inside a shoebox and buried it on the shores of Lake Bob. Farahn was crying again. Something was not right.

I was about to go talk to her when a few students came over to talk to me.

"I heard rumors about it last night," said one.

So this was not about the fish.

Someone was getting expelled. No, five people were getting expelled, or maybe three. A couple of them were Farahn's friends. Rumor was that the boys had been caught drinking, smoking, abusing prescription painkillers, and possibly cheating on exams. No, wait, they hadn't been caught. They had been turned in by one of their roommates. He had written a long letter to the dean of students. Now everyone who knew the students was "shaken" and "scared" and "paranoid" and afraid their friends weren't really their friends. Already a couple had been stopped by the local police for loitering; they were watching a movie in the car because they were afraid if they watched on campus, someone might turn them in.

"Who wrote the letter?" I asked.

"Nathan Poe."

"Nathan Poe?"

"I know," one student told me. "It kills me. I can't figure it out."

Since the college had passed the pro-snitching policy that year, I'd been waiting for this moment. The lure of glory was just too great. But Nathan Poe was not the name I had expected. There were plenty of Patrick Henry students with NARC practically tattooed on their foreheads—kids who spent their evenings scanning other students' playlists for songs with inappropriate lyrics, or who volunteered to help the tech department come up with new and efficient ways to monitor who'd been looking at porn. But Nathan Poe was not like that. He was a regular kid. He wore Dickies urban-cowboy shirts to class under a corduroy jacket and occasionally smoked clove cigarettes. On his twenty-first birthday, he'd had his father fly in from San Diego so that he could drink beer in the open. (College rules allowed drinking in the presence of parents.) He complained constantly about how the school rules were juvenile and imprudent, and the punishments were erratic and unfair. When CNN came to campus to film a segment about Patrick Henry, administrators put Nathan forward as the new enlightened face of evangelical youth: "We can't just be pigheaded Christians, fundamentalist Christians who just say, 'Well, this is what it is, this is what the Bible says. And I'm sticking to that,'" he'd told Judy Woodruff.

In the 2004–2005 academic year, Nathan had been an honorary member of the "den of sin." A group of boys had worked the roommate-selection process to commandeer one wing of a dorm. With the door to the main hallway closed, it served as a kind of safe house. They would bring in six-packs and store them under the bed, or stash packs of cigarettes in someone's guitar case. The hallway looked like any nineteen-year-old hipster's room: a *Pulp Fiction* poster showed Uma Thurman with generous cleavage holding a cigarette; ticket stubs from *Life Aquatic* and a Nada Surf concert were taped on the wall, along with handwritten poetry and the current month's schedule for the Black Cat, a nightclub in D.C. On one day I visited, an ironing board was piled high with empty Krispy Kreme boxes.

The wing had served the same purpose as an embassy in a foreign country. If someone came back too drunk to risk running into an RA, he could dry out in one of the rooms. If someone found himself wondering, even once, whether any guy he knew had ever been attracted to another man, he could ask that question there. The wing recognized "pants off" days, and Farahn had warned them that everyone thought they were gay, but the thrill was only in the subversion. In *Godfather* fashion, they had an oath: Anyone who got caught snitched only on himself. LOOSE LIPS SINK SHIPS read a poster hanging near one of the doors.

Nathan had spent many late nights in that wing, and he seemed like one of them. He would come in looking for a place to sit, wanting to ask endless questions and argue about whatever movie, book, or fussy abstraction had captured his fancy that day. Sometimes he would come in complaining about an outrage committed by the Patrick Henry administration. And sometimes he didn't turn down a smoke or a beer. If any of the boys ever suspected he'd snitch, they showed it only by feeling the need to remind him several times of the pact: "Nathan, don't get that guilty look. If you need to tell, tell on yourself. Nathan, swear before God. If your ass goes down, only *your* ass goes down."

The den of sin had disbanded at the end of that year, but one year later, Nathan's letter had given the administration the clues to hunt down its former denizens one by one. One of the guys sat him down on the stoop and asked him, "Why did you write that letter?" Nathan just put his hands over his face and started to cry.

"I still want to give him the benefit of the doubt, I really do," his friend told me. "I mean, it's the system that pits people against each other like this, right?"

A few days earlier, Chris Tuggle, a junior who was Nathan Poe's roommate, had gotten a call from Dean Wilson. "Hey, I heard some things. I'd like you to stop by my office." Chris didn't think much of it; he was an RA, and RAs frequently got called into Wilson's office for one thing or another. When he got there, Wilson laid it out: "Hey, I heard you've been smoking and drinking. Is that true?" Chris took a few seconds to assess the situation before answering. Chris thought Wilson seemed casual, not accusing. It sounded as if he'd heard a rumor but didn't have any hard evidence. In fact, Chris was a regular smoker and went out drinking often, although not nearly as often as he had the previous year when he could take cover in the den of sin. But if he told Wilson that, he'd be risking too much: He was an RA, a star on the debate team, and an excellent student with political ambitions. In that CNN segment, Chris was featured as the other cool kid, a future senator who could charm Woodruff. Besides, Chris was interested in intelligence work, and when the CIA came to campus to do background checks, Wilson was known to speak his mind about a prospect's "character."

"No, sir," he said. "It's not." And he left.

Wilson knew Chris and his family well. If Chris had lied, Wilson would be quite disappointed in him, especially because Chris was an RA charged with enforcing the rules. Wilson set his twin goals of figuring out whether Nathan's accusations were true, and if they were, helping Chris "regain the credibility he'd lost by lying." He went about the fact-finding like a homicide detective building a case. He already had the letter from Nathan, although he hadn't mentioned it to Chris. Instead he tracked down the other four suspects, one by one, and leaned on them to tell the truth. Randy Wanis got the call just before dinner on an already terrible evening. He had gone to pick up an uncle who worked at the Defense Language Institute to bring him to Patrick Henry for a lecture on "The Mind of a Jihadist." When he got the call on his cell phone, they were pulled over by the side of the road with a flat tire and a spare that didn't fit.

Randy also had a lot to lose: He, too, was an RA with a rare profile the school valued: He came from an Egyptian family; he had transferred to Patrick Henry because of the security intelligence program and was planning to go to the Middle East that summer to study Arabic. A smart, swarthy, patriotic evangelical who speaks Arabic would be a prize for the CIA. But Wilson told Randy about Nathan's letter, so he had no choice but to tell the truth, at least about himself.

"Do you know if Chris Tuggle was involved in any of these activities?" Wilson followed up.

"I have no idea what Chris was doing," Randy said.

Wilson tracked down the other three guys and leaned on them, too. All of them said the same thing: "Chris? I've never seen Chris smoke or drink."

He told them all to report to his office the following evening, which was the eve of election day. Chris and two of the other guys spent the day working the polls in Loudon County for the Virginia governor's race; by then they'd all talked and shared what they knew about Nathan's letter, so they waited "that whole long day for hell to unleash its fury," said Chris. Randy tried to study, "my mind circling at a hundred miles an hour."

At around nine that night, Chris and Randy made their way to

Wilson's office, on the first floor of Red Hill dorm. Upstairs they could hear some boys playing Halo, but no one else was around. They stood on one side of the office, away from Nathan. Nathan's eyes were red; the other three boys were stone-faced.

One by one they confessed. I drank on two different occasions, but I never smoked; I don't like the taste of tobacco. I just drank some pumpkin punch at a Halloween party at an alum's house, but those painkillers were actually prescription. I smoked on a couple of occasions and drank a Newcastle Brown Ale at a bar. Cheating on exams turned out to be a false rumor; no one brought it up. They all confessed to drinking with each other, but no one mentioned Chris. By normal college standards, they were describing a boring Wednesday night at Sigma Chi, but from the atmosphere in the room you'd have thought their fingerprints had just been discovered on the murder weapon.

Nathan had written that he'd seen them come back to their rooms obviously drunk, and that he'd smelled smoke on Chris's clothes on several occasions. He accused Chris and Randy of rigging a system to cheat on chapel cards so they wouldn't have to go every morning and turned himself in for helping them do it. By signing the student honor code, "you have pledged to obey the provisions," he'd written. "I love you guys, and I'm praying for you."

The boys waited for Chris to make his decision. Nathan was crying—he cried through the whole meeting. Now another one of the boys was crying, too. A third looked as if he wanted to kill Nathan.

Chris said nothing.

And then he said: "I did do it. And I'm sorry I lied."

In a cop show, this would be the moment the lead detective leans against the wall, spent, his triumph muted by encountering, once again, the endless supply of evil. "I think you all owe Poe a huge apology for putting him in this position," said Wilson. Chris and Randy muttered their apologies. One boy hugged Poe and later hated himself for it. Another said, "You know, Poe, I may want to forgive you later, but right now I want to punch you in the face."

Wilson released them each with a hug and a prayer. "I love you," he said, and sent them off. Chris stayed on to talk to Wilson: "I want to apologize for breaking my word. But I feel I was pushed into it. If you had sent Poe to talk to me the first time around, I would have been able to confront my accuser, and then it all would have come out. I realize that's no excuse for lying, but the way it came out was pretty negative."

Chris recalls Wilson gave him a "hurt father, you broke my heart" look and sent him away.

The meeting's conclusion did not bring the expected catharsis. Instead the atmosphere began to feel even smaller and more oppressive. Roommates were afraid to talk in front of each other. Friends became suspicious of friends. The campus felt like a Chinese village at the height of the Cultural Revolution or a theocracy in its dying days. A girl talked about her romantic exploits on a debate trip, and a boy made a joke about them; a fellow debater reported the boy for sexual harassment. Wilson, ever suspicious, took the girl's side, and Farris threatened to take away the boy's debate scholarship.

Two best friends argued over whether one would support the other as president of the College Republicans. After their argument, one turned in the other for having gone out drinking with some young Republican friends in D.C. Farris was upset, but not with the snitcher. At a meeting in his office, he called the drinker a "political hack."

"When I ran for lieutenant governor, I had twenty volunteers who would do anything for me because I didn't have alcohol at the hospitality suite and Ollie North had alcohol," Farris told him. "Never drink. It hurts you politically."

Two clearly opposed sides began to emerge on campus. On one were Dean Wilson and Farris. Wilson was upset with the boys for not being "man enough" to tell him the truth. He was deeply sad that they were "undermining their personal integrity" by breaking rules they had agreed to enforce. When I visited him in his office one afternoon, he shook his head at their being "Addicted! Addicted to that behavior! I did not coerce them. They chose to lie. I was arguing in here how much I love them. It's just a shock, a shock!"

But ultimately he did not blame the boys. During the crisis, Wilson had had a "lightbulb moment," when he could see clearly who was maneuvering in the shadows. "I came here pretty naïve, thinking everyone was on board with Mike's mission," he told me. "But I'm slowly figuring out the game they're playing,"

"They" were the handful of charismatic professors who were most popular with the students—among them Bob Stacey and Erik Root. In Wilson's view, the students had arrived at school from the bosom of home, clean and gossamer-white. Their parents had sent them to Patrick Henry because they expected the professors to act as their substitutes and to continue the education they had begun. But instead the professors had begun to "subvert the parents" by encouraging the students to rebel against their upbringing, Wilson surmised.

"They are teaching them that if you don't challenge the rules, you'll never be a culture-changer," he said about the professors. "They are setting up a battle between stupid moral people and smart immoral people."

He gave me an example I might relate to: "If you hired me to babysit your kids, you wouldn't want me to tear down what you believe. If you say, 'Don't let my baby eat bananas' and then I immediately run to cut up bananas as soon as Mama's out of the house, well, then, you'd find another babysitter."

"Not that I'm saying these kids are babies," he quickly added.

By the end of our meeting, Wilson was quite upset. He resented having been turned into the "whipping boy" in this situation—Billy Sunday on a campus of intellectual snobs. He had spent the hour with me convincing himself that he had done the right thing: "You and I know that teenage boys drink. But the reason I treat it as different is because I see these kids as different. To those who much has been given, much shall be required. We have a great responsibility teaching the best and the brightest, and we can't play games."

He wanted to convey to me that he was a loyal soldier on a campus crawling with Judases. "I love Mike," he said, before he gave me a hug.

In the meantime, the professors had caught on that they were being turned into the villains in this tale. More than anyone else, Stacey was responsible for stitching together a curriculum that met the impossible twin demands of Farris's mission: intellectual rigor and a sound Biblical worldview. Now Stacey was fast losing his patience. "They say, 'I want you to shape the culture and lead the nation,' but then they say, 'Shut up and do what I tell you,'" he said. "What the college pushes away with one hand, it embraces with the other."

The rules instructed students to report infractions by faculty as well as fellow students, and the faculty feared one of them would be next. They worried something they said in class or during office hours might jeopardize their jobs. They also worried that they were getting paranoid, afraid of being treated like nineteen-year-olds.

But then it happened: After class, Erik Root, who taught political philosophy, joked with two of his students that they could get around the rule prohibiting couples from kissing on campus by breaking up. Another student overheard the joke and told Wilson, who sent an e-mail saying he wanted to see Root. Root was highly irritated: "We should be able to say the word 'sex' in the classroom without everything falling apart," he said.

The professors spent a lot of time huddled in Root's glass office with the shutters down, talking about academic freedom. After class they escaped to a cigar bar for more of the same. They considered skipping the staff Christmas party but changed their minds. The occasion was universally described as "awkward" and "grim." Farris showed up, and no one would talk to him except Jennifer Gruenke, the biology professor. He cornered her and pleaded, "I don't understand why they're so mad at me." The faculty watched the conversation from behind a table of cookies.

Just before winter break, the administration handed down punishments in the Nathan Poe affair. All five boys were suspended for a day. The three RAs lost their positions and had to return their salaries. They also lost their campus-security jobs. The student senate, which, absurdly, is made up of one-third of the student body, moved quickly to impeach the boys, all of whom were senators. The prevailing view was that they had "failed to be models for Christ." In their defense, one senator stood up and read Jesus' famous injunction: "He that is without sin among you, let him cast the first stone." Shaken by the whole incident, Nathan declined to testify. The vote was delayed until the following semester.

In a special session Farris addressed the student senate and clarified the mission of God's Harvard: "We will not go the way of other great colleges who have lost their way spiritually. By rejecting God, all of their foundations will eventually crumble." One student senator asked if he was not being too "legalistic," the insiders' polite code word for fundamentalist. "Find me a college someplace that has kept its spiritual moorings and not been somewhat legalistic," he answered.

Wilson conveyed Farris's request that Chris and Randy make a public apology. Randy refused. He acknowledged that he had signed the honor code and vowed to enforce it as an RA, but he also wanted to be true to himself. "Some of my best times here were when I'd been out drinking three cans of Foster's and we got to talking about God," he said. Chris, however, more mindful of his reputation, agreed to the apology.

The following Wednesday, chapel began in the usual way—a few announcements, some singing. Then Dean Wilson came up to the podium looking chagrined. "Chris would like to bring up something that's been laying on his heart," he said. The freshmen crowded the front row as usual, and they had no idea what was coming. Years later, they might remember this moment as an object lesson in political damage control, a model of the Washington apology. Chris structured his speech as a testimony, moving from pride to fall to recovery. He was brilliant at accepting blame and then deflecting it completely. A close listener could have parsed the speech as an act of prostration before the school with a middle finger raised behind the back.

"When I was fourteen was the first time I got drunk. Initially, it was out of an adolescent desire for acceptance. But then you quickly learn to depend upon it. If you're stressed out, you smoke; if you're depressed, you drink. . . . I hope I can be an example to all of you—a reverse example."

Chris went on to describe how he'd continued to live a "double life" in college; "double lives are easy, double lives are fun." And then he told how he had lied to Wilson: "You can't imagine the self-loathing."

Then came the "powerful and good awakening." And finally the twist: "If you are breaking the rules, stop, but don't use that as a measure of your righteousness. Whether or not you can stand blameless before the Lord, I would ask you to examine your own lives. You can judge me, it's okay. But now put yourselves in the judgment seat and turn those same eyes back on yourself and say, Am I blameless before the Lord?"

I saw the speech in person and then later watched it on video. (The chapel had been filmed by a documentary crew.) Close up, in a suit at the podium, his tone contrite but never broken, Chris came across as a master in action, a young Bill Clinton adept at packaging pain. A few days later, the boys celebrated Chris's twenty-first birthday at a friend's house off campus, and there was plenty of Foster's at hand.

Patrick Henry or no Patrick Henry, Chris would have a future in politics.

For a while, Nathan Poe, the snitch, stuck to the elevated platform at the fringes of the cafeteria, eating alone and hiding behind the newspaper. At the best of times he wore a kind of hangdog expression that was now punctuated by bloodshot eyes. "It was pretty bad," he said. "I felt awful, they felt awful." When, in his initial meeting with Wilson, Chris had blithely denied the accusations, Nathan had snapped, thinking to himself, "Am I going crazy? Could I have made this all up for some weird psychological reason?" He thought he was committing a brave, selfless act, and he really didn't think Chris would lie.

He was hopeful that a couple of his ex-friends would eventually forgive him. That's the way it was supposed to work: Hold a Christian brother accountable and he should thank you. But that's not what happened. For two weeks he'd had to sleep in a different bed every night because he'd heard one of his "friends" wanted to pummel him, and he was afraid. One of the guys put him on a mailing list for the Victoria's Secret catalog. Everyone started quoting the Al Pacino character's speech from *Scent of a Woman,* where he defends his college friend for not being a snitch. And the neologism "to Poe," meaning to rat, came into common usage on campus. Nathan's friends no longer talked to him. The conservative types on campus didn't really trust him, either. "I'm not one of them," he said. He wasn't one of anyone's. Or at least anyone's on campus.

Lately, Nathan had been spending a lot of time at the Catholic church down the road, the same one where kids sometimes went to make out. He'd befriended a priest there who'd taken him to Bible studies. He wasn't the first to drift that way; after a year or two of Socratic questioning by Bob Stacey, certain students would drift toward Anglicanism for its liturgy and tradition. Nathan was going one step over the line. He was studying the canonization of Scripture—a heretical notion to evangelicals, who balk at any cleric's telling them how to read their Bible.

In his first meeting with Wilson, Nathan told him he'd done it because he'd begun studying Catholicism over the summer and had become convinced of the importance of authority. He still considered the rules juvenile and imprudent, but he didn't think they were too harmful, either, so he had decided he would submit and follow them. "If I am going to faithfully live out my Catholicism, then I have to recognize the authority in my own life," he'd told Wilson, who had always considered Nathan one of the rebels.

If Nathan kept flirting with Catholicism, he would have to leave Patrick Henry. Catholics and evangelicals have a long history of animosity, and Patrick Henry continues that tradition. The school's statement of faith emphasized that the Bible is the "only infallible and sufficient authority for faith and Christian living." Catholics would understand that as a rebuke to their tradition of drawing on other authorities, such as the pope and early church fathers. Nathan was prepared to take a year off if he needed to, and he had a Catholic friend in town he could stay with if he got kicked out before the end of the year. Nathan had talked to Farris about this, and Farris was heartbroken. Farris tried his best to win Nathan back, taking him to lunch and calling him whenever an appropriate Bible verse popped into his head. But Nathan lived according to his own rigid understanding of intellectual integrity, so it was difficult to change his mind. For Christmas break, he had convinced his family to go to Rome instead of Paris, and he was looking forward to midnight mass with the pope.

Several times during the rest of the year, I asked Nathan why he'd turned in his friends and set this disaster in motion. He always gave me the same dry, inscrutable, legalistic answer—the kind of answer you'd expect from a fresh, earnest law-school graduate with a strong sense of duty but no common sense or human experience. "I was obligated. I may not agree with the rules, but I was obligated."

CHAPTER 8

From Humanzee to Liger:
A Brief History of Evolution

In 1926, a year after John Scopes was found guilty of teaching that "man had descended from a lower order of animal," Soviet researcher Ilya Ivanov set out to prove the jury wrong. He traveled the world with vials of human sperm looking for a recipient with suitable characteristics, in short, "a hairy quadruped, furnished with a tail and pointed ears," as Darwin once described man's closest living ancestors. In the tabloids and other press that followed Ivanov around the world, the anticipated offspring was known by the name "humanzee."

Despite many attempts, the offspring never materialized. Ivanov ended his career in disrepute, exiled to a labor camp in Alma-Ata. Eighty years later, a sizable segment of the American population still hasn't warmed to their hairy ancestor. In fact, a group of American scientists has taken Ivanov's idea and thrown it back in his face, showing off what could be called the humanzee's revenge.

One morning, Patrick Henry biology teacher Jennifer Gruenke unveiled a photo of the strange hybrid beast in a classroom in the basement of Red Hill. The class was filled mostly with freshmen who had waited eagerly all semester for this segment on creationism and evolution to begin. Gruenke displayed an impressive feline, too big even for a big cat. He boasted the enormous loping belly of the lion, but his mane was sparse. His fur was striped like a tiger's, but only faintly. He looked noble but estranged from the animal kingdom, more a product of some Hollywood animation studio than of nature's jungle. And the students responded to him the same way Lucy does to Aslan, with a mixture of awe and childish delight: "It's a liger! It's a liger! It's a liger!" yelled Derek Archer, who was sitting in the front row.

The liger was followed by a parade of hybrid animals one might expect to find only in Narnia, or Dr. Seuss, or in the annals of petting-zoo horrors: the geep, a sorry-looking creature from Botswana whose woolly fur stops abruptly above scalded-looking legs. A wolphin, an overstuffed sea mammal with a cantilevered head, the daughter of a bottlenose dolphin and a false killer whale who "met on the job at the Whaler's Cove Show," as the promotion for Sea Life Park in Hawaii explains. The tigon, a small housecat-looking creature once presented as a gift to Queen Victoria by an Indian princess. And finally, the ever-familiar broccoflower, available from your local Whole Foods.

What the spotted owl is to environmentalists, the liger is to an obscure collection of creationist scientists known as baraminologists. Unlike Ivanov, baraminologists do not travel the world foisting reluctant mates on each other; they merely rejoice whenever a blessed event occurs. The word "baramin" is itself a mutt, coined in the 1940s from the Hebrew *bara* (created) and *min* (kind). Gruenke's understanding of the natural world began with Genesis, which she accepted as a literal recording of history. Although she'd probably rather you didn't ask, if you did, she would say the earth was created in six twenty-four-hour days and is just about six thousand years old, the amount of time disdainful geologists say it takes to create one inch of limestone.

Most baraminologists consider themselves a subset of "young earth" creationists, but a more accurate name might be "young life." By their reading of Genesis, God created different types of organisms instantly and independently (winged birds, great creatures of the sea, every creeping thing that creepeth upon the earth). Each baramin represents one of these kinds and all its descendants. Microevolution can happen within the baramins and can lead to different species; horses, zebras, and donkeys all belong to the same baramin, as do whales and dolphins, and goats and sheep. But there is no evolution across the boundaries. Unlike in traditional evolutionary biology, birds and reptiles could not share the same ancestors. Over the last few years, baraminologists have begun the task of reclassifying millions of species under these new headings and finding the boundaries between the groups.

Recently one of the baraminologists devised an algorithm that measures a species' characteristics and helps place it in the correct baramin. But the simplified method, accessible to a freshman biology class, is the one Ivanov tried: Can it mate with other creatures in their baramin and produce live offspring? Hence the excitement surrounding the liger.

"Some students are impressed when they hear answers to destroy evolutionists, but that's not the purpose of this course," Gruenke told the class. "It doesn't do any good to attack if you don't have your own system. What I see as my role as a Christian biologist is to build up something positive."

"Dr. Gruenke?" Derek asked. "Can you go over the definition of 'transposons' real quick?"

A secular biologist would see the baraminologists' chore as akin to wrecking a large, carefully constructed house only to rebuild it according to your own peculiar specifications. Likely he would approach the project with a large degree of suspicion and dread.

But this view misses much of the theory's enduring appeal. Gruenke and her colleagues behave like scientific pioneers who have stumbled upon an unexpected discovery. A secular biologist is forced to carve out a tiny niche to study. But the baraminologists are more in the position of the young Darwin in the Galapagos. Before them lie vast swaths of virgin territory waiting to be mapped. Like kids with new crayons, they draw and redraw the boundaries of the animal kingdom, sharing the results in e-mails and annual meetings. With so much exciting work to be done, who has time to bicker with evolutionists?

Since the national humiliation of the Scopes trial, creationism has gone through its own dramatic evolution. Rare is the creationist these days who just ticks off verses from the Bible when asked about the origin of life. Instead, they point to scientific "proofs" that, say, dinosaurs and men lived at the same time, all corroborated by one of the handful of scientific creationism institutes that have arisen over the past fifty years to support this research.

Scientists have always been confounded by the enduring popularity of creationism in the United States. Polls show, for example, that 80 percent of Americans believe that "God created the universe." Perhaps even more puzzling is its hold on a growing number of credentialed scientists. The scientific advances of this century seem to have had no effect on the popularity of scientific creationism; in fact, quite the opposite. The birth of the modern scientific creationism movement dates to about the time of Sputnik, the first artificial satellite launched into space.

The more scientific orthodoxy hardens, the more the subculture of educated creationists seems to thrive. Around the time of the Scopes trial, creationists could not point to any credentialed biologist as their ally. Now there are hundreds of creationist scientists with degrees from respectable universities, according to Ronald Numbers, in his definitive history, *The Creationists*. Gruenke got her Ph.D. in cell biology from the University of Virginia. The movement's star is Kurt Wise, a Ph.D. in paleontology from Harvard who studied under Stephen Jay Gould, the nation's most famous opponent of creationism.

"Young earth" creationism, the most extreme wing of the movement, is entirely a modern phenomenon; William Jennings Bryan, the most famous prosecutor in the Scopes trial, was never hung up on the age of the earth; life was created "in the manner and time recorded in history," he would say vaguely, implying that "day" described in Genesis could have a less-obvious meaning. Only around the 1960s did a significant number of creationists begin to insist on six to ten thousand years as the age of the earth and to build a massive research infrastructure to prove it, partly funded by Tim LaHaye.

These days, the new elite breed of creationist scientists is most closely associated with intelligent design. Proponents of this theory argue that certain biological features are so complex that only a divine agency could have created them. But the baraminologists and other young-earth creationists do not associate with the intelligent design crowd. ID people do not necessarily take a position on the age of the earth; a few take pains to mention that the earth could be billions of years old and life could have developed from a common ancestor. When asked what the "divine agency" is, there are a few among them who might even mention aliens as a possible candidate.

Baraminologists instead opt for an impossible twin purity: pure faith married to pure science. Genesis is literally true, and they will prove that by using standard scientific methods. In that way, baraminology is the perfect kind of science for Patrick Henry, a way to speak the modern idiom without conceding anything.

In class, the weird hybrid of these twin orthodoxies—exacting science and strict Biblical literalism—made for jarring transitions. One minute Gruenke was describing the technicalities of subduction, and the next she was making a point about God's rainbow of promise. "The hot mantle contacting all of that ocean water could easily account for the opening of the floodgates of heaven," she said.

Gruenke grew up homeschooled in a religious family in Alaska, "pretty much a great place for encouraging a young biologist." For her graduate work, she studied the hemagglutinin protein, which allows viruses to enter cells. At thirty-one she was slight and fair, and preserved the same air of quiet curiosity she must have cultivated as a young girl who spent her time alone in the backyard, pressing and labeling wildflowers. During the stressful time when several of her colleagues were on the brink of quitting, Gruenke soothed herself by perfecting the aquatic environment of the fish tank that sits on her desk. You could say that science was her most constant companion. "I guess at some point I made the choice to do this instead of getting married and having kids," she said.

Gruenke did not assign her students reading from any creationist textbooks, because "there are no good ones." Instead, the class used the standard college textbook titled *Biology*, written, of course, from an evolutionary perspective. The book includes a lengthy section on the evolution of primates in which it calls chimpanzees "the closest living relative of humans." It estimates the age of the earth as 4.6 billion years and describes the early conditions on earth with no mention of Adam and Eve. The words *baramin, liger,* and *wolphin* do not appear anywhere in the index.

"I want them to understand what evolutionary theory is and what I disagree with. You can't ignore the data. That's a valuable lesson about science in general, and not something most creationists understand."

When a student asked Gruenke a question, she would often answer on two levels, one for the secular world and one for Christians. "If I'm talking to an atheist, I'm not going to quote Scripture to them because it won't make sense to them." When a student asked if on the final exam she should quote Scripture, Gruenke advised her against it: "Well, I hope Genesis would inform your thinking, but you don't need to put it in your answer. I'd prefer you to explain it in terms of the scientific model." Even when she talked about purely biblical events, Gruenke maintained a no-nonsense attitude and warned her students against jumping to conclusions. "We don't actually know or have any evidence about where the Garden of Eden is, so I wouldn't assume that," she answered one student.

From their homeschool textbooks, the students had often

learned a cruder version of creationism, arguing, for example, that scientists had not discovered any so-called "missing links"—transitional species between, say, sea and land animals. Gruenke made a point of correcting this impression: "Well, it's sort of a sliding scale," she said, when one student asked her about it. "It's not as common as some evolutionists would have us believe, but it's much more common than many creationists would have us believe. It's certainly common enough that creationists need to address it. We certainly don't want to ignore the data."

When polled, nearly half of Americans agree consistently with the statement: "God created human beings pretty much in their present form at one time within the last 10,000 years or so." But a Christian university with intellectual pretensions does not normally perpetuate this view. The statement of faith for Wheaton College in Illinois, for example, says that the "Scriptures are inerrant in the original writing," that "God directly created Adam and Eve" and they are "distinct from other living creatures."

But when it comes to pinning down the age of the earth, the school balks. Wheaton has a strong geology department. Its professors argue that the Bible makes no specific mention of the age of the earth. They belong to the Geological Society of America and wring their hands about the "geo-literacy of the Church." In lectures and papers, their professors gently take evangelical parishioners by the hand, issuing long tracts comparing the various methods of radiometric dating and showing that they all agree: The earth, indeed, is over four billion years old. Every once in a while, the department head proposes hiring a young-earth creationist and the professors revolt, fearing taint by association.

Politicians, too, meet the prevailing public opinion only halfway. Despite what their constituents might think, no politician who expects to have a career will get drawn very far into a public debate about Noah's Ark and the dove and the fallacies of carbon dating. Instead, they resort to the standard noncommittal construction that George Bush used with Texas reporters who asked if he thought creationism should be taught in schools. "Both sides ought to be properly taught . . . so people can understand what the debate is about," he said. "Part of education is to expose people to different schools of thought. . . . You're asking me whether or not people ought to be exposed to different ideas, and the answer is yes."

Given these realities it would seem that Gruenke was doing a disservice to the aspiring young congressmen and Supreme Court justices in her class by teaching them that men used to live to be nine hundred years old and frolic among the dinosaurs, that light from distant galaxies is just a divine illusion, and that all these "facts" can somehow be verified by the scientific method. Should they be publicly embarrassed by these views one day, they might resent her.

But at the moment her lessons are not received that way. Biology class is filled with freshmen, many of whom have just come from homes where evolution might as well be a cussword. In this class, they face the monster right in the eye, armed with their own data. The exercise makes them feel empowered, on par with secular scientists and even more so, because they are privy to a special body of scientific knowledge known only to an elite few. As the freshmen see it, Gruenke has given them the gift of the Sword of Excalibur: truth married to righteousness.

"Why do we as Christians study biology?" Gruenke asks her class. "Why does PHC force you to take classes where you learn about cell photosynthesis and ecosystems? Because in order to lead a meaningful life and be able to shape the nation in the name of God, you have to know where the world is in terms of biology. If you're going to be a politician, you have to follow debates on stem cell research and scientific advances. And when you're talking to the secular world, you have to be able to defend your positions on scientific grounds."

"This really opened my eyes," Derek said one day after class. "Here is a genuine scientific account that fits almost perfectly with the Bible. Even though I wasn't struggling with this, it really strengthened my views."

EVERY SUMMER THE Baraminology Study Group holds its annual conference at one of the handful of "old earth" creationist schools with science departments. This year it was held at Cedarville University, a campus that in its architecture gives off the opposite impression of Patrick Henry: low, flat, undistinguished midcentury buildings with no pretensions to deeper history. The school was emptied of students, so the BSG members were just about the only ones around; they numbered about fifty scientists and theologians—and the director for content development for the new creationist museum opening in Petersburg, Kentucky. Gruenke, who came in her PHC sweatshirt and wore her hair in a girlish ponytail, was known as the "virus expert."

At lunch on the opening day of the conference, they bonded over their favorite topic: the dunce-cap creationists. The baraminologists see themselves as the bad boys of ICR—the Institute for Creation Research—mad geniuses who will soon leave those amateur scientists in the dust. "Man, the notion that someone spends hours of their time posting that nasty stuff on the Internet," someone said. "It's just slop before swine."

"It's slop *from* the swine," corrected Todd Wood, who got his Ph.D. from the Department of Biochemistry and Molecular Genetics at the University of Virginia. "Most of us tend to have advanced degrees; we have a couple of chemists, geologists, an astronomer, a bunch of biologists, a math whiz," Wood continued, turning to me.

Whereas creationists tend to be?

"Uhhh. Profoundly uneducated?" Wood answered. "Oh, I don't know. I think a lot of them just repeat some bad information they found on the Internet. It's frankly appalling to see a so-called creationist and evolutionist go at each other and hack and slash for hours. I think sometimes they do it just to fight."

A creationist who makes it through a respectable graduate program has two options: Stay undercover or come out and fight. Although she never tried to hide her beliefs, Gruenke took the quiet road in graduate school, keeping her views mostly to herself and sticking to cell research. The fighter among them is Kurt Wise.

Wise is the kind of mentor every graduate student wishes to have. He is up for conversations late into the night about any topic you wish to bring up, and at the same time he is briskly dismissive of idiots. He holds court with stories of such precise vividness that you'd be amazed if every detail held up. His endless supply of Wild Cherry Pepsi seems to fuel an imagination with no discipline or restraint; every half hour out pops a new theory as to why Noah outlived his grandson or dinosaurs died out, followed by a brief, surfer-style self-congratulation: "Whoa, that's beauteous" (about Noah living long enough to tell stories pre- and post-flood), or "Wow, that's cool" (about divers finding preserved cockroaches in the Spanish galleons).

As an undergraduate studying geophysical sciences at the

University of Chicago, Wise cowrote a paper about the relationship between sea-level changes and mass extinctions. Three of his professors, including David Raup, strongly recommended Wise to Harvard for graduate school, and he was accepted.

The way Wise tells the story, the weekend before school was about to start, he got in his car, dropped his sister off in Greenville, South Carolina, and then drove through seven states in fifteen hours until he got to Cambridge. He was coming from rural Ogle County, Illinois; he'd been the first person from there ever to go to the University of Chicago, and now he was the first to go to Harvard. "It had been my childhood dream to go to Harvard and study invertebrate paleontology, but I never thought I'd get in," he said.

When he arrived, it was after one in the morning. "I was bleary-eyed and I didn't know where I was supposed to be. It was too late to get a room, so I just get out of my car and run smack-dab into Stephen Jay Gould."

Raup hadn't told Gould that his advisee was a creationist when he recommended him, but later Raup had broken the news this way. "Steve," Raup had said. "Hypothetical situation. If a creationist student applied for a position in your lab, would you accept him?"

It was 1981. Gould had just won a MacArthur Foundation "genius" grant and published the bestselling book, *The Mismeasure of Man*. He'd also spent the summer preparing expert testimony for a case known as "Scopes II," the first legal test for scientific creationism. The case challenged an Arkansas law requiring public schools to give "balanced treatment" to evolution and creationism. After his testimony, *Newsweek* would put Gould on the cover as the symbol of opposition to creationism.

Still, Gould said, "In Harvard we don't ask for photographs, and we don't discriminate. If a person is willing to do the science, then yes, we would."

"Good," Raup had said. "You just did."

Now, at a parking lot near Harvard, Wise got out of his car and said hello. "And as soon as he [Gould] saw me, he started screaming, 'You lied to me! You deceived me!' I honestly can't tell you what else he said. I was horrified. This was exactly what I was afraid of. It seemed like we stood there forever."

The tirade lasted twenty minutes. Then, in Wise's telling, Gould walked away and didn't bring up the subject for two years.

Gould supported a handful of the most accomplished graduate students every year with his numerous grants. They were a tight group, and they slowly began to pick up on Wise's views. One of the junior professors would set up pizza parties where the other graduate students would gang up on Wise. All of them had to serve as teaching fellows for Gould's immensely popular "History of the Earth and Life" class. They were encouraged to improvise, and they focused on topics such as feminist geology or the rocks of Harvard Square. Wise stuck to very narrow topics, which some of his fellow graduate students interpreted as his way of avoiding showing his hand.

Once or twice a fellow student asked how he could hold such views and be part of a secular department. According to fellow graduate student Warren Allmon, Wise answered, "It's just like playing Monopoly: Play by the rules, move the pieces around, get play money."

Allmon recalled finding a letter Wise had mistakenly left on the copy machine. The letter was written to a fellow creationist and dealt with an old creationist standby about finding gold chains embedded in coal. Wise was advising the person that the example had no validity. For the sake of the movement, he wrote to his friend, they had to "act like scientists."

"I walked into his office breathing heavy," recalled Allmon, now the director of the Paleontological Research Institution in Ithaca, New York. "How do you sleep at night?" he yelled. "How can you sit here in this building next to all of us, using our computers?"

"Don't you want to hear my side of the story?" Wise asked.

"No," Allmon said, and walked out.

Allmon and others considered Wise to be Gould's misguided social experiment, an unfortunate outgrowth of his naïve liberalism. Gould could have kicked Wise out at any moment, but he didn't. Wise wrote his thesis about the fossil record's being incomplete. The thesis is typical of work done by creationists at secular institutions. The incomplete record is a standard problem in geology. Researchers propose different mathematical models to approximate how much of the whole any given sample of fossils represents.

But it is also a weapon used by creationists to prove that there are large mysterious gaps in the record that cast doubt on evolution. One of Wise's fellow graduate students failed to pass her orals. When Wise passed his, she was furious, Allmon recalled.

Before Wise graduated, Gould checked on the results of his own social experiment.

"Do you still believe that same way?" he asked Wise.

"You mean, about being a creationist? Yes," Wise answered, and they left it at that.

After he graduated from Harvard, Wise sought out Walter ReMine, an engineer and inventor trained at the University of

Minnesota with a side interest in biosystematics. Wise knew that ReMine was working on a new baraminological model, and he wanted to help him perfect it. Remine was reluctant to use explicitly biblical terms, so eventually they parted ways, with ReMine agreeing to let Wise use some of the terms for a new creationist model.

In 1989 Wise got a job at Tennessee's Bryan College, named after William Jennings Bryan and located just down the road from the court where the Scopes trial took place. There he started the Center for Origins Research, an outpost for young-earth biologists. On a creationist Web site he came across Todd Wood, whose views were similar to his, and a decade later, recruited Wood to Bryan. Gruenke had been an undergraduate student at Bryan and remembered her time there fondly—the stuffed monkey in the basement, everyone arguing at Wise's house about Baumgarten plate tectonics late into the night. In 1995 Wise, Wood, and several like-minded scientists turned an Internet discussion group into the BSG.

In the Scopes II trial, when creationists would repeat that evolution was only a "theory," Gould famously replied: "Nonsense. Evolution is as real as gravity. Whether you believe in Newton's, Einstein's, or someone else's explanation of it, the fact is that the apple still falls." Baraminologists, like most creationists, operate from that same logic, only with a different fixed point. The Bible is the falling apple, clear and true. Any facts that contradict it must on their face be incorrect. And if they can't understand why, well, then they just haven't looked hard enough.

Because the baraminologists have been exposed to so much standard science, they don't allow themselves the usual blind spots of other creationists. Instead they operate with tortured honesty, taking on the questions that most directly contradict their views. "Data is never the enemy. It just has to be explained," Gruenke liked to say.

Wise's first presentation included a slide of a fossil sequence that moved from reptiles to mammals, with some transitional forms in between. "It's a pain in the neck," he said. "The fossil sequence fits the evolutionary prediction quite well." A few of the other researchers in the audience offered theories, but they did not satisfy him. "I'm concerned because I don't want to explain this with some ad hoc thesis. This is unacceptable!" he said, half joking.

Throughout the conference he brought up the contradictory evidence staring him in the face, and either explained it away with one of those "ad hoc theories," or else just declared it "weird" and filed it away for a later date. The similar DNA of humans and chimps? "Oh, yeah, Todd and I think we were created with the exact same DNA. We haven't mentioned it to the other creationists because they'd find it too disturbing." Carbon dating? "We've got no one with merit working on that. We need a nuclear physicist with us."

So how did he think about it?

"The same way I think about everything else. Weird."

"Yeah," said Wood. "He's not scared of it."

"My approach is to keep finding weird stuff and eventually I'll be able to explain it."

Young-earth creationism made a brief appearance in the 1830s and was revived in the early 1900s by George McCready Price, a farmer's son, high school teacher, and self-published author. Price was raised as a Seventh-Day Adventist, a religion that preached the imminent end of the world and promoted worship on Saturdays to respect the six-day creation. On his own, Price began to study geologic ages and struggled to reconcile them with the teachings of his religion. Until then, creationists followed various theories to reconcile the text of Genesis with geological time but Price felt these theories involved too much intellectual "dodging and twisting." Eventually, he concluded that the standard geological columns were "the devil's counterfeit." To explain how so much change could happen in such a short time, Price focused on Noah's flood. Through "flood geology," Price could explain mass extinctions and geological shifts happening in a short burst of time; he called his innovation the "new catastrophism."

Price's work went mostly unnoticed until it was picked up by Henry Morris, a Texas engineer, in the 1950s. In his book *The Genesis Flood,* Morris updated Price's new catastrophism. Morris proposed a worldwide flood that had deposited most of the fossils; he argued against multiple ice ages and the existence of the geological column. Morris included the bombshell that remains the favorite cartoon image of creationists: giant dinosaur footprints found alongside human ones. If he could establish the Flood as the third event dominating human history, after Creation and the Fall, then evolution just "vanishes away," Morris wrote, and the rocks become a tremendous witness to the "power of the living God of creation!"

"Creation" is an uplifting term that brings to mind God's majesty and beneficence, uncanny little stick insects and giant elegant beasts. But the flood is the "watery grave," a reminder of God's holy wrath. During the Flood, Gruenke told her students, the normally slow geological processes careened out of control like a train jerked over a cliff. In a few weeks' time, glaciers formed, and then mountains. Deserts were suddenly drenched; the Middle East became a "land flowing with milk and honey." Viruses entered the gene pool, spreading disease and the rapid aging that had already begun after the Fall.

Get them going on the Flood, and they sounded like a bunch of late-night stoners who have talked themselves into a fun house they don't want to leave. "I mean, we have no idea how much technology there was before the Flood," offered one of Wise's groupies in a late-night marathon session.

Technology?

To most scientists, doing science confined by the Scriptures would feel like working in a straitjacket. But for the baraminologists, it has the opposite effect. They behave like scientists in the pre-Darwinian era, unfettered by the tedium of peer reviews and microspecialization and academic credentials. Each of them can play at being biologist and paleontologist and ocean chemist and nuclear physicist, and at each moment be touching on the very deepest of questions.

With Wise, there was never a dull moment. "Come on, guys, let's stretch, let's stretch," he called out, if his colleagues were trotting out the same old theories. In half an hour he jumped from ferns to hypsodonty to chimp DNA to carbon dating, and still it wasn't enough. "Sometimes I think we just haven't gotten weird enough," he said.

Among themselves, with no one to judge them, the creationists crowed about their successes. Michael Matthews talked about the plans for the new $27 million Creation Museum set to open the following summer, with a sister museum in Hong Kong. "With just a little money, a handful of young scientists have done what the other side has done in over two hundred years," Matthews bragged. "Poor little thing called evolution."

Wise told the story of his latest talk at an annual conference of the Geological Society of America. They had asked him to come speak on a panel about the threat of creationism in the classroom. Wise was the single defender of the approach. He had stood up before a room of ordinary geologists and tried to spook them. "In the sixties, you could count the number of creationists who were scientists on one hand," he told them. "But in the last decade, the number of creationists with graduate degrees has increased exponentially. And they're getting more and more sophisticated. Soon you are going to have more creationists in your classroom who are immune to your arguments. And approximately by the year 2050, they will outnumber you. So I can understand why we scare the hell out of you."

Later, during the conference, he ran into Allmon.

"Hi, Warren," he said.

"How's the game of Monopoly, Kurt?" Allmon asked, and then, by his own account, Allmon lost it. He had just helped to write an obituary for Gould. And he'd just read a complete account of Scopes III, a case testing the legitimacy of teaching intelligent design then being heard in Dover, Pennsylvania. Two decades' worth of resentment exploded.

"Don't you know you're an icon? You are the only creationist in the world who can say, 'I was Stephen Jay Gould's graduate student.' So all of us who worked with him have to carry around your sorry ass every day. If the Dover case goes the wrong way, you will bear unique responsibility. It could be the end of science as we know it, and I'm not kidding."

Wise was befuddled and contrite. "What you want me to do? Go home and give it all up?"

"That would be a good start."

By the end of three days, however, the bluster showed through. The conference added up to shards of unfinished theories, grand projects conceived but unfunded, studies submitted to mainstream science publications and never accepted in those places because, of course, they were discriminated against. "I've had various theses I thought were true and I've rejected all of them," Wise would say about a particular problem. Or "I'd hate to try it out. It would be another one of my ideas I'd have to throw away if I tested it." Wise turned out to be too extreme even for Bryan College. "No secular institution will hire you. No old-earth creationist school will hire you. I sent out thirty-five letters and I got one response." He now teaches at Southern Baptist Theological Seminary in Louisville, Kentucky, as the only scientist on staff.

Dover, of course, went the way of the other Scopes trials; a federal judge ruled that intelligent design was merely "creation relabeled," and told the school board it was unconstitutional to present it in a public school. The goal of creation scientists has always been to establish a "grassroots movement across the United States to demonstrate how creation can be taught in public schools," Henry Morris said in 1970, when he was hired by LaHaye to start the Creation Science Research Center.

On the ultimate goal, they have failed so far. But they have easily sustained a grassroots movement. Each year scientific creationists convince school boards in various parts of the country to try new ways to include creationism in science curriculum. Each year, the number of creationists with college degrees grows. To them this is victory enough: In Christian terms, "grassroots movement" is just a political term for the main goal of any evangelist: saving souls, one by one.

Late at night, Wise and his admirers sat around the fireplace eating hot dogs and chips. One of them told a story about a friend and fellow scientist he'd tried to convert. He'd always talked to the friend about creationism, thinking that must be the stumbling block. But it turned out, "All he needed to hear was the straight-up gospel."

"Oh, man, you hit it in the heart," said Wise. "People don't really believe because of facts. Faith is what saves," he said, paraphrasing C. S. Lewis.

"Did you ever talk to him about the gospel?" someone asked, and everyone understood "him" to mean Stephen Jay Gould.

Creationists have always felt a kinship with Gould and tried to appropriate his work. More than others, his model of "punctuated equilibrium" looks like "new catastrophism," with change taking place in abrupt fits and starts instead of one smooth evolution. But Gould always made his position clear. "I am not a believer," he wrote in *Rocks of Ages,* his meditation on religion and science. "I am an agnostic in the wise sense of T. H. Huxley, who coined the word in identifying such open-minded skepticism as the only rational position because, truly, one cannot know."

Nonetheless, Wise said he'd always detected an undercurrent. "Steve was working out his own spiritual issues through the Cambrian explosion," he said. "It really bogged him down because it looks so much like an argument for creationism. He couldn't rationalize it, and it just bugged the beejeebers out of him. It bugged him deep in his soul. It's clear God kept shoving the Cambrian explosion in front of him, saying, 'I created. I created. I created.' And it's just so poignant. If anyone pressed him on it he would just become irrational and start screaming. But he was always drawn to it. When I read *Wonderful Life,* I just cried. He has a paragraph about the Great Token Stringer and it's amazing. He's describing Creation!"

The room was hushed now. No one was crunching on their potato chips, and they'd let their hot dogs grow cold.

"Do you ever think he might have had a deathbed conversion?"

"I don't think it's impossible," said Wise. "He certainly knew the gospel."

Half an hour later, the fireplace, too, went cold, so they moved all the furniture right up against it. I left them there, several grown men and one woman, climbing on top of couches and upended chairs, scouring the stones by the mantel for fossils. Jennifer came with me, through the door into the girls' side of the dorms where we were staying.

"You must think we're so weird," she said.

CHAPTER 9

The Fifth Quadrant: Hollywood Finds God

Considering that the weapon was a FedEx tube covered in black tape, the boys were doing a decent job with the fight scene. They jabbed and swiped and threw each other convincingly murderous looks until they both ended up on the damp grass, covered in dead leaves and bits of dirt. Then one of them pulled out a little green capsule of deadly "Stalin Gas" (a paintball tube), threatened to break it open, and said in his best deadpan: "This is it, Fox. The end of the road."

The speaker was Daniel Noa, a.k.a. Hitman, the star of a twenty-episode series shot entirely on the campus of Patrick Henry. Noa was also the director, which in scenes like this made for an awkward combination. (He had once directed a scene while handcuffed to a chair.) But two weeks from finals and three thousand miles from Hollywood, Patrick Henry's resident aspiring filmmaker couldn't be too picky.

For two years, Daniel had done his best to turn this dignified campus into a seamy underworld complete with assassins, hostages, torture chambers, and girls with guns. For him and crew of friends, *Hitman* was like their favorite video game come alive. Ski masks and fake Uzis transformed nerdy coeds into trained killers ready to shoot on sight. Night shots turned the front doors of the dorms into the Counter Terrorist Unit, or CTU, a rip-off of *24*. Sunglasses and a black leather jacket turned Red Fox, Hitman's nemesis, into a homegrown Jack Bauer, a hero haunted by inner demons. Creative angles turned the thin line of trees behind the campus into a dense forest, convenient for staging a rebel attack or hiding a body.

For the girls who participated, *Hitman* greatly expanded the universe of accepted gender roles. With the help of a black turtleneck and some lip gloss, a prim PHC girl could transform herself into a gang moll, ready to shoot, torment, flirt, or just lounge around a poker table. Chivalry is not a priority. In one scene Hitman takes a sassy redhead with whom he is romantically linked and chokes her from behind; when she begs for mercy, he shoots her in the foot and leaves her to be captured by rebels.

The series was inspired by a trip Daniel's friends took to Wal-Mart. The friends bought Daniel some BB guns for his birthday, and they rode back to campus pretend-shooting out the window. That road trip pretty much determined the spirit of the show. *Hitman* opens with a one-minute clip called "The Assassin." A man in a black ski mask sneaks into someone's bedroom. He points his gun at the sleeping body. Just as he's about to pull the trigger, someone shoots him from behind.

Daniel plays Hitman as a vacant sociopath. When his protégé questions something Hitman has done, Hitman smiles as he shoots him in the gut. The camera lingers on the arc of his body falling into the grass. But Red Fox, Hitman's enemy and the hero of the series, is no angel. Over four seasons, Daniel pushed Red Fox dangerously close to the dark side. His brother is killed, and he is betrayed by someone inside CTU, a weasely double agent played by none other than Nathan Poe. He has an argument with the president and walks out against orders. He throws Hitman over the balcony and then tortures him using a hypodermic needle filled with snake and scorpion venom. He grows so bitter and dispirited that he nearly lost the support of his campus fans, for whom lack of hope is the doorway to sin. Now, moments before death, comes Red Fox's last chance to redeem himself.

"I've signed your death warrant. Have you ever heard of Stalin Gas?"

"Yes." (Splutter, cough.)

"This is it, Fox. There's no cure. There's nothing you can do. Fox, you're a condemned man. You're like me. Our destinies are one." Hitman breaks the capsule.

Daniel had always said he wanted to use the art of filmmaking to "impact the culture" for God. But it wasn't obvious how he was doing that. In the scene he was filming that day, he got a little closer to showing his hand, although if I hadn't been paying close attention, I might have missed seeing it entirely.

The scene involved the kind of code-speak that's used by the growing number of Christian filmmakers working in Hollywood; they tell a story that's understood one way by a Christian audience and another way by everyone else. The method has been tried by young Christian directors in many genres—comedy, horror, spaghetti western, even low-budget action series like this one. It's the cinematic equivalent of "evangelese," the language politicians speak when they want to reach out to a Christian audience without ever mentioning Jesus.

Jeremiah Lorrig, the actor who played the director of CTU, walked into the scene.

"How do you want me to play him?" Jeremiah asked Daniel.

"Larger than life. A father figure. And a friend. I want all the shots up, almost like he's coming down from on high," said Daniel.

"It's not too late," said the CTU director, picking up the empty shell of the capsule. "We'll find a cure."

"I deserted you. I defied you. I abused our friendship. I broke our trust," answered the rapidly fading Red Fox. "And you'll still try to help me?"

"Yes, I will."

"You'll take me home?"

("Do it soft, but strong," Daniel directed.)

"Yes, I'll take you home, Fox."

If you don't know your Bible, you might think of this as the moment our hero gets called back from the dark side: Luke breaking away from Darth Vader, Frodo after the ring is destroyed in Mount Doom. Red Fox did not get down on his knees and pray. The CTU director did not tack on a white beard and float up into the clouds with a halo and a staff. But if you were a student at Patrick Henry, you'd catch it immediately: echoes of Cain and Judas, the all-knowing, all-forgiving voice from on high calling you home. Yes, the dialogue came straight out of a comic book; but still, Daniel Noa is onto Hollywood's favorite new kind of crossover marketing.

Daniel's outlook changed during his freshman year, when he and some friends went to see Mel Gibson's *The Passion of the Christ*. The movie opens with a spooky shot of the moon. "To open a

Jesus movie on something as simple as the moon. I loved it. I'd never seen that kind of look in a Bible movie. That's something from sci-fi or horror, *The Blair Witch Project* or *Werewolf.* I knew immediately: this is going to be a real movie, not some perversion of a gospel flick."

Daniel was used to the treacly gospel films from his church youth group: a stylized crucifixion, a Jesus with shiny hair who flutters up to heaven. *The Passion* is relentlessly violent, in a way Daniel and his crew, nicknamed the "Mod Squad" on campus, could appreciate. Jesus is whipped and kicked and spat on; close-ups show flesh ripping and an eye so bloody it looks like a rotten tomato. The mostly unknown actors speak a language almost no one alive understands because Mel Gibson wanted it that way. The lesson for the young Patrick Henry filmmaker was powerful. Gibson stayed true to his very particular traditionalist Catholic version of Scripture and still made a very successful movie. He did it despite being ostracized by a Hollywood elite that considered him deranged and anti-Semitic. He did it because God told him to.

"You get signals. Signs. 'Signal graces,' they're called," Gibson told Peter Boyer of the *New Yorker.* "It's like traffic lights. It's as clear as a traffic light. Bing! I mean, it just grabs you and you know you have to listen to that and you have to follow it."

Gibson used his own production company and created his own audience. He arranged private screenings at churches he thought might be sympathetic. He specifically targeted groups that felt estranged from Hollywood and popular culture, and avoided the theater: people like the Patrick Henry parents. Church groups bought blocs of tickets and filled the theaters. In the end he got his revenge in a language Hollywood understood:

The movie grossed $370 million. Nine months later, Bush beat Kerry, Hollywood's chosen favorite; the industry had to adjust.

Producers began talking about "*Passion* dollars" and "Christian values" without irony. In the weeks after *The Passion* opened, major studios greenlighted *The Chronicles of Narnia: The Lion, the Witch and the Wardrobe,* Disney's adaptation of the C. S. Lewis classic and *The Exorcism of Emily Rose,* a horror movie with improbably strong Christian overtones. New Line Cinema assigned a hot new director to *The Nativity Story,* a prequel to *The Passion.* Studios began courting young graduates of Act One, a new screenwriting program for Christians run by Barbara Nicolosi, a former nun.

"Didn't you know?" one producer told Nicolosi. " 'Christian' is the new 'gay.' "

Before this, movies were marketed according to quadrants: men, women, younger than twenty-five, older than twenty-five. After *The Passion,* "faith groups" became a "fifth quadrant." For Hollywood executives, this was an untapped gold mine: Any movie that was family-friendly, mentioned God, or seemed redemptive in some way fit the bill.

A new breed of consultants rose up to help Hollywood navigate this foreign demographic with increasing sophistication. A typical Hollywood person's knowledge of "Christian" does not stretch far beyond Jerry Falwell or Pat Robertson. But the people at Grace Hill Media or Motive Marketing, who worked on *The Passion,* know that the Christian world has moved beyond that. They know that, like everyone else, Christians shop for opinions online, and someone like Daniel Noa is more likely to read the movie reviews on movies.ign.com or Google news than he is to watch *The 700 Club.*

When Daniel went home to Los Angeles for the summer, he

saw confirmation everywhere that he was wanted; spirits and angels rose up on billboards, touting the new fall TV season, proof that Hollywood, if not born again, was at least enthralled with the realm beyond: *Ghost Whisperer,* a sort of *Bewitched* from the dark side; *Three Wishes,* a canceled reality show starring Christian rocker Amy Grant as an earthly angel, doing good deeds for needy families just because it's a nice thing to do; *The Book of Daniel,* a show about an Episcopal priest who takes frequent breaks to check in with Jesus (also canceled).

Rare was the pop-culture phenomenon that rocked Patrick Henry, but Narnia was the exception. A month before the December 9 release, the mania on campus had gotten distracting. The bookstore was stocked with new titles: *Finding God in the Land of Narnia* and *Aslan's Call.* At chapel, the freshmen started to sit in the back so they could show each other the supertrailer on their laptops. Debates broke out on whether the kids could see it in the theater on opening night, which fell right in the middle of finals. Rumor had it that one sophomore had ordered one thousand posters and planned to plaster his dorm with them. A poster was already hanging in Dean Wilson's office, confirmation that the movie was campus-approved. What more proof did the Patrick Henry students need that they were not at the fringes of culture but at the very center?

Because of their religious undertones, the Narnia books are considered required reading in modern evangelical households, and many Christians regard Lewis as the greatest writer of the past century. Daniel's father read the whole series to him, starting when he was around six. Daniel's first stab at acting was putting on a crown and playing King Peter, battling the White Witch of his imagination.

Disney and its collaborator, Walden Media, set out explicitly to reach a Patrick Henry–type audience. They hired Motive Marketing to do outreach to churches and held a publicity event for thirty faith-based groups in an attempt to create buzz for the film. Director Andrew Adamson checked religious symbolism with Douglas Gresham, C. S. Lewis's stepson, to ensure that *The Chronicles of Narnia* didn't portray anything "theologically incorrect," Adamson told me.

Expectations among evangelicals ran so high that the studio had to explain, with great delicacy, why the movie was not, in fact, presented as explicit Christian allegory. "To me, the books didn't overwhelm with any religious or spiritual references," Adamson said, though he acknowledged that such references were there if you looked for them. As one of his actors told him: "I don't remember the bit in the Bible where Jesus kills the White Witch." The Christian press closely tracked Adamson's search for the actor who would supply the voice of Aslan, the lion. In the novels Aslan's life parallels the Resurrection story, and Christians wanted Adamson to hew to the character's Christlike aspects. Ultimately, Adamson explained, he opted not to make Aslan "too omnipotent," because "then he would be inaccessible." He said, "Those who want to look deeper can find more in the story. Those who don't want to look deeper can just enjoy it."

Patrick Henry became a distant outpost of the fifth quadrant. Motive Marketing gave out dozens of reduced-price tickets to the students for a special preview held two days before the official opening night. For days, Peter, a freshman, sat in the cafeteria studying for finals ringed by a crimson halo of tickets. By the morning before the show, he'd sold them all.

The outing served as Patrick Henry's version of *The Rocky*

Horror Picture Show. In groups of six and eight, the students filled up the Leesburg theater. Some of the girls wore velvet capes they had last worn to *Lord of the Rings.* Daniel went with some of his friends. Being self-appointed film critics, they all found things to complain about. They complained that Aslan didn't quite reach the level of "raw power" they would have expected in a Christlike figure and that Peter, who was supposed to fill the leadership role, was too soft on Edmund. But fundamentally they were in love. Here, after all, was a movie glamorizing a group of kids who never seem to go to school and are nonetheless very clever. They remain presexual for an inordinately long time and play out their emotions through their siblings. They are heroes of a self-devised adventure, guided lightly by a kindly, eccentric professor. By remaining both courageous and innocent, they are able to rescue a cursed world.

Before he was out of the theater, Daniel started to do the calculations, counting forward through sequels. "Let's see. Two years times six. That's twelve years. In twelve years they'll be doing the Space Trilogies," he said, referring to Lewis's more obscure works, which were Daniel's favorites. "And by then I'll be ready to direct them."

RELATIONS BETWEEN Christians and Hollywood have often been called antagonistic, but that fails to convey the current of deep envy that runs between the two communities. When the medium first appeared, evangelists saw it as a potential new tool for their trade—a vivid, portable passion play. One of the earliest movie hits was the nineteen-minute *Passion Play of Oberammergau,* shot in New York in 1897. Filmmakers welcomed the association.

The first movie theaters were built to look like nineteenth-century cathedrals, with ornate gothic facades and high arches leading you into the show. The architecture implied that the movie house was another kind of sanctuary; in the dark, cavernous space a viewer could expect to feel awe, and a sense of mystery, and experience something close to transcendence.

The illusion of mutual reinforcement lasted until about the twenties, when Cecil B. DeMille began making his Biblical epics. DeMille recognized the cinematic potential of Scripture stories, but he warped them to fit the screen. In his hands, Bible characters turned into divas, and pagans provided a good excuse for an orgy. He cast Mary Magdalene as a peevish teenager and Moses as the object of a girlish crush. "Oh, Moses, Moses, you stubborn, splendid, adorable fool!" cries Nefertiti, played by a kittenish Anne Baxter in Bettie Page bangs. One critic compared DeMille's epics to a nine-and-a-half-foot showgirl: "Great to look at, glittery, a bit naughty, but excessive."

With his 1932 extravaganza, *The Sign of the Cross*, DeMille went over the line. He shot the movie with an extended orgy sequence, including a long seduction, "Dance of the Naked Moon." He lingered on a deranged day at the Coliseum where naked girls were fed to alligators and a lascivious gorilla, as women in the bleachers gawked. The censors cut both those scenes, but they left in another, now-infamous one: the Empress Poppaea invites her Christian girlfriend to join her in a milk bath. "You'd better take off your clothes, come in here, and tell me about it," she purrs. The camera lingers on her naked back and legs.

DeMille held mass on the set and invited important church leaders to screenings, but his outreach efforts failed. A year later, the Catholic church started the Legion of Decency to launch a "vigorous campaign for the purification of cinema, which has become a deadly menace to morals." Other denominations followed suit. For decades to come, the Christian establishment allied itself with the censors. Every time a filmmaker tried to sneak a titillating scene into a movie, the Legion threatened to boycott unless the censors clamped down.

John Updike portrays this zero-sum battle for souls in his novel, *In the Beauty of the Lilies.* The story opens in the spring of 1910 in Paterson, New Jersey. D. W. Griffith is filming *The Call to Arms* when Hollywood's first starlet, teenage Mary Pickford, faints in the heat. Across town, Reverend Clarence Wilmot stands at the pulpit of the Fourth Presbyterian Church, feeling "the last particle of faith leave him." The realization hits him like a dull slap: *There is no God.* The story follows four generations of Wilmots as they are jerked from Christ to Culture. Clarence's son Teddy stops going to church. His daughter, Essie, is enthralled by movies and becomes the Hollywood star Alma DeMott. Her son pays the price for her debauched Hollywood life; he joins a Branch Davidian–like cult. Hollywood can't substitute for church and provide people with meaning, but there are no longer any giants of faith to fill the role, either.

By the sixties, churches had lost the power to dictate content and were forced to come up with new ways to compete with the enormous influence of Hollywood. With his Worldwide Productions, Billy Graham acknowledged the "power of film." He began pumping out dozens of what Christian director Scott Derrickson calls "Godsploitation" movies designed to give a lowbrow church audience a "cheap theological fix," writes Derrickson in his essay "A Filmmaker's Progress."

The movies took a series of stock characters—juvenile delinquent, unwed mother, alcoholic—and ran them through the conversion mill. By the end of the movies, each miscreant ended up down on his or her knees, eyes facing heaven. Graham hoped to turn the theaters into actual churches by having the audience walk up the aisle to meet the characters onscreen and receive Christ.

One subset of this genre was the infamous End Times movies from the seventies. Many a Christian remembers the horror of being forced to sit through *A Thief in the Night*. The series follows Patty, a genial housewife who is not a believer, through the cataclysmic events of the Tribulation. In the last of three parts, Patty is prepared to receive Christ, but it's too late. Patty wails hysterically as the Antichrist's minions drag her to the guillotine—yes, the guillotine—*CLANG!* She is beheaded! (After which the assembled Christian youth are asked if they would like to be saved, or end up like Patty.)

In his essay, Derrickson, a graduate of Biola University who directed *The Exorcism of Emily Rose,* runs through the other schools of Christian thought he encountered in Hollywood during the eighties and nineties: the Content Assassins, watchdog groups that tallied up instances of sex, violence, and cussing, and boycotted movies whose tallies were too high; the Battalion of Value Changers, who cheerfully set out to "conquer Hollywood for Christ"; the Monastery of Harmless Entertainment, who proposed inoffensive G-rated fare as the solution; the Uplifting Movies Theme Park, which allowed in some non-Christian movies as long as they had a redemptive theme (*Chariots of Fire, The Shawshank Redemption*).

Ultimately Derrickson settles with the "Quality Club." This is the place many in this new generation of evangelicals land after they realize that the Christian subculture is a pale imitation of the real thing. Like Derrickson, they love movies, and they can find truth in even the darkest of them—Ingmar Bergman, *The Godfather,* or horror flicks (Derrickson's preferred medium). Doing excellent work is their obligation, and moving people toward the Good is their privilege, Derrickson explains. As Christians, they follow the rule outlined in Proverbs 22:29—"Do you see a man skilled in his work? He will serve before kings; he will not serve before obscure men."

When Daniel Noa was a teenager, his father taught him a version of that lesson. They'd gotten a VCR and had rented some action-adventure movies from the church library, but they all had that "tacky eighties look," and the acting was dreadful, Daniel recalled. "My dad was big into quality. He would always say, 'There are no Christian movies and no Christian books. There are only books written by Christians and movies written by Christians, and they are good or bad.'"

The Noas moved from New Jersey to Los Angeles when Daniel was nine years old, which was about the same time as the Southern Baptist Convention decided to boycott Disney for its pro-gay company policies. Daniel's dad, Jorge, who had come to the United States on a freedom flight from Cuba when he was six, wanted to get into acting. But Daniel was not allowed to watch TV or see many movies. Back east, the family's church had sponsored an "Unplug Your TV" month. His mom liked the experiment so much that she never plugged it back in. Jorge Noa's most prominent role was playing a street thug in *Bad Boys,* a Sean Penn movie; Daniel watched parts of it on a demo reel but still hasn't seen the whole thing. Whenever his dad appeared in *Days of Our Lives* or one of the other soaps, his mother took the kids to a friend's house, or to the local mall to watch.

When Daniel was a teenager, his grandmother snuck him some tapes of the old Batman shows from the sixties, and he watched them at a friend's house. They included promos for *Mission*

Impossible, and Daniel asked his grandmother to send him those, too. At home, his parents relented and let in some black-and-white movies: the Marx Brothers and Fred Astaire and *Casablanca.* However, Daniel's taste ran to action adventure. His mom tried to keep violence at arm's length—no toy guns, even water guns—"But I gave him drinking straws, and you know what he did with them."

At sixteen, Daniel borrowed a video camera and made his first short, a *Star Trek* rip-off he edited on computers at a local Boys and Girls Club of America. By then the Southern Baptist Convention's boycott had cooled, not because Disney had changed its policies but because attitudes in the Christian community had changed. Among his fellow homeschoolers in the Hollywood-attuned L.A. suburbs, Daniel's new ambition was greeted with a shrug: "Oh, sure, you can do that for God."

During the summer, I visited the Noas at their home in Valencia, forty-five minutes north of Los Angeles. They lived in an upscale development with cream bungalows all facing a man-made lake. The streets were quiet and empty, and Hollywood felt very far away, although in a truck outside the house a blond model type was making out with the gardener, with no one to notice but me.

The Noas homeschooled in the California style, which meant you couldn't pick them out in a crowd. Daniel's mother was an Italian Catholic from New Jersey and she looked it, with her dark complexion, long dark hair, and dark eyes. On the afternoon I visited, she was in a typical working mom's frenzy—talking to me with sweeping hand gestures as she made dinner, in preparation for leaving for her afternoon shift as a histologist. She was wearing a lace undershirt under a tight sweater accented by a heart-shaped diamond necklace.

The family's unplugged days were long over. A big TV dominated the living room, with digital cable, and Daniel's two sisters sat in a side room doing their homework and watching the Disney Channel on a second TV. They came out every once in a while for snacks, looking like typical California teenagers in tank tops and jeans. Daniel's dad, who now worked at an infomercial company, breezed through later on his way to the gym. There wasn't much Christian paraphernalia around, just a marriage binder from Awana, a Christian youth and family ministry, next to a coffee-table book titled *Beatlemania* and the latest copy of *GQ.*

Daniel and his writing partner, Brandon, had spent the summer making a movie, their first one with a real budget of $5,000 raised from family and friends, real actors, and a real production crew. "Daniel's a Christian and I'm a Christian. But who you are and what you do doesn't matter to me," Brandon told the crew on the first day of shooting.

The movie, a thriller about a girl who smuggled Bibles into Romania, was called *Smuggler's Ransom.* "Our goal was to make something like *Bourne Identity,* a spy thriller with Christian elements," Brandon told me. "There are good Christian films, but there is yet to be a cool Christian film. It's cool. I've never felt like I've been on the cutting edge of anything before."

For the role of the father, they got Anthony Tyler Quinn, from *Boy Meets World,* whom they met at church through Brandon's boss. Daniel intentionally wrote the leading role as a flawed character whose missionary work puts her father in great danger, "so heavenly minded she does no earthly good." He did include a conversion scene, but he modeled it on what he imagined a good sex scene might look like—"a lot is implied."

Daniel took some inspiration from *The Last Samurai,* one of his favorite movies. "If other religions can get their point across in movies without sounding like a Billy Graham sermon, I don't see why Christians can't do it," he said.

After knowing Daniel for a while, I started to think there were two irreconcilable Daniels. West Coast Daniel was a cocky young director trying to learn the rules of Hollywood and break his way in. East Coast Daniel was more like a conservative Christian audience, still somewhat wary of the temptations of "Satan's vineyard," as Hollywood used to be known. East Coast Daniel was a hindrance to West Coast Daniel's success. His conservative tastes had left holes in Daniel's cinematic knowledge. He would never see *Midnight Cowboy* or even *Braveheart*. ("I've heard there's upper female nudity.") He hadn't seen *The Sopranos* or heard of *The Wire*. Judd Apatow's version of family values would never reach him (too much cursing and bathroom humor).

He would think hard before putting a sex scene in one of his movies because he was "worried about what he'd be asking the actors to do." In campus politics, Daniel and his Mod Squad, most of whom were senators, played the role of James Dobson, the right-wing conscience of a Republican campus. They'd led the charge to impeach the members of the den of sin for drinking, and they were staunch supporters of the new honor code. "I wouldn't want to be surrounded by girls in spaghetti-strap tops," he said, although his sisters routinely wore them. "I'd feel uncomfortable."

Like many Patrick Henry students, Daniel and his friends spent a lot of time worrying about how to "guard their minds." They dissected each movie, TV show, and video game with the same earnestness and intensity that college students in the sixties must have expended on the iconography of their clothing. To them the mind was like a delicate piece of silver that could easily corrode in bad air, and they were determined to keep themselves in a state of high polish. "Garbage in, garbage out," one student summarized it for me, repeating his grandmother's favorite phrase.

Students would sometimes pass copies of DVDs with a sex scene cut or warn each other in advance which scene to skip. At one point, *The Emperor's Club,* a movie about a prep school was making the rounds, and everyone was warned about the part where the teenage Sedgwick Bell flips through porn magazines. ("You have to be careful," read a Post-it attached to the DVD.) The students were especially annoyed when what they called "superfluous sex" or "language" was inserted into movies they really wanted to see, such as *Cinderella Man* or *Mr. and Mrs. Smith.*

When I was growing up in the eighties, I recall my guy friends rewinding, over and over, the close-up in *Fast Times at Ridgemont High* of Phoebe Cates jumping off the diving board. At Patrick Henry they did the opposite: If they decided to watch the offending movies, they fast-forwarded over exposed flesh.

"As Christians we don't focus on what we can get away with. We focus on God," one of Daniel's friends told me. "We can learn what's going on in the culture without soaking ourselves in evil."

The rules encouraged students to consider "how much is too much violence," but on this score Daniel and his friends had a harder time resisting temptation. One Hollywood firm, Market-Cast, discovered that conservative Christians were more likely than other groups to see movies rated R for violence. Campus habits confirmed that finding. Once a homeschooling mother recommended showing a five-year-old a *Spiderman* video she had on hand. "But there's a disturbing scene about halfway through," she warned the other mom, by which she meant not the dozens of beatings, the death by impalement, or the multiple lethal bombings that led a British reviewer to declare the movie "the most violent film ever aimed at young children," but the famous upside-down kiss.

When discussing violence, the students sounded like alcoholics justifying just one more drink. " 'Too violent' is anything more violent than what I'm currently watching," joked Ben Adams, author of the chastity letter and one of Daniel's close friends. Video games posed a particular problem. No one would go so far as to play *Grand Theft Auto: Vice City* because the game encouraged you to kill innocents, even if they were street thugs and prostitutes. *Halo,* however, provided hours of blood-spurting fun. The boys justified it because it involved a modicum of sociability (they played in teams) and the combatants wore uniforms. Also, they swore the thrill came not from blowing heads off but from "hunting and stalking," as Ben put it.

"Be in the world, but not of it" is the standard Christian formula for how to engage with mainstream culture. But in a world hypersaturated with information, that was a difficult stunt for tech-savvy teenagers to pull off. There are no specific instructions in the Bible on how to avoid a foulmouthed Jack Black skit calling to you from YouTube, or another glimpse of Scarlett Johansson's lips. Even for the most conservative students, even in the controlled environment of Patrick Henry, cracks appeared. A senior became addicted to andrewsullivan.com before he realized that Sullivan was gay and a strong proponent of gay marriage. A sophomore who'd sworn off movies visited friends off campus and found them watching *Pulp Fiction.* He joined them and became a Quentin Tarantino devotee.

Ben Adams couldn't get enough of *Spore,* a video game that lets you guide a cell through millions of years of evolution. A girl couldn't stop checking the raunchy daily updates on gofugyourself.com.

The most uptight freshman I met got a girlfriend sophomore year, and next thing I knew, he was dancing to Beyoncé. Farris's warning may have rolled around in their heads—*Hath not God made foolish the wisdom of the world?*—but the world was just two mouse clicks away.

Sometimes it took only ten minutes of Top 40 to reveal the truth: "The Christian subculture was nothing but a more commercialized rip-off of the mainstream, only manically sanitized, and suckier," one sophomore told me. From some friends at Patrick Henry he discovered the 9:30 Club in D.C., which he told his mother was a "dance hall." Before, he had hated cigarette smoke with almost a moral passion; now it clung to his clothes and made him feel "alive."

If Patrick Henry parents worried that exposure to pop culture could warp their children, their fears were confirmed not by Daniel Noa, but by senior Mark Shane, the resident prodigal son. Mark was either Patrick Henry's greatest success or its biggest failure, depending on how you shaded his story. He was over six feet tall, smart, and "really, really, ridiculously good looking," as he wrote on his Facebook page, mock-quoting the Ben Stiller character in *Zoolander*. He was also in possession of some magic charm that gave him entry into the powerful mainstream institutions that Farris longed to take over. On this tiny campus, Mark should have been prom king.

And indeed Mark had done exactly what Patrick Henry demanded of him, and more. His sophomore year he got a White House internship at the Office of Intergovernmental Affairs, which handles relations with the governors. There he befriended a high-level Bush adviser, who invited him over to watch football games and drink beer. The following summer, through his White

House connections, Mark got a job in Hollywood working for the publicity department of one of the major networks. He figured at least half of his colleagues were gay. They spent their days gawking at celebrities, staying at the Beverly Hilton, shuttling around Lindsay Lohan or the Black Eyed Peas. He dated a thirty-two-year-old actress who'd had a cameo on *Desperate Housewives.* "What are you doing tonight," she asked. "Not sleeping with you," he answered.

And yet Mark's success at infiltrating both nation and culture seemed to boomerang when he got back to campus. No one ever pinned anything specific on him, but when he returned, he was a marked man. He lost his RA position. He haunted the short path between the dorms and the cafeteria like a shadow, huddled in a big black overcoat. He ate lunch by himself, reading the paper. Once in a while, his brother or his roommate joined him. He wasn't on the student senate or the debate team. He didn't go to parties or hang out with his friends off campus on weekends. He didn't have a girlfriend on campus. A typical senior might have one foot out the door, but Mark was almost invisible. And his invisibility only pushed him faster toward where he was inclined to go.

Most weekends his senior year, Mark hung out with a friend he'd made during his White House internship. Jay was a Jewish guy who grew up in Dallas. At George Washington University he was the resident hustler, pulling in $600 a night organizing parties at downtown clubs. Jay and Mark had a mutual fascination. They were both tall and made an impression, and both were going places. "He's even more ambitious than I am," Mark said. "He wants to go to China and make a million before he's twenty-seven." Late at night, Mark would hang out with Jay and his friends in Jay's apartment in D.C., splitting a bottle of Grey

Goose and talking about their plans. "Money is a priority, and producing something of value," said Jay. Transforming the culture for Christ never came up.

Jay found out Mark was a Christian only when they drove to Atlantic City one day and Jay found a Christian rock CD in Mark's car. "What is this crap?" he asked. Until that point, Jay's closest encounter with evangelical Christians had been driving past the Baptodome, a monster church in Plano. But Jay didn't mind. "To me it plays as a joke: 'Oh, Mark. He goes to that super Christian college,' and then he's embarrassed." Sometimes he would call Mark's voice mail, scream: "You're not Jewish!!!" and hang up.

Jay introduced Mark to a whole new vocabulary: hookah bars and $12,000 VIP tables—jackets and ties, please—at the Ritz-Carlton. "Most of the time you go to a club and it's weak," Jay said. "But I like to bring my own music, my own liquor, and my own crowd. Socially, I create my own environment. And I make money." Mark hung out with Jay's crowd nearly every weekend, but he set himself some rules: He could drink and smoke, but no drugs and no sex. The others made fun of him for being a virgin and for not smoking pot, but in a way it made him a different breed, and superior, especially when *he* was the one to figure out a way to get some coked-up congressman's kid home.

Once I went with Mark to one of Jay's parties. It was supposed to be in the VIP rooms at Love, D.C.'s premiere red-velvet-rope club, but something went wrong. Instead we ended up at Karma, a downtown bar way too small for this crowd. The occasion was GW's first-round win in March Madness, the college basketball playoffs. The party was on the debauched end of college normal, but by Patrick Henry standards it was downright demonic. Girls in handkerchief tops and skinny jeans kittened up to the bar to decide between kamikazes and orgasms. Patrick Henry had always struck me as eerily disembodied for a college campus; even on the first warm day of spring there was no giddy baring of legs, no bikinis on the grass, no holding hands. Here at Karma, you couldn't avoid flesh unless you levitated up to the ceiling. Once the music started, the place was as dense as a mosh pit, backs pressed against breasts, thighs up against thighs. A female bartender—no doubt older than Mark's mom—poured vodka into her mouth half the night and screamed, "Happy Fucking Birthday!" in an effort to foment the general atmosphere of anything goes. Around midnight, the basketball team showed up. They walked up onstage and picked out girls from the crowd, the ones with the biggest breasts. Then they started grinding in earnest, working their hands easily up under those loose halters (*Shake . . . yer . . . laffy taffy*).

Above the noise, Jay tried to talk to me about his plans for spring break. He was taking Mark and some of his other friends on a road trip through Texas for a "week of debauchery." He mentioned parties and bars and prostitutes in Mexico. He said MTV's *Spring Break* had called to ask if they could film the trip, but the boys turned it down, in case one of them ever wanted to go back to the White House.

As we talked, Mark stood at the far end of the bar drinking a Corona Light. For most of the night he and Jay had stayed at opposite fringes of the party like bookends; a Jew from Dallas and an evangelical Christian, outsiders both. There was a Sikh guy at the party, too, whose appearance made him conspicuous, but Mark didn't have to bear that cross. In his blazer and jeans he looked like any other college kid, if a little more clean cut. "Juvenile," was his commentary on the scene. "A whole bunch of underclassmen trying to live it up. I'm past that," he said, although he'd never really passed through it.

Mark didn't exactly fit in here, but he didn't exactly fit in at school anymore, either. He seemed like Farris's worst nightmare, the kind of changeling Patrick Henry most feared creating. He talked about the college as if it were the Betty Ford Clinic, a place to dry out. "This place is good for you," he would say to me when I saw him in the cafeteria. "It's like working out." Or, "A normal college would give you condoms for free. Here, whether or not I'm inclined to have the discipline, it's forced on me." After graduation he was headed straight back to Hollywood. But for the moment he was happy to "have an umbrella over my head."

Once I'd asked him about the two Marks, and how he could live with them both.

"I don't know. Maybe I can't," he said. "Everyone else just gets to decide what they feel is right and wrong at any particular moment, and I have to follow what the Holy Spirit says. If I'm sitting where people are partying and the Holy Spirit says, 'Get out,' I have to get out."

I asked him about the two Marks again right after the party at Karma, and this time he was annoyed.

"I don't know," he said in a leave-me-alone voice. "I'm only twenty-one years old."

IN HOLLYWOOD I met some extremely successful evangelical Christians who were working in both film and television. They all subscribed to the Quality Club and aimed to do the best work they could do. But as a group they were tortured and guilt-ridden, frustrated with insular Hollywood, frustrated with a Christian community that couldn't seem to get it right.

Dean Batali was one of the lead writers for *That '70s Show,* a long-running sitcom that was literally about sex, drugs, and rock and roll. The day I visited him, he had two things on his desk: the first line of a script he had to complete ("Fez wakes up in bed with a forty-five-year-old woman") and his Bible, which he read every day despite the mockery of his colleagues. If he was given a sex scene to write, he didn't "get into the mechanics" the way another writer would. Instead he used wordplay. "Does that change the culture and bring more people to the God of Abraham? No. But it's a tiny grain of salt." In the Batali household, the Hollywood execs were known as Pharaoh and that's how he got through his days. Joseph, too, had served an unrighteous ruler so that one day he could be in a position to serve God. But when that day would come, who knew?

Scott Derrickson was where Daniel Noa wanted to be in ten years. He'd gotten his break making one of the Hellraiser movies and then hit gold with *The Exorcism of Emily Rose,* which was the top-grossing movie the week it opened. Yet even with all his success, he never went into a pitch meeting saying simply "I am a Christian." Too much baggage: close-minded, Bush-lover, judgmental. Instead he said, "I am a Christian, but . . ." and explained his views.

Emily Rose is based on the true story of a Catholic priest who in 1976 was called to exorcise demons from a college-age girl in rural Germany. The girl died during the exorcism, and the priest was put on trial. The movie cuts between her possession and the priest's trial. Derrickson said he modeled it partly on Spike Lee's *Do the Right Thing,* meaning he wanted to put both sides on trial— relativism and religious conviction—to "force the viewer to examine his own beliefs." The movie ultimately sympathizes with the priest and the reality of possession, but this comes across more as faith in the palpable presence of evil than faith in God.

Still, reviewers remained suspicious. They did not appreciate the horror genre being hijacked by a philosophical lecture. They mistrusted Derrickson for what A. O. Scott of the *New York Times* called "propaganda disguised as entertainment," and a "fascinating cultural document in the age of intelligent design." Another reviewer called it "Karl Rove" cinema. "That was crushing to me," said Derrickson, who described himself as anti-Bush and anti–right wing.

From the other side, Derrickson had to defend himself against Christians who thought horror movies were Satanic and accused him of "dwelling in the darkness," as one Christian reviewer put it. On Christian Web sites he got drawn into long arguments with his accusers: "To me, this genre deals more overtly with the supernatural than any other genre, it tackles issues of good and evil more than any other genre, it distinguishes and articulates the essence of good and evil better than any other genre, and my feeling is that a lot of Christians are wary of this genre simply because it's unpleasant. The genre is not about making you feel good, it is about making you face your fears. And, in my experience, that's something that a lot of Christians don't want to do."

Pious as he could be, Daniel Noa also suffered for his art. Parents who saw *Hitman* were often alarmed that he would cast the women of Patrick Henry as killers and seductresses. In one of his other short films, a girl who looked like she was wearing pajamas was shown brushing her teeth in a boy's bathroom. Parents complained that Daniel had portrayed a clearly unmarried couple as living together. (He hadn't.) Daniel's filmmaking created an air of suspicion around him, particularly to the parents of Patrick Henry girls, who unfortunately included his girlfriend's father.

The father was a missionary in Africa, and Daniel got the impression that he was worried about Daniel's morals. Why did he dress girls up in tight black T-shirts? Why did he let them hold guns? Why did he play a character who choked a girl?

There were other factors, but the end result was the demise of the relationship. Daniel found out about this over the phone just before Thanksgiving. The unraveling proceeded in a nineteenth-century fashion. The girlfriend came down with pneumonia and had to leave school. Daniel was asked, first by her father, and then by her, not to contact her again. In his own mind, Daniel was one of the campus incorruptibles, but now the ground was shifting beneath him, as he wrote in an e-mail to a friend:

> Today I find myself unhappy, discontent, sorely missing a woman who meant so much to me. The natural assumption is that God must have some sort of plan. What's eating me up is impatience. I'm sitting here, and nothing seems to be happening. My relationship with her isn't being fixed; there is no new Ms. Right in my life to prove that I was mistaken. Nothing.

Today I Met the Boy
I'm Gonna Marry

One afternoon in February, Elisa Muench was sitting in the cafeteria killing time before she started her shift at the coffeehouse. Her boyfriend—now she could use that term comfortably—was away in Israel on a weeklong trip organized by the International Fellowship of Christians and Jews. But Elisa had gotten to see Aaron the night before, on television. A local ABC crew had filmed a fifteen-minute segment on Patrick Henry that, naturally, featured the student-body president and, naturally, got everybody gossiping.

The students agreed that Aaron was good at doing "voice of the establishment" and explaining the school's mission to train "future leaders for Christ." When an interviewer asked about women's roles in this project, Aaron had answered: "We don't want to eliminate suffrage or racial integration or anything."

"Oh, thanks, Aaron," Elisa joked, repeating what she'd said to her friend while watching the interview. "Let's not go back to *Leave It to Beaver* days."

At that moment one of Aaron's friends stopped by: "Elisa, there's a box waiting for you in your mailbox," he called out.

Graduation was only three months away. At a nearby table, a girl wondered whether it was too corny to write on her White House application that her parents were the people who had influenced her most. Her friend wondered whether it was better to take a job answering phones in Congress or opening mail at the White House. At another college, some portion of kids might have been buying Eurailpasses or sending home for snorkeling gear. But here the pressure weighed heavily to find a job that furthered the mission or, for the girls, to marry someone who would. In these final months, the seniors were quoting that great career consultant, Jeremiah, whom I'd often heard used to defend a woman's traditional role in marriage: "I know the plans I have for you," declares the Lord, "plans to prosper you and not to harm you, plans to give you hope and a future."

But how would they know those plans, the seniors wondered. How would they know they hadn't chosen the wrong future?

Like many of her classmates, Elisa was praying for guidance, but not in a feverish way. Among this end-of-year turmoil, she seemed as content as I'd ever seen her. "There are so many different options," she said. "I don't know how things will turn out with Aaron. But it's a daily comfort to know as long as I'm seeking, my life will not fall apart."

She was considering the Department of Defense, the State Department, and possibly Congress. She was working all her old White House contacts. She was considering joining her best friend on Lynn Swann's campaign for governor of Pennsylvania. Even though she and Aaron were officially courting now, when she talked about her plans, she seemed automatically to assume that she'd be the one running the show. "He'll have to come visit me because a campaign is really, really tough and you work all the time," she said. "But the White House is what I really want."

There are certain Bible passages believers turn to when darkness is closing in and they need blanket comfort: "Though our outer man is decaying, yet our inner man is being renewed day by day," or simply "Rest in the Lord." But the verse that was calling out to Elisa these days was Judges 6:37. Gideon has already asked God for a sign. He says he will leave a piece of wool on the threshing floor. If there is dew only on the fleece and not on the floor, he'll understand that God will use him to save Israel. God answers, drenching the fleece but not the floor. But Gideon is a classic type A, the kind of guy who organizes his CDs by genre and then by an artist's last name. Even though he already has his answer, he asks God for another sign: This time would He please leave the fleece dry and cover the ground with dew?

"All the options look good and I'm thinking, Please, God, please give me some guidance, a sign," said Elisa. "Maybe take some of the options away?"

Aaron's friend came around again.

"Elisa, the box!" he insisted.

"Okay." She rolled her eyes and made her way down to the basement where the mailboxes were.

She came back with a small box marked ZALES.

Of course. Saint Valentine. Who was jailed for refusing to stop marrying Christian couples. Who left a mash note to the daughter of a prison guard right before he died.

Inside was a necklace with a diamond-studded gold heart. Elisa was flushed, suddenly full of purpose but light, like a hummingbird.

"I guess I better reconsider the photo album I got him," she said, jingling her keys. "Maybe I'll get him a shirt. But then he'll think I'm trying to give him a makeover. Which I am!" she yelled over her shoulder, as she fluttered out of the cafeteria.

Aaron and Elisa had spent Thanksgiving together at Elisa's best friend's house in Pennsylvania, which had made the courting official. They'd gone skiing together over Christmas break and visited each other's parents. Over time, Aaron had changed Elisa's mind about him.

"It just takes time to get to know someone. I think you've made some assumptions about me," he'd assured her. "I really don't mind if you work."

Back at school, they worked for the same organization—the Center for Equal Opportunity, an anti–affirmative-action group. Each of them combed through a different data set looking for racially determined scholarships and benefits in an attempt to "ensure color-blind opportunities," as Aaron put it. They had other hallmarks of coupledom as well. They sat close and even touching on a love seat at the coffeehouse, he reading Plato and she engrossed in foreign-policy handouts. They held hands or sat together or kissed good-bye on the cheek, but that was all. Elisa had once joked that a movie about Patrick Henry could be called *Never Been Kissed,* but this time around she was following the college's courting rules for the most part. She didn't necessarily believe in involving her parents heavily, but she did believe in "exercising caution" and not putting herself in a compromising situation. She and Aaron had spent plenty of time alone together, but they weren't "making out in the backseat of a truck" or anything. Like many Patrick Henry couples, she and Aaron planned to save their first real kiss for their wedding day.

These days Elisa talked about "the time we were broken up" as if it were ten years ago. She browsed wedding dresses online, compared a friend's bridal-flower arrangements to those she might someday order herself. Still, she worried about the campus buzz about her and Aaron. "People say he's ultra-ultraconservative," she told her best friend, who answered, "But how conservative could he be if he likes you?"

"Yeah, but they get around that by saying, well, Elisa's changed," Elisa fretted.

In some essential ways, Elisa and Aaron were very similar. They'd been raised in the same way, believed the same things, wanted the same future. Even on this campus of preternatural adults, they stood out as mature. Already they liked museum and movie dates, dining in elegant restaurants. True, Aaron could parrot a party line without self-consciousness, while Elisa often spoke in quotation marks, but she charted this difference in his favor. "He's so optimistic, and I have enough pessimism for both of us," she said. "He tells me to have more faith in people, and I tell him to have less."

But Elisa was wrong about the campus buzz. It was starting to shift. Lately, the line on Elisa was that what she'd really always wanted was not to run for office herself, but to be First Lady of something—the fantasy of many a Patrick Henry girl. After all, she loved those biographies of First Ladies. This year she had prominently displayed only one Bush administration poster—the one for Laura Bush's book festival that was hanging above her desk. Her favorite show was *Commander in Chief,* but she accepted Aaron's criticism that the Geena Davis president character did a poor job of balancing work and home life. And wasn't it a clue that both guys who had courted her had been Patrick Henry presidents?

Aaron's campaign slogan had been simply "Ideal." And he was, really. Maybe he wasn't exactly charismatic, but he fit the Patrick Henry image of a leader. He was blond and blue-eyed, a star on both the soccer and basketball teams, and he'd been raised on a farm. After graduation he would begin basic officer training at Quantico, a marine base north of Fredericksburg, Virginia. At twenty-six, he was older than most of his peers. He was clean-cut and mature, the opposite of frivolous.

The campus political establishment had already rewritten the unofficial history of the election to give Elisa a critical behind-the-scenes role. "I was somewhat talked into running," Aaron had said, and everyone now assumed it was Elisa who had done the talking.

With someone pushing him, he could be groomed office by office. "It started to mean more to me," he said. "I learned how to promote myself without being self-aggrandizing. I'm not a recluse and I'm not the life of the party, but this forced me to seek out contact with people. I learned how to phrase things diplomatically, how to communicate clearly without alienating people," he said. "I'm not a person who just revels in the spotlight, but I'm comfortable standing for and communicating what I believe"—the sound bite of a reluctant future senator who could prove to be a rock in uncertain times.

During the campaign for student-body president, he'd exhibited an unusual combination of ambition and reserve. Fast-forward fifteen years and Aaron has now ticked off all the boxes. He's worked on several campaigns and congressional offices. He's served overseas with the marines. He's married to a wonderful woman, and they have four lovely children. Together they teach Sunday school. The campaign bio writes itself. Aaron Carlson. Farmer.

Marine. Husband. Straight-shooter. Christian. Yes, he lacks the raw ambition, the charisma, and maybe the guts for a political fight, but that's where Elisa, his shrewder half, comes in.

Already at Patrick Henry, Elisa had taken bold steps as the campus's unofficial First Lady. When her name came up for a committee, she was not diverted to secretary. In a quick, silent vote, she was chosen as the female representative for the student-life panel reviewing the school rules. In a public meeting, she sat on stage with a group of professors and Dean Wilson. In khakis and a trench coat, she had her Hillary Clinton moment, suggesting the following change: "If you're expecting your child to be parented while they're here, then this is not where you should send them. We do not follow the policy of in loco parentis."

One Sunday I went with Aaron and Elisa to Grace Community Church, a nondenominational church in nearby Ashburn beloved by many PHC students for reasons that quickly became obvious: Services were held in the auditorium of the local high school, jeans were the norm, and the pastor looked exactly like Tom Cruise. Elisa told me several times this would not be her first choice; she preferred her church a little more buttoned up. But Aaron had started going to Grace with a friend the previous year, after they'd broken up. And in a Patrick Henry relationship, it was often the man who chose the church community.

On the way over, Elisa and I chatted a little. At a lingerie shower, she'd recently seen two friends who had graduated, one the previous year and one two years earlier. They'd both been married nearly a year "and they were still working," one at the White House and one in Congress. "That really encouraged me. They didn't seem to be having kids right away."

Unlike the other Patrick Henry kids at the service, Aaron was wearing a blazer and khakis and Elisa was in a chocolate brown skirt and pointy shoes, with her trench coat over her lap, her Bible out, and a pad for taking notes. Aaron rested his hand on Elisa's arm, and she adjusted her skirt shyly. Because many Patrick Henry couples avoided physical contact, their relationships often appeared to move in reverse. When they were courting, they seemed as if they were already married—poised in a comfortable tension. Then when they married, they went through that first year of dating, when they couldn't keep their hands off each other.

Right now, Elisa and Aaron seemed to have more in common with the new parents Pastor Bob had just called up onstage than with their classmates, who roamed the aisles in packs. "Our modern society does not esteem the family," said Pastor Bob. "They think of the child as a burden. We disagree. We accept it as a gift. We resolve to raise this child to love Jesus Christ."

The PHC kids, born after the age of the televangelist, had always raved about Pastor Bob and how "on fire" he was. In town he had a reputation for turning teenage skateboarders into zealots, and I could see why. Change the jeans and the rumpled oxford shirt into a suit, and it was Jim Bakker holding the microphone. He turned on his bug eyes and lowered his voice to a whisper and intoned, with impeccable horror-movie timing, "Stick with Jesus or you're useless. Shriveled. Dead."

His sermon ran from pregnancy centers to the recent tsunami to feminists to Freud ("He disgusts me"). He ended with a personal story:

Three days ago I was sitting at home and the doorbell rang. The children were running around, and the dog was slobbering everywhere. I thought it was some sales person. I looked out and saw someone showing my wife a copy of the *Watchtower* magazine. I was deeply saddened. In my heart, I thought, This message is driven by lies. I dismissed my family, and I told this Jehovah's Witness, "I am a born-again Christian. I believe God sent His only Son to cleanse us of our sins. You teach that good works can get you to heaven, and that is wrong! Please stop distorting the word of God! Please stop spreading heresy! Please flee to the Lamb of God! And by the way, have a nice day."

As soon as they left, I gathered my children and prayed for them: "God, my eyes have been open to the truth. Jesus is the Son, the Savior of the world. Why do I know the truth, while they subscribe to lies? God, there is a world of enemies knocking at our front door. We're not better than anyone. We're not better than any heretic, or proponent of false religion. We've just come to know You."

Liberation!

He was screaming now. A guy in a wheelchair next to us was going crazy. I was wondering if Pastor Bob had set up the cameras to catch him from all the angles. "Be free of torment! Confess your sins!"

"Judgment is coming! Yes! Yes! God save us! Judgment is almost here!"

After the sermon, we wished some strangers a blessed day and headed back. Aaron waited for Elisa to get back in her Jetta before he got into his red pickup with some guys from his dorm. He reminded her that she had to stop for gas. He drove ahead of her at the speed limit—he always drove at exactly the speed limit—and pulled into the gas station with her. He was respectful, protective, and chivalrous. She looked radiant, her cheeks full of color, her hair pulled back. The church might not have been what she would have chosen, but it wasn't such a sacrifice either, given everything else.

WHEN ELISA WAS ENTERING her preteen years, "courting" was turning into a youth revolution. In 1993 the Southern Baptist Convention launched the True Love Waits campaign. Christian teenagers gathered by the thousands in youth groups, festivals, on the National Mall to sign a pledge that read: "Believing that true love waits, I make a commitment to God, myself, my family, those I date, my future mate, and my future children, to be sexually pure until the day I enter a covenant marriage relationship."

The movement's name wrote its own headlines. Profiles of radiant Christian couples who held hands but nothing more appeared in every newspaper. "It's awesome to be a virgin," seventeen-year-old David Medford told the *New York Times*. The pledge was followed by the Pure Love Alliance and the Silver Ring Thing (which was meant to hold the place of a future gold one), along with bracelets, T-shirts, and key chains. But the gimmicks worked only up to a point.

By sociologists' standards, the movement was pretty successful: During that period, nearly 85 percent of teenagers who attended church weekly said they would wait until they got married to have sex, and nearly 25 percent reported actually signing the pledge. Teens who took the pledge lost their virginity later, had fewer sexual partners, and were less likely to cheat than nonpledgers. But from the pastors' point of view, it was a disaster. The majority did not live up to their vows; at best, the pledges delayed premarital sex by only eighteen months. When the results were reported, the news media picked up on two findings: Men who took the pledge were slightly more likely to report having had anal sex and were less likely to use condoms.

"They encourage, um, to save sex for marriage and stuff like that. But that's pretty much it," fifteen-year-old Megan told researchers who were conducting a study on sex and religion in the lives of American teenagers. And therein lay the problem. True Love Waits asked kids to stay virgins, but didn't tell them not to make out, not to be alone in a car together, not to take off their clothes. For a seventeen-year-old, this proved difficult. The movement had built a house with no foundation.

True Love Waits needed new rules, new habits, and new love songs, with a troubadour to sing them. In the mid-nineties, he appeared. Josh Harris first surfaced through *New Attitude* magazine, which he published with his brothers from their house in Gresham, Oregon. He was the first celebrity of the True Love Waits generation, an eighteen-year-old celibate heartthrob, a pinup boy for Christian virgins everywhere.

New Attitude was the coolest thing many homeschoolers had encountered to date. Its covers looked like a cross between Soviet constructivist design and *Wired* magazine. It read like a zine produced in somebody's basement. Its message was on the extreme end of devout, but it had been written by someone who clearly sneaked peeks at MTV. "I hate homeschooling," read a cover that showed a girl with pouty red lips who'd chucked her books on the steps of her house. "To Know, To Do, and To Dare" was the magazine's motto. To a homeschooler starved for hipness, this smelled like teen spirit.

One cover story, "Emotional Fornication," featured a ghoulish James Dean–era couple locked in a formal dance position. In this and other similar stories, Harris began to lay out the manifesto that would make him famous in Christian conservative circles: "Every Friday night, millions of single Americans crowd the movie theaters and live out their romantic/sexual fantasies by observing the action on the screen. Many in the audience leave the theater yearning for intimacy (or at least the backseat) and, in effect, say to their date, "Let's go out and try what we just saw," or perhaps, "If only you could be like that!"

He urged his fellow Christians to resist. Replace the cycle of "Dating! Engagement! Marriage! with Friendship/Courtship! Marriage!" Giving up sex was not enough; Christian teens needed to start a "revolution in relationships," he wrote. In 1997 Harris expanded his ideas in *I Kissed Dating Goodbye*. The book spread like a fever through the homeschooling communities and beyond; Elisa read it, Aaron read it, Derek read it, everyone read it; their parents read it to them first and then the kids snuck it into their rooms and read and reread the sections on Jeff and Sheena and Kara and what happened to them when they failed to keep their hands to themselves. Boys wanted to be like Josh. Girls wanted to change his mind. He sold one million copies and eventually wrote three more books.

Harris used anecdotes that hit home with his generation. He confessed to making out with three girls in one night, stealing porn, engaging in heavy petting with a Christian girlfriend, meeting cute, wholesome Chelsea in a stairwell at Christian leadership-training camp and then corresponding obsessively with her, one letter ending in a bright, bubbly "I love you in Christ." "It's a miracle that I remained a virgin," he wrote. That, plus the photo of him on the back cover—slim, feline good looks, lips slightly parted, waiting, in his slouchy overcoat, on a deserted street for someone to show up—was enough to melt any homeschool girl's heart.

Harris asked his fellow teenagers to reel back to what at the time seemed monkish extremes. If you knew you weren't going to marry your girlfriend, break up with her. Don't kiss, don't touch, don't share secrets, don't cross the line of platonic friendship unless you were thinking of marriage. On second thought, avoid platonic friendship altogether. Girls, dress modestly. "Get rid of anything in your closet that might cause a brother to stumble." Boys, control your lustful thoughts. Don't masturbate, don't even watch shows that "mock your beliefs about purity. Tune it out, turn it off."

"Guard your heart," was the core of his advice. For the wary, sophisticated Patrick Henry generation, this was the phrase that replaced the airy jingle, "True Love Waits."

Harris repackaged the patriarchal rules of his parents' generation in hipper terms. A man should initiate romantic expression, and a woman might "match but not outpace him." Send her an e-mail to let her know you're thinking about her. Give her flowers or leave her notes. Women, make him brownies and have his favorite ice cream waiting in the freezer. Then, "Watch, wait, and pray." If he got the right signs, he could deepen the friendship by, say, asking her to teach Sunday school with him. Soon it would be time to "put yourself on trial" by talking to her parents. Get to know her some more, then ask her to marry you.

Harris saved the bomb for midway through the book. Erik and Leslie were already married, but Erik never took his eyes off her. They held hands in the car, even though she was in the backseat and he in the front.

Their secret: "Our first kiss was at the altar," Erik told him.

"My jaw dropped," Harris writes. "'You didn't kiss until you got married?'"

"'Nope,' Erik said, beaming. 'The most we did was hold hands.'"

Didn't kiss? How could they not kiss? Didn't they watch *Arrested Development*? Didn't they read *Glamour*? Didn't they have any hormones?

In a comprehensive study on abstinence pledges in high schools, researchers made a surprising finding. If an abstinence pledge was too popular at a school, its effectiveness dropped. The pledges worked best when a critical mass of students took them—but not too many students. Their conclusion was that an abstinence pledge worked by embedding kids in a self-conscious minority that perceived itself as special, even embattled. American teenage culture worships the First Kiss. But Christian kids could subvert peer pressure and create their own cool. Now the "cool girls" were virgins.

Among the many storybook courtships at Patrick Henry, that of Matthew du Mee and Christy Ross stood out as a model. Before they began spending "exclusive time" together sophomore year, Matthew called Christy's father to ask his permission. They took long walks together on the bike path behind school and talked. "Still, I felt like I was getting a 'wait' signal from God," Matt recalled. Later he accepted that as one of the "small miracles of their relationship."

It turned out that Christy had written at sixteen in her journal, "I don't want to spend my life having crushes on different guys." She had pledged to "love Christ with my whole heart and not fall in love with a guy for five years." ("But don't you want to get married?" her mother had asked. "Goodness, I just feel like there's more to life than having crushes on different guys!")

Matthew's courtship proposal came exactly five days before her five-year pledge expired. "But I got a lower grade on my

SATs," she responded earnestly. (Matthew had scored a perfect 1600.) He reassured her and wrote her father an eighteen-page single-spaced letter telling his life story. "My name is Matthew du Mee and I was a good kid," it began.

Courting didn't speed up their physical relationship; it just meant they began to talk about things most teenagers divulge in the first five minutes of an IM session. Usually on their walks they'd stop at a certain point and turn around. "Let's keep walking and see what's around the next bend," Matthew said now. They talked about their families, their friends, and their future. "I used to say what was going on but not how I felt about it," said Christy. "Once we started courting, I could be more open." When they were apart, their e-mails got longer and longer

Over Christmas break of their senior year, Matthew drove through a snowstorm to Christy's house in Evansville, Indiana, to propose. Christy, her parents, and her five siblings were downstairs in the basement, watching television. Matthew showed up wearing a suit but no socks; he'd changed and shaved at a gas station, but couldn't find his socks in his suitcase. He kneeled in the middle of the room, her family all around and recited:

> Christy, you love Jesus Christ and you point me to him.
> I didn't come here on some simple whim
> I love you, I need you and all that you give.
> I want to serve you as long as you live.
> Christy, will you marry me?

Christy dropped to her knees and hugged him. "Yes—absolutely. Yes." They hugged for a while, but didn't kiss.

They told me this story in April 2005, in a Burger King on the way to a debate trip in Indiana, a few months after they were engaged. Dean Wilson, the debate coach and Matthew's mentor and confidant, teared up at hearing the story again. "I think we have a very special love story," Matthew said. "Especially because God wrote it," Christy added and leaned her head on his shoulder.

In the 2006 contest for best courting couple, Farahn would not be a participant. Jared was now an occasional blip on her text-message screen—an "I will always love you" that made her sigh and turn off her phone. Over break he had been sitting with her whole family watching TV when a commercial for the upcoming NBC drama *Revelations* came on. Jared had chuckled and said, "Well, that's not really gonna happen," and the family went dead silent. Another time he told Farahn homeschooling "was for re-tards." Once he yelled at her for missing an exit on the highway.

On that visit to her parents' house, he had sulked in his room for two hours because he felt Farahn wasn't being affectionate enough. That was the last straw. "When he leaves, you're going to break up with him," her mother had said. Farahn did as she was told, and then put her fate in other hands: "If God wants me and Jared to be together, we will be, and there's nothing Mom can do about it. And if God doesn't want us to be together, then there's nothing I can do about it."

With her boyfriend out of the picture, Farahn was sounding more like the old Elisa. Just as her mother had hoped, Farahn was focusing more on her studies and had become one of Bob Stacey's best students in "Freedom's Foundations." In class, Farahn's wari-ness came across as a canny sense of political strategy; she seemed to understand Machiavelli all too well. She decided she was des-tined to become a political consultant, or maybe the next Condi Rice. She started looking for summer internships on the Hill.

That left the total number of engaged Patrick Henry couples

at eight, most of whom would be married between June and August. "Gosh, what's in the water?" Elisa said, repeating the slogan of her junior year. But this time there was no nervous edge. "It makes sense. They have the same values, the same upbringing, and the same morals. Isn't that cool!"

One Friday Aaron skipped classes and disappeared for the day—to pray and think, he told Elisa. Some wary part of her thought he might break up with her; it was not like him to skip classes. But she hoped that wasn't true. She hung out at Borders to read her Bible and write in her journal: "Now I've changed in a way that couldn't be my doing," she wrote. "I do know, without a shadow of a doubt, that he's the one I'm called to."

On Saturday Elisa was sitting at her desk studying when she saw Aaron drive by in his truck. She hadn't heard from him all day Friday or Saturday morning. Then at 4:15 he called. "Do you want to go for a drive?" Elisa didn't get dressed up. She just grabbed her trench coat and headed out. She didn't ask where they were going, and he didn't say. She didn't really want to pry about his alone time.

After about ten minutes, they came to a familiar spot. It was an old Civil War bridge in a secluded spot in Middleburg where she and Christy, who was a close friend, used to take walks or study. Maybe he's lost, she thought. She'd never talked to him about this bridge, and she was pretty sure Christy hadn't, either. The sun was setting soon, and she felt tired. She'd been stressed out by Aaron's sudden disappearance and didn't know what to expect.

Aaron stopped right by the bridge, took her hand, and led her to it. He said he'd been praying, and that had led him to the story of the prophet Elijah. In 2 Kings 19, God tells Elijah to stand at the top of the mountain, for the "Lord is about to pass by." Elijah hears a "great and powerful wind," but God is not in the wind.

Elijah feels an earthquake, and then a fire, but God is not in those, either. Finally comes a "gentle whisper."

From this, Aaron concluded that he'd been waiting for some blaring signal from God about Elisa, but that signal would never come. God, like Aaron himself, "speaks quietly," he told her. Then he got down on one knee.

That night Elisa called her family and some friends who'd already graduated, including Christy, who said Aaron had e-mailed her for the exact location of the bridge. She updated her Facebook status to "engaged!" and scanned a photo of the ring, a diamond-studded band that had to be resized. She didn't tell anyone at school outside of her roommates, but word got out quickly. "LOTS of people getting engaged these days," another girl wrote on her Xanga site. "The world must be peopled! And what a beautiful way to people it, too. :)"

Her friends on campus kicked into action secretly. A Patrick Henry engagement occasioned two separate rituals—one for the man and one for the woman. The man had to undergo a "Bobtism." One night, while he was studying or hanging out in his dorm room, his friends would hustle him out and throw him in the lake behind the dorms. Until 2005 he also had to suffer through a beating with a wooden paddle, but the school administration declared these "engagement spankings" embarrassing and barbaric. (Matthew du Mee was the last recorded victim.)

A woman went through a much gentler process. A boy on campus was told about the engagement. He sent out a mass e-mail announcing it, but without saying who the parties were. In the evening, the girls gathered in one of the dorms. They passed around a ring on a candle. When it reached the right girl, she put it on her finger and everyone came over to hug her.

Scott sent out an e-mail to all the girls on campus: "There's a candlelight ceremony tomorrow in Mt. Vernon." Elisa knew what came next. She didn't want the usual dried roses and violins, so she planned the music for a swing-dance kind of vibe: "Love Potion Number Nine" and "Today I Met the Boy I'm Gonna Marry."

At about eight in the evening, forty or so girls showed up in the lounge. Elisa told the story of how she and Aaron had met, broken up, and gotten back together. She read from Isaiah 41, when God says to Jacob:

> *So do not fear, for I am with you;*
> *do not be dismayed, for I am your God*
> *I will strengthen you and help you;*
> *I will uphold you with my righteous right hand.*

She ended with a snippet from her favorite letter from Aaron: "It's good spending time with you. You're addicting, and I'm hooked. And I don't want any rehab. I love you, youngster. Love, your old man."

CHAPTER 11

Obey, All You
Little Children

Just before class, someone pointed out the window, where you could still see the outlines of last night's moon. "Please take your seats," said Bob Stacey, sounding oddly formal. In honor of spring, someone was wearing a bow tie dotted with daisies; someone else was wearing a lime green polo. But Stacey didn't joke about those things, or anything else. He waited up at the front of the room in his olive green button-down shirt and khakis, looking much like himself, but different. In his hand he was holding not the Gettysburg Address or any of Lincoln's other writings that were on the syllabus for the day. He was holding a copy of the 2005–2006 Patrick Henry student handbook. His expression was difficult to interpret, beyond sober.

But when he began to read, it was in a shaky voice the students had never heard before. "The mission of Patrick Henry College is to prepare Christian men and women who will lead our nation and shape our culture with timeless Biblical values and fidelity to the spirit of the American founding."

He seemed too exposed, like a father who'd come home from work one day to tell his children he'd lost his job and to seek their reassurance. But as he continued, his voice steadied, as if he was finding himself in the words he was reading. "Educating students according to a classical liberal-arts curriculum, and training them with apprenticeship methodology, the College provides academically excellent baccalaureate-level higher education with a Biblical worldview."

He looked up. "I agree with that statement. But if anyone here feels conflicted about whether my teaching is inconsistent with anything in this statement, I would urge you to leave the class. You can be excused without the usual penalty for absence. I would not expect you to tolerate teaching in error. In fact, if you believe that, it is your duty and obligation to leave."

Silence, although the puzzled faces implied a million questions: *Why are you asking us? What can we do for you? Are you leaving?* But no one said anything, and eventually Stacey resumed where he'd left off the previous lesson, with the Gettysburg Address. But no one took any notes. "Please God, let it be all right," one girl sitting in the back whispered to herself. And for about ten minutes, it was.

Then another girl sitting in the middle of the front row raised her hand. She was pale, with reddish hair, and she was known to hang out with the Mod Squad. In class she talked a little, but not much. Her trademark was her velvet cape, which she tied on mostly for Tolkien-related affairs. "I'd like to be excused," she said. She picked up her things and walked out.

One of Daniel Noa's friends found her in the hallway. At first she seemed only quietly agitated, but when they spoke she seemed to be in a state of "emotional hysterics," he reported to another friend on his cell phone. She explained that she was not against Stacey. Who could be? But she just couldn't quite read which way the Holy Spirit was guiding her. So she walked out.

Her friends suggested she talk to Marian Sanders, the dean of academic affairs, and then to Farris. By lunchtime she made her way to Farris's office, still shaken, and reported what had happened. Farris seemed sullen at hearing the news. This latest development left him with only bad choices. Farris did not want to take on the beloved Stacey with only six weeks left in the semester. But he couldn't let a professor put his students in this position. He told the girl not to worry. As soon as she left, he sent for Stacey.

When Stacey walked into Farris's office, the students were already asking themselves the critical question: What kind of school was this going to be, Virginia Bible U or God's Harvard? Were they going to take back the nation or bicker among themselves?

A few people saw Stacey walk out of Farris's office after half an hour, chat with some students, and head out to the parking lot. By mid-afternoon, the rumor had gelled: Dr. Stacey had been fired.

On student blogs, in voice mails, on text-message screens, one phrase reappeared: "It's 9/11 here at PHC." The students were used to living under a direct chain of command that ran from Dr. Stacey to Dr. Farris to God. They loved Stacey, but "God raised up Dr. Farris as our leader," as they liked to say. In their rarefied lives, the patriarchal confusion hit with the force of the Last Days. People huddled at cafeteria tables in small groups, praying through sobs. The lady serving lunch asked, "Did something happen in your country?"

The cafeteria crowd divided into the forces of light and the forces of darkness. On the light side, people clung to a very literal definition of Christian hope, which translated loosely into "Things are never as bad as they look."

"Lord, You knew this would happen in the year 2006 at PHC, and I pray we'll be able to trust You and rest in Your arms."

"I see a very bright future for PHC. Even though it's going through rocky times, I believe God will bless PHC."

"We need to stay calm. God is in control last time I checked. He created the world. I think He can handle this."

"Dear Lord. You are good. You love us and You love kindness."

Jeremiah Lorrig, who played the God figure in *Hitman,* appointed himself the spokesman for the forces of light. Already he'd seen positive results, he told me: Boys had been raised into positions of leadership, people were praying more. "We can despair short term, but if we despair long term, we're in sin. God won't jerk us around. If God says stay at Patrick Henry, we'll stay. If He says leave, we'll leave," he said, as if God were the safety patrol.

In another corner of the cafeteria, a group of students treated the breakdown of order as a demonic liberation. Although it was still officially "business hours," they were out of dress code, wearing flip-flops, T-shirts, or black "mourning" outfits more appropriate for a nightclub. In public, not caring who heard them, they talked about their evening's adventures like ordinary college kids.

"No way! You drove last night? In your condition?"

"We took turns."

"Did you throw up?"

"Well, a little."

A group of girls checked other colleges' Web sites to see who had rolling admission—Calvin? Hillsdale? Claremont McKenna? Their moods raced from giddy to distraught. "Our professor is gone? Dang it. Well, what's the homework tomorrow?" one said, making fun of everyone else.

"I just want to go to Stacey's house and sit at his knees and say, 'Plato, Aristotle, teach me,'" said another.

"I'm going, right now. Who's coming?"

"No. Let's just go to my house and watch *Dead Poets Society*."

"If we burn the school down, should we call you?" they asked me.

A friend of Farahn's who had graduated the previous year and was in town visiting came by to see her. He found her alone, having just come from the gym, watching old *Seinfeld* reruns, and eating stale Goldfish and grapes. She'd been a mess since the tension with the professors began—one car accident, one bad fall that had left her limping.

"Stacey's my beginning and end of PHC," she told her friend. "There are so few people I can talk to, and he's one of them. What am I gonna do? What am I gonna do?" Once she thought she would be a dancer, but she was already nineteen, and that winter the Rockettes had turned her down again. Political consulting was still on her mind, but that interest came from her connection to Stacey and how much she'd enjoyed his class. Her friend said that talking to her was like talking to someone who'd lost her identity.

One thing she was sure of: She was not coming back to Patrick Henry next year. "I don't care," she said. "The only thing that makes me happy is getting out of here."

Around dinnertime, a student was driving out one side of the circle that led off campus when Farris's SUV swerved back around it, nearly hitting him. Naturally, the student followed him, and he was right behind Farris when he burst through the door of the cafeteria, his face red, breathing hard.

"By now most of you have heard the rumors, and I want to

correct them," he said to the forty-or-so people still there. "I did not fire Dr. Stacey. I asked him to apologize, and he asked for time to think about it. I told Dr. Stacey he had until Monday morning." He said Stacey had acted unprofessionally and treated the students like kids caught up in a divorce who needed to choose sides. "Figure out who you trust," Farris told them.

The girls in the dorms passed the night huddled in the RAs' rooms. Just past the lake, a gray mass was jerking around in the sky, and they wondered if it was a tornado, and if God was angry with them.

Early Saturday morning, Stacey stopped by his office. He was worried Farris would change the locks, and he wanted to get his books and photos out. His phone had already been cut off the day before, he discovered; and his e-mail account came back "no access." As far as he was concerned, he had already been fired; a student had even called his wife Friday and reported that to her. He and his wife prayed a lot Friday night, not about whether Stacey would stay or go. They already knew he couldn't stay. Instead, they prayed about whether God would see them through the rocky stretch ahead.

Stacey was obviously not going to apologize. That Saturday morning, a student who was helping him pack picked up the pile of midterms on his desk and put them on top of a box of books. Stacey considered leaving them there, in the empty office. But he took them out of the box, and then changed his mind and put them back in. "It's hard for me to say how much teaching at PHC has meant to me in the last years," he told his students over the next few days. "I've had a chance to know some of you since freshman year and I've seen you come to fruition, and I can't ask for more than that. It's a great job and I've been grateful for the time I've had.

"I will miss you all very much. We shared something special, as if we were comrades in arms, and that's special. I encourage you to remember that.

"Remember that in an important way we have succeeded. We haven't compromised on what's important to us and that means a lot."

On Monday morning, no one showed up to lead chapel, and there was no explanation. Leaderless, the students sat for a while listening to the lawn mower outside, until someone started off in prayer. "Lord, I had all my plans all laid out. I expected to take these classes next semester. Lord, will there be a school to come back to?"

At 10 A.M. the students headed to class. Instead of Stacey they found Sanders at the front of the room. She was, unfortunately, perfectly cast in the role she was being asked to play. She looked like a fifties-era schoolmarm in her kelly green suit and pumps and her chocolate meringue of a hairdo. All she lacked was the cat-eye glasses.

"Good morning," she began. "This will just take a minute or two. As you know, Dr. Stacey has been fired, based on what transpired. It's a sad thing for you and for us. Dr. Stacey gave time and effort, and he's made a valuable contribution. We are optimistic we can get a replacement, but we can't make a promise that it will be this day or that day."

The students had showed up to class in jeans, sweatpants, and sneakers. They were slouched in their seats like the high school misfits of *Welcome Back, Kotter*. As Dean Sanders talked, they texted each other jokes: "What do u think shes hiding up there in that hair?" And: "Can u be a virgin and still be a slut?" Farahn, who had written OBEY in big letters on the board behind Sanders, fixed her with a cold stare.

"Just so you know, this is a service we've paid for," Farahn said. "With all due respect, how exactly does the administration expect us to respond?"

"Remember, God is fruitful in all circumstances," Sanders answered. "No matter how bleak they appear to the human eye."

After she left, they translated her sentiments: "When life hands you a bucket of warm spit, you make lemonade."

"And sell it to other people."

Out of nowhere, Farahn commented that when she was home for spring break, all her old friends wanted to know if she was still dancing. "Yeah, at Twin Peaks," she said now. "Drinks, half price."

Before Farahn left, someone went up to the board to elaborate on her graffiti. OBEY, ALL YOU LITTLE CHILDREN.

EXPERIMENTAL COMMUNITIES almost always implode. One faction wants to hold on to the purest version of the mission while another begs for a little fresh air. The men fight for power, while trying hard to project an image of unified authority. But eventually, their adoring subjects catch on.

That day they called "9/11 here at PHC" was significant only because the truth had filtered down to the students. Stacey and his fellow professors had already made it clear to Farris a few weeks before that they were leaving. In retrospect, the breakdown seems inevitable, even from the first weeks of that year.

Every semester, Patrick Henry held a one-day Faith and Reason seminar, part of the school's effort to cement its own barely minted traditions. Classes were canceled, and a professor or guest lecturer spoke on this timeless Christian theme. The idea was for students to reflect for a day on the twin pillars of a Patrick Henry education and rededicate themselves to the school's mission. The speaker could address the topic from a philosophical, theological, or modern political point of view. For the fall seminar, the honor had fallen to Todd Bates, a rhetoric and theology professor.

Bates prepared a lecture on St. Augustine and the liberal arts. The day before the seminar, he e-mailed a copy around; his colleagues made a few comments, mostly positive. Farris had an entirely different reaction. "I have no quarrel with what you say," Farris told him. "I have a quarrel with what you left out. There's no acknowledgment here that the Bible is the ultimate source of truth. If you want to speak at Patrick Henry, you've got to integrate the Bible."

Bates was surprised by this criticism. St. Augustine's writings showed up in many classes at Patrick Henry. On the first page, his lecture talked about Scripture's insights into life; he'd written that when Augustine converted to Christianity, "his restless soul found its rest in one who is the Truth."

But this was not enough for Farris. "What's at stake here is, do we regularly affirm the Bible as the ultimate source of all truth, or is it an unstated assumption lurking in the shadows?" Their exchange got testy enough that at one point Farris threatened to call off the lecture.

In the end, they found a version they could agree on, and Bates spoke. Farris said that he was satisfied, but on the day of the lecture, the professors felt that he was hassling them. David Noe, an assistant professor of classics, recalled Farris walking up to him and saying: "Hey, I hear you think Augustine is a Christian." He said to a group of professors, "Augustine is roasting in hell," and complained that much like Calvin, Augustine "burned people at the stake—and I have problems with people who burn people at the stake," according to several of the professors. He showed up at a breakout group run by Stacey and delivered what Stacey considered a crude, wrongheaded lecture on Augustine's heretical notions. The way the professors saw it, the president of the college had conducted himself like a heckler intent on disrupting proceedings.

Farris was not saying anything they hadn't heard before. He was making age-old arguments against general revelation—the concept that you can know something is true apart from the Bible. Christians have argued over this question for centuries. But it had been a long time since disagreements on the matter were considered a firing offense at a Christian university with any ambitions. At Wheaton College, a professor might still get fired if he converted to Catholicism. But no one would question him for failing to make an academic lecture sound like a sermon, with Bible verses sprinkled liberally throughout.

The professors began to worry that maybe they had misunderstood what Farris meant by Christian liberal arts. If Augustine was a problem, then what about Kant, Nietzsche, or Marx? "We can appreciate any human who contributes to learning without seeing them as an enemy to be defeated," one said. But in Farris's view, they were all enemies to be beaten back with the Bible. Maybe the press was right: Once a fundamentalist, always a fundamentalist.

After the incident, nine professors, including Stacey, Root, Noe, and Bates, had made a pact. "If one of us goes down, we all go down." They didn't flesh it out or draw up a contract. They didn't think much about the consequences, even though all but

Root had young children at home and wives who didn't work. They came collectively to the realization that they were vulnerable and needed to stick together.

Soon the band of brothers was put to the test. Farris had received a letter from a freshman girl's father who was upset by what he'd heard in Root's class. Root had asked the students to imagine that two people were clinging to an inner tube in the middle of the ocean. The inner tube could support only one of them, so someone had to let go. The example was part of a discussion on the state of nature. "What would Hobbes and Locke have to say about this?" Root had asked the class.

One student answered by quoting John 15:13: "Greater love hath no man than this, that a man lay down his life for his friends."

"That's great, but it's too simplistic," Root recalled having told her. "Can we flesh that out?"

Root did not want to stop with just the verse. He wanted his students to think about the questions raised by this student's answer: Was God really saying you should kill yourself, which was "against the law of nature and the Word?" If not, then what did God mean by "lay down his life for his friends"? Further, Root's example involved a state of nature, in which true friendship is not really possible.

But the girl's father did not dwell on the nuances. In his letter, he accused Root of using the lifeboat example to "confuse the class on the moral issue and clarify the value of one's right to choose life even if it meant someone else's death." Farris took the father's side. "That's a well-known trick of the moral relativists," he fumed. "You'd have to be tone deaf to use that!"

Farris wrote Root a letter that read like a notice to appear before the heresy board. He asked about the lifeboat example. He asked six more questions about an article Root had written about St. Augustine in the school newspaper. He accused Root of using postmodernist, feminist logic, and quoting a "well-known Darwinist."

I happened to be in Farris's office on the afternoon he drafted the letter, and as he turned it over in his mind he became more and more irate. "He cites a Darwinian! What was he thinking? How can a Darwinian help you? I've used—what's his name?— Immanuel Kant in an argument. But that doesn't mean I advocate his views. You can't leave it to inference. You have to be clear!

"You know, there's a sense that in teaching these things we've lost a sense of our Christian mission. And I wouldn't say it that strongly, except that I am seeing signs. Signs of a lack of clarity in people's thinking. It comes from an arrogance, from being in love with the intellect.

"I don't believe in drinking from the font of human wisdom. I don't care if it's Billy Graham or C. S. Lewis, but no human authority is the equivalent of the Scripture."

Farris informed Root that he was temporarily withdrawing Root's contract for the following year until he received satisfying answers to his questions.

The band of brothers was now on alert. "It's scary to work for a guy who can hire and fire at whim," said Noe. "How do we know we won't be next?" If Root was to be questioned, they wanted it done openly before a board, not in Farris's office.

In this trio, Root was the hyperactive freshman, always slamming his desk, comparing Farris to Saddam Hussein. Stacey was the grave, disappointed senior. "I actually believe in the mission," he said. "'Tragic' is the word. For tragic, something good has to be lost." In the early evenings, Stacey, Root, and Noe disappeared to a cigar bar to hash out strategy over a glass of scotch. *"Shhh, don't tell anyone,"* Root whispered. *"We're going to a bar."*

By the second semester, none of them was speaking to Farris. They were like estranged relatives living together in a tiny house, communicating only through written notes. The professors tried to clarify their positions in e-mails and articles in the student paper that only inflamed Farris. In mid-March, chaplain Raymond Bouchoc wrote a five-page sermon lecturing them on the "harmful implications" of their beliefs and e-mailed it to all the staff and students. The letter was "fully endorsed" by Farris. That was it. Stacey felt particularly offended by having his faith questioned in public. He decided that whatever happened to Root, he couldn't stay.

This was turning out to be the most calamitous semester of Patrick Henry's brief existence. In semesters past, Farris had lost a professor or two over disagreements or his own bad temper. But this semester, it looked like one-third of the staff might decide they were not coming back, and all of them from the good third, the most popular with the students. Farris was in his car on his way to speak at a Reclaiming America for Christ conference in Fort Lauderdale when he got the call from Sanders. Stacey, Root, Noe, and one other professor had handed in letters that morning saying they wouldn't be coming back. In a letter explaining why, they accused Farris of creating "an environment hostile to the teaching of Liberal Arts." They quoted him saying things that would make his mentor Tim LaHaye proud: "I've [sic] read seventy pages of the *Iliad* this weekend and it's rubbish; it's all about adultery. I can write better than that." And: "We study Plato for opposition research. Even a broken clock is right twice a day."

A few nights after the professors had turned in their resignations, one of the previous year's graduates who still lived nearby threw them a party. At that point only one of them had a job lined up; the rest did not even have any prospects yet. For much of the night, they stood outside on the porch, shivering, smoking cigars, drinking whiskey, and marveling at the hell they had just escaped.

"How do you write a legal brief, Mike?" one taunted. "That's not in the Bible."

"I have an announcement," Stacey said. "We homeschooled our kids for six months, and we can't take it anymore."

At some point a student at the party rushed up to the porch, a little tipsy, and yelled, "It's the Patrick Henry wake! It's the Patrick Henry wake!"

Back at school, with nothing more to lose, Root had let himself off the leash. "Is there a future for the evangelical college?" he asked his class. "Maybe it's an oxymoron."

In addition to the Bible verses he occasionally recited at the beginning of class, Root conducted one-man poetry slams, reading barely coded protest poetry. One day it was the St. Crispin's Day speech from *Henry V*, meant to convey what Root experienced as "the terrible struggle for liberty" and the sacrifice involved.

> *We few, we happy few, we band of brothers;*
> *For he today that sheds his blood with me*
> *Shall be my brother; be he ne'er so vile*

Another day it was William Blake's "A Little Boy Lost" suggested to him by a sympathetic student who identified with the lost boy:

> *The Priest sat by and heard the child;*
> *In trembling zeal he seized his hair;*
> *He led him by his little coat,*
> *And all admir'd the priestly care.*

263

And standing on the altar high,
Lo, what a fiend is here! said he;
One who sets reason up for judge
Of our most holy Mystery.

The weeping child could not be heard,
The weeping parents were in vain;
They strip'd him to his little shirt,
And bound him in an iron chain;

And burned him in a holy place,
Where many had been burned before;
The weeping parents wept in vain,
Are such thing done on Albion's shore?

By the last few weeks, Sanders was sitting in on Root's classes to monitor what he said, and Root was tape-recording. On the final day of class, three students surprised him by standing up on their desks, although two were wearing heels and skirts. ("Get off the desks!" Sanders yelled.) They took turns reading Walt Whitman's elegy, "O Captain, My Captain."

O Captain! my Captain! our fearful trip is done,
The ship has weathered every rack, the prize we sought is won,
The port is near, the bells I hear, the people all exulting,
While follow eyes the steady keel, the vessel grim and daring:
But O heart! heart! heart!
O the bleeding drops of red,
Where on the deck my Captain lies,
Fallen cold and dead.

THE WHITE TENT was back up. It was graduation day, and the campus looked like a Fourth of July barbecue from a different era. The Ingalls clans were once again strolling around campus, braids trailing from straw hats and toddlers stuffed into velvet dresses. Elisa's and Aaron's families stood by the buffet tables, hashing over wedding plans. Aaron would be commissioned as a second lieutenant on June 3; Elisa's father would have the honors. One week later Elisa and Aaron would be married.

Farahn had some friends graduating, but she was no longer welcome on the campus. Once she had decided to leave the college, she had let herself be quoted in the local paper as the voice of the opposition and had even posed on the front steps for a picture. Hearing that some of the departing students planned to disrupt the ceremony, Farris had hired several plainclothes guards. So far the protest amounted to a couple of students who'd dyed their hair green and one graduate standing across the street with a big sign that read WHAT ABOUT BOB?

People who knew him well said Farris looked like he'd aged ten years. He had stopped me in the hallway one time to talk about the bright new future—a new student center, a new president, new professors—but he couldn't quite keep it up. He sat on the bench and started fidgeting with some pennies in his hand. "Maybe the divide was inevitable, but why did it have to be so nasty?"

But humility is not Farris's natural state. In the roster of speakers, he followed Brit Hume, a Fox News commentator who delivered a breezy manual on how to survive in Washington. (Have good telephone manners. Suck up to everybody. Be patient. Be positive.)

I'm not sure what the crowd expected of Farris—perhaps, if not an apology, then some kind of rounding off, some closure. But Farris had not yet moved to the Christian phase of reconciliation.

In fact, he was still completely in the grip of the ordeal, a man obsessed. Just that day he'd berated a girl for intentionally breaking the rules by wearing a miniskirt. He lectured her on the sin of rebellion and blamed the professors for corrupting her with their altar of intellectualism: "You have been taught lies from the pit of hell," he told her, "philosophical and factual lies." Speaking "as a dad," he added that her skirt was appropriate only for a cocktail lounge. After that he drafted another letter to Root, accusing him of having attended a party where he'd witnessed students drink, uttered the "f word" in their presence, and urinated in front of female students.

Now, at graduation, Farris spoke as if these nice parents in their floral prints and summer suits had gathered under this tent on a beautiful spring afternoon to decide on somebody's excommunication. Jennifer Gruenke was tearing up about the point I dropped my pen in amazement, which was just when Farris recited the anchor verse of his speech.

"Some have said that we should not be particularly concerned that there is error in a text written by a non-Christian writer, we should simply seek to discover whatever truth is there," he said. "I categorically reject this notion." Those who disagreed, he continued, would suffer the fate outlined in Romans 1, a favorite of angry preachers everywhere:

> Furthermore, since they did not think it worthwhile to retain the knowledge of God, he gave them over to a depraved mind, to do what ought not to be done. They have become filled with every kind of wickedness, evil, greed and depravity. They are full of envy, murder, strife, deceit and malice. They are gossips, slanderers, God-haters, in-

solent, arrogant and boastful; they invent ways of doing evil; they disobey their parents; they are senseless, faithless, heartless, ruthless. Although they know God's righteous decree that those who do such things deserve death, they not only continue to do these very things but also approve of those who practice them.

On the receiving line, a senior who had dyed his hair green for the occasion even though he'd had no previous alliance with the rebels said, "Thank you for ruining what was supposed to have been the best day of my life."

CONCLUSION

When I caught up with Derek Archer in the spring of 2007, he greeted me with a friendly hug. In two years at Patrick Henry, he had shed much of his awkwardness and come into his own. He was wearing a black felt cowboy hat that he'd picked up at a Republican booth at a fair in Ohio—his first-ever original fashion statement. "I know. Me, buy clothing? Can you believe it?" He'd fixed the AC in his car and now drove routinely on highways. He'd gotten a cell phone, and he was using it to carry on a fairly regular conversation with a girl.

Yes, a girl. In his wallet he carried her photo: a pretty, smiling coed with long sandy hair, a red blazer, and a backpack. THE MOST BEAUTIFUL WOMAN IN THE WORLD TO ME, read a note tucked next to the picture. They had crossed paths three times in their lives. Derek's parents told him they had been playmates as children in New Guinea, where her parents were also serving as missionaries. The families had a reunion when Derek was eleven, and again when he was fifteen. After the 2004 Bush campaign, Derek saw an e-mail message from her family, who was still overseas, to his. Her face popped into his head, and "I felt an impression in my heart," he told me. When she moved to Washington state to live with a relative, he started up a separate e-mail correspondence with her and then, one day, "nonchalantly obtained her phone number." Thanks to his new cell phone, he was now calling her once every couple of weeks.

Following the advice of an older woman at his church, Derek wrote an e-mail to the girl's parents, asking for their blessing to get to know their daughter better. After two weeks (which felt to him like two years), they wrote back: They could not yet sanction a "romantic relationship" but they could give their approval for a friendship. The answer from the girl herself was as warm as he could have hoped for: "At this point I feel I can give you a 'yes,'" she said about the friendship. "And if God wills that something else should come of it, we'll have to see that."

Derek was thrilled. He arranged to get a summer internship at a conservative think tank in Olympia, about an hour's drive from where she was living. "It's amazing," he said, "how certain people would push me at just the right moment, and then the Lord would just open it all up!" Whatever came of it, his conscience was clear because "the whole thing is completely submitted to God's will."

In two years, Derek's political views had shifted, too. None of the campaigns he had worked on while at Patrick Henry had lived up to his Bush experience in 2004. In the 2005 Virginia governor's race he'd worked on, Tim Kaine's victory had become a case study in how Democrats could recapture the faith vote.

In the 2006 midterm election, Derek had placed his hope in Republican Kenneth Blackwell, an African American former football star with a preacher streak who was running for governor back in Derek's home state of Ohio. To Derek, Blackwell was a dream candidate. At church rallies, Blackwell talked about "forces that were running God, faith, and religion out of the public square."

Derek volunteered and gave the campaign his all. He worked eighteen-hour days in an unheated conference room assembling phone lists and flyers for teams of Generation Joshua kids. He walked into the "victory" party an hour after the polls closed, pumped, until he ran into some local Republicans who were already discussing Blackwell's concession speech. True to his optimistic nature, Derek covered his ears. "He could win. He could win," Derek told himself. "What do the polls know?" But Blackwell lost by 23 percentage points. Other titans of the Christian right lost that year as well: Rick Santorum in Pennsylvania, Jim Talent in Missouri, Jim Ryun in Kansas. Bush's approval ratings plummeted to record lows.

The Patrick Henry kids were forced to acknowledge that "taking back the nation" was not going to be so easy, that the cozy proximity to power they enjoyed during the Bush years might sometimes elude them. Students described the Wednesday-morning chapel after the 2006 election as "like a funeral." Students were crying and quoting Old Testament passages about evil rulers taking over the land.

In the months after the election, Derek acknowledged a fact he'd long avoided: Republicans were not all good Christian men. There had been the scandal involving Republican lobbyist Jack Abramoff and House Majority Leader Tom Delay. In March 2007 Derek was shocked to hear Newt Gingrich, one of his heroes, admit to having had his own affair while he was fighting to impeach Bill Clinton for lying about Monica Lewinsky. "He's trying to lead the nation and he can't even control his own life? It's sad."

Monica Goodling's story was a lesson to him as well. She was a thirty-three-year-old ambitious Christian conservative who worked at the White House. She'd graduated from Regent University School of Law, founded by Pat Robertson in 1978 in much the same spirit as Patrick Henry had been. (One hundred fifty of Regent's graduates have worked at the White House.) Now her loyalty to Bush and her zealous defense of her values had landed her in the middle of a Justice Department scandal.

Then Derek nearly dropped his hat when he learned that the two leading contenders for the Republican presidential ticket, John McCain and Rudy Giuliani, had five marriages between them. "To be honest with you," he told me that spring, "I've become in some ways disenchanted with national politics."

A historian of the Christian right might perk up at the phrase "disenchanted with national politics." In the past, Derek's sentiment would have been a sign that evangelicals were about to go back into the wilderness, that we could soon expect to hear a modern-day evangelical prophet telling his flock to drop out of mainstream culture, to see a boom in the homeschooling movement and a dip in the number of Bible-quoting politicians.

But this time around, the cycle is unlikely to repeat itself. Evangelicals are far too entrenched in American politics and culture to drop out en masse. It took the conservative political movement thirty years to become a fixture in American politics, and it's taken evangelicals about the same amount of time. Like conservatives, evangelicals may remain chronically ambivalent, afflicted with a persecution complex despite their obvious successes. But they now controlled enough interest groups and think tanks and state and federal offices and movie-production companies to employ bright Christian interns for generations to come. They are secure enough in their power to know that they can respond to trying times without falling apart as a movement.

One of the Patrick Henry graduates already working on the Hill called me the day after the 2006 election because he'd heard that students had cried at chapel, and he thought it was ridiculous. "That's just wrong," he said. "It takes only a few months in the real world to realize the end-all and be-all is not returning America to 1776." Instead, Patrick Henry students should aim to be "realistic idealists." Almost all of his friends on the Hill drink pretty regularly. Women in his office curse. Some young staffers sleep with each other. It "sucks," he says, to be surrounded by so much temptation, but "welcome to Washington," he says. Much as they wish they could, none of them actually thinks they will get laws passed within the year to end all abortions.

"It's worthwhile to live for certain ideals," he said. "But sometimes you just have to stand back and realize the limitations."

Jim Ryun's son Ned, who runs Generation Joshua, could not imagine sending his kids to work on campaigns for any of the early crop of Republican presidential candidates, like McCain and Guiliani. But he balked at the idea of sitting out the election. At some point, he figured, the Generation Joshua activists would settle on some candidate they could live with. "We're not fundie nuts," he said. "We're actually rational human beings. Politics is not the art of the perfect. It's the art of the possible."

My guess was that most would hold on to their political views, but get better at presenting themselves and choosing their battles. The National Association of Evangelicals hasn't stopped fighting to end abortion. The group just does not make outrageous headlines anymore; it operates like any other lobbying group—quietly and behind the scenes.

Even Derek did not want to drop out of politics entirely, just national politics. Unlike some of his classmates, he knew he would have a hard time muting his faith to appeal to a broad audience. "I have a burning desire to proclaim the gospel to set someone free, and I don't see that a lot in national politics," he said. If he ran for local office, maybe city council or mayor, he figured he might be able to make it work. "With local politics you can build relationships," he told me. "They'll know I'm not some crazy religious wacko. They'll say, 'Oh, this guy's a Christian but he's a good guy.'" Already he'd tried his hand at community organizing. In the fall, he'd sent his fellow students an e-mail asking them to boycott the local Wal-Mart for joining the National Gay and Lesbian Chamber of Commerce, saying that he couldn't shop there "any longer with a clear conscience."

Much as I marveled at the Patrick Henry students, I doubted that any of them—not even the most rebellious of the campus rebels, not even the least-conservative kid there—would ever moderate their views enough to win my vote—not for president, congressman, or even city councilman.

Toward the end of my reporting, my recalcitrance began to bother the students, and I could feel their frustration. After two years of long, intense, often personal conversations with me, they hadn't managed to move me much. Much as I hated to disappoint, I remained constitutionally incapable of the modern conservative Christian's brand of certainty.

I still didn't really believe what the Patrick Henry kids told themselves—that everything happens for a reason. I believe only that it happens, and we muddle through. I suppose in some way I fundamentally believe in chaos, less in a grim Nietzschean spirit than a casual bohemian one. If this makes me a postmodern nihilist, so be it. I certainly don't feel hopeless most of the time. I just feel more at home with the God of what they call the Old Testament, merciful one moment and cruel the next, but fundamentally unpredictable. To me this is much closer to life as we live it.

I could see Patrick Henry graduates shaking their heads in sorrow as they read that last paragraph and resolving to pray for me. As they see it, my values are based on nothing but whim and circular logic: It's wrong because I think it's wrong. "Intellectual suicide!" one of the graduates warned me. But underneath the arrogance, there must have been some concern for their own predicament: If they couldn't take back one friendly reporter, what about the rest of America?

But whatever doubts they had, they drove right through them. After Patrick Henry students graduate, the command to "shape the culture and take back the nation" haunts them even more strongly than it did while they were in school. Some try to duck it, but they can't. They're soldiers who've gone AWOL, restless and running scared. One graduate worked as a waiter at the Chili's in his Oklahoma hometown for a while. He enjoyed drinking beer with the locals after hours, but he was ill at ease and couldn't really show his face among his Patrick Henry friends. Finally, through some local contacts, he got a job on the Hill with his senator. He was answering phones and writing congratulations letters to constituents, with a half-hour break for lunch. But at least he had a direct view of the U.S. Capitol.

The most ambitious graduates can't relax until they get accepted at Georgetown Law School or get a job at the Heritage Foundation, a conservative lobbying group, or the White House, even if it's in the mailroom. Even the least ambitious find a way to comply. One 2006 graduate who hadn't let go of her prairie-girl look over four years said she would contribute to the mission by raising "godly children." Then she thought about it some more. "Maybe, God willing, my husband will be President and then I can be the First Lady."

Farahn actually followed through on her impulse from the spring to become a political consultant. After she dropped out of Patrick Henry, she got a summer internship with Bobby Jindal, a young Louisiana Republican congressman much admired on campus. I visited her a month into the job. She already had a reputation as smart, efficient, and bold. "Let's face it. Farahn stands out," said one of her new officemates. She was wearing a pink sweater and gold flats and had her hair up in a bun. She handled a lot of calls from Louisiana constituents asking about federal aid, and she wanted to tell them, "Go get a job. Since when do Republicans just throw money at things?" As we walked to the cafeteria, everyone we passed seemed to know her, and she greeted them with uncharacteristic sweetness. ("I can definitely do the Southern-charm thing," she said. "But it's definitely a turn-it-on, turn-it-off kind of thing.")

Farahn was turned off by the Republican frat-boy partying on the Hill and the lack of intellectual heft. "They read John Grisham, not Harvey Mansfield," she complained. She'd had the same realization that overtakes all Patrick Henry grads after a month on the Hill: "You think everyone working in politics is so idealistic, but it's not like that. Maybe 90 percent of what Democrats do is ridiculous, but at least 50 percent of what Republicans do is too." But she was not giving up on the ultimate goal. In fact, being surrounded by "your basic kids" who live for dollar draft beers at happy hour actually made her miss Patrick Henry—not in its oppressive details, but in its broad view: "The whole mission of the school has become really important to me, and I'm kind of amazed at how little people actually care about it in the real world." First, however, she would finish her degree at Wake Forest University in Winston-Salem, North Carolina, among "just your basic kids—parties, pop music, MTV."

Elisa worked on the Hill, too, as a staff assistant and legislative correspondent for Todd Akin, a conservative congressman from Missouri known for his work against abortion, gun control, and taxes. She loved being up on the Hill even though it meant an hour-and-a-half commute to and from Quantico, where she and Aaron were living, and even though she had to sometimes call and tell him to "put something out for dinner" because she'd missed the 6 P.M. train and would get home late.

But her life as a workaholic Washington staffer would last only a year. In June of 2007, Aaron was scheduled to start at a Pensacola flight school and then she would have a whole new set of worries: Where would they live? Would she make new friends? When he was ready to deploy, would the Iraq war still be going on? Would he miss their kids' first steps? And, lastly, what would she do with herself now? "Being a military wife is not conducive to some things, there's no way around that," she said. "But I want to make sure I have an impact somehow. I don't need to have a huge career off the bat, but I do need to feel productive, even if it's small." She was considering getting a master's, "but I'm not sure in what yet," she said.

After graduation in 2007, Daniel Noa planned to head back to Hollywood. He was applying for a creative job in a production company and looking for a distributor for his completed film, *Smuggler's Ransom*. A couple of his friends planned to travel around

Europe for the summer, but he couldn't do that. "That's nice, but I gotta do something." He and his girlfriend never got back together, and he joked about growing old as the childless and unmarried "rich Uncle Daniel" from L.A.

Mark Shane was already working in Hollywood at one of the major networks. He had a prize job as an assistant to two vice presidents—the kind of position that usually went to people ten years older than he was. In his office, it was a cliché to say you loved *The Wire* or *Brokeback Mountain*. Even when his boss mentioned a family member who was a preacher, Mark didn't bring up his own faith. "I don't want to be the local curiosity—'Hey, check out the homeschool freak,'" he told me when I saw him in the summer of 2006. He spent his days reading and commenting on scripts and figuring out how he could make his first million by producing one of his own. If he could pull it off, he wanted to make his mark with something Christian-themed, or at least redemptive. "People here say, 'Oh, they hate Christians,' but it doesn't matter," he said. "If I tell a good story, it will sell."

Bob Stacey got a job at Regent University teaching government. "The administration does not meddle in the details of each professor's work," he said. He was living the drama-free life of a normal professor—writing op-eds and book reviews, working on a book about balancing liberty and security in an age of terrorism. Root moved to North Carolina and did some adjunct teaching at Regent, as well.

Root's question from his final semester: "Is there a future for the evangelical college?"—hung over Patrick Henry in the year after he'd left. In *The Opening of the Evangelical Mind,* Alan Wolfe concludes by urging evangelical academics to be less defensive and show other religions respect. They're not doing themselves or America any favors by "fencing themselves off," he writes. But this is easy to say from the outside. Even after the trauma was long over, the school seemed to live in mortal fear of becoming "Christian in name only," of damning its students into "conscious torment for eternity."

At the end of the 2006–2007 year, the school was accredited by the Transnational Association of Christian Colleges and Schools. At the same time, a couple of the fired professors' remaining allies left, including biology teacher Jennifer Gruenke, who was an old college friend of Stacey's. Farris meanwhile dreamed up an even more idealized form of his mission. He created a group called Tyndale's Ploughboys, a kind of Rhodes Scholarship within God's Harvard. A select group of students was asked to apply. Then he—playing the role of Tyndale—mentored them personally, inviting them to accompany him to speeches and meetings on the Hill.

Creating the perfect Joshua—pure and hungry for power— seems an increasingly elusive goal. But it can be done. Matthew du Mee had graduated with a straight-A record and in his final semester had sealed his legacy by beating a moot-court team from Oxford University for the second time in two years, in a debate judged by three Virginia Supreme Court judges. "If the rebellious kids had his gifts, it would be scary," said Dean Wilson, who was Matthew's best man at his wedding to Christy Ross (Matthew being the kind of old young man who asks the college dean to be his best man).

In April 2006 I visited Matthew and Christy to see how a model Patrick Henry couple might fare out in the world. After graduation, the newlyweds had moved to Phoenix, where Matthew had grown up. Their apartment was what you'd expect for a young couple—a two-bedroom in an undistinguished stucco complex at the edge of the city, next door to a self-storage unit. But it was their corner of paradise. Christy had decorated it like one of the Patrick Henry lounges, with artificial ivy and dried roses strung over flimsy bookshelves, and a seashell motif in the bathroom. Biblical phrases adorned the walls: As FOR ME AND MY HOUSE, WE WILL SERVE THE LORD. I could imagine their house in thirty years: much the same, only bigger. It looked immaculate to me, but they apologized for its messiness. "We'd rather spend time with each other than clean," Matthew said, and squeezed Christy's hand. Christy is fair with straight blond hair she flipped and then tucked behind her ear. She was always proper and restrained, so it was surprising to see the screen saver on their computer that sat outside the kitchen: a large photo of their first kiss, which took place at their wedding—a passionate full-body affair, with Christy's whole body swallowed up by Matthew's.

Matthew is tall, with searchlight eyes and ears that stick out a bit. He was once a contestant on *Wheel of Fortune,* and he fit right in, with his big head of sharply parted hair and goofy, wholesome locutions. Now he worked at the Center for Arizona Policy, the major Christian-right organization in Arizona. Right inside the door of his office hung a framed editorial written by Len Munsil, CAP's founder, titled "Legislate Morality: Why Not?" On the opposing wall hung a huge poster showing an empty crib, with the slogan "Abortion Changes Everything." Just as at Patrick Henry, the staff of CAP began every morning with prayer.

Phoenix is one of the fastest-growing cities in America, and CAP wanted to make sure it didn't turn into a Las Vegas. CAP lawyers and activists were fighting against porn entrepreneurs, gambling moguls, "homosexual activists," and teachers who assigned "dirty books" in class. Matthew played a reconnaissance role. His job was to comb through newspapers and alert the staff to developing issues. He sent the info out under preset headlines: "abstinence," "bestiality," "don't ask, don't tell," "gay gene," "euthanasia." In a year or so he planned to go to law school, "But not so I can join a multimillion-dollar law practice." Instead, by his late twenties, he planned to run for the Arizona state house. After a few terms in state office, he'd try for Congress.

Even by the standard of Christian conservative organizations, CAP was pretty unevolved. The group functioned like an old-fashioned vice patrol, defending even archaic sex laws on the books. ("We need those!" Matthew explained. "A few days ago they found a dead dog that was sexually abused.") Its library contained alarmist pamphlets with titles like "The Homosexual Agenda in Public Schools." Matthew and Christy spent their weekends collecting signatures for the state's marriage-amendment referendum.

But Matthew did not see himself as outside the political mainstream. When I once used the phrase "weirdness of Christian evangelicalism" in an article, he had asked me it if wouldn't have been more accurate to write "weirdness at the fringes of Christian evangelicalism." After the disappointment of the 2006 election, he spun for me a scenario of how "values voters" like him could be decisive in the 2008 presidential election. This is what made him the perfect Patrick Henry graduate. Despite significant political experience, he was not yet willing to make Derek's compromise. In his mind, he could remain exactly as he was and still go all the way. He knew enough to know to ask me what I thought of the final episode of *The Sopranos,* even though he'd never seen it and never would. A few months after my visit, he got accepted into Harvard Law School. Despite their antagonism toward the Ivy League, the news was received at Patrick Henry with much rejoicing (and some jealousy).

In the evening of my April visit, Matthew and Christy changed into matching red polo shirts that made them look like waiters at Chili's. In fact, these were the uniforms for Awana, the Christian youth group they had volunteered to lead one evening a week. On the drive over to the church, they asked about my kids, which naturally led to the subject of when they might have theirs. Their closest friends in Phoenix were just about to have their baby, and Matthew wanted kids right away. But Christy was not eager. "I've been around kids all my life, and for me it's not a big draw." When Christy was sixteen, her mom had become bedridden with a mysterious illness, and Christy had to take over raising her six siblings. She'd woken up at 5:30 A.M. to cook, clean, and then homeschool them and herself. "That probably has to do with my lack of enthusiasm for kids."

When I first met Matthew and Christy in the winter of 2005, just before they graduated, they were equals in every way. But now Matthew's former debate partner had taken a backseat to his ambition. Christy worked as a paralegal at a law firm that helped to plan estates. She followed up on letters written by the lawyers to their clients and made sure they were prepared for meetings; she was neat and organized and responsible, so she was good at her job. But it was a job, not a career. She liked it because her boss seemed open to having her work part time in the future, or even at home, and she knew that someday she would have kids—probably three or four. "It's just not terribly exciting for me. I don't know, Matt, what would you say?" she asked. He didn't say anything, just gave her a squeeze on the shoulder.

We arrived at the church just as the sun was setting. In a small classroom sat about two dozen Awana "Sparkies," the five- and six-year-olds who would soon take their place at the tip of the spear. This was Silly Hat Day, and the kids had risen to the occasion, donning Dr. Seuss hats and unicorn horns and contraptions made of newspaper. Matthew met them at their level, joking with them as they entered. He led them through limbo and kickball and a game where they played dead and he made goofy faces to get them to laugh. Christy seemed to have no desire to muster the silly theatrics that the situation called for. She stood at the back, more patient than bored, like a teacher waiting for recess to end.

When it was time for Scripture recitation, Christy, or Mrs. du Mee, as she was known here, took her place at the front of the room.

"Are you ready?" she asked the two little girls seated before her.

"Lying lips are an abon . . . abomin . . ."

"Abomination," Christy urged the halting girl, and finished the verse. "But those who deal truthfully are his delight. Sparkies, I need you to quiet down. Can you tell me what an abomination is?"

No one raised a hand.

"I know it's a big word," she continued. "But I want you to re-member it. 'Abomination' is something really, really bad. Not like a food you don't like, but something bad, something God doesn't like. Like when you tell lies. Even if you're good most of the time, but you lie to your sister, or you disobey your mom, you're still a sinner."

After they recited their verses, Christy read them a story. It was about Bartimaeus, a beggar who couldn't see "because of the darkness in his heart." One day, Bartimaeus heard something loud. "Who's coming?" he asked. Jesus was coming.

"*Whoa!*" the kids gasped.

Christy was a clear, confident reader. She kept their attention right to the end, when Jesus came to heal Bartimaeus.

Christy told them to close their eyes and bow their heads. "If you've never asked Jesus to take away the sin in your heart, I want you to tell me that. I want you to tell me and Mr. du Mee."

Five kids raised their hands and came over to whisper to her. She sent four away and kept one, a five-year-old girl—exactly my daughter's age—who'd come with a friend. Throughout the evening, the girl had been one of the bossy chatterers. She was wearing a sassy cheerleader's outfit, and her hair was tied up with sparkly purple ribbon.

Christy led her to a private room and asked her to repeat a prayer.

> *Dear God*
> *I have sinned*
> *and my heart is dark.*
> *Thank you for sending Jesus*
> *to take away the darkness.*
> *Thank you for saving me from the punishment of sin.*
> *Amen.*

The girl looked up at Christy, the spell broken.

"Now you're God's child!" Christy told her, showing her first bit of enthusiasm. "Welcome to the family!"

The girl went back to the main room and blinked. All the other kids were looking at her. They applauded and surrounded her, shouting, "Welcome!" "Welcome to God's family!" "See you in Heaven!"

Her expression stayed blank, and she seemed a little off balance. At one point she looked down at her pink T-shirt, which read GIRLS RULE! in bubbly script.

She quickly zipped up her white sweatshirt and left the room, looking down at her sneakers.

ACKNOWLEDGMENTS

Be kind to strangers is the first lesson taught at church, and I can attest that most people I came across had absorbed it. Michael Farris trusted me enough to let me back on campus after my *New Yorker* article ran. He always treated me as a friend as much as a reporter and let me interrupt his own research so he could help me with mine. Although they surely must have been weary of the stream of visiting reporters, the students of Patrick Henry also treated me with graciousness and respect. They shared their stories, insights, gossip, papers, and sofa beds. They patiently explained countless times what I'm sure they felt was the obvious.

I am especially grateful to the students and professors who agreed to be singled out for the book: Derek Archer, Elisa Muench, Farahn Morgan, Daniel Noa, Bob Stacey, Jennifer Gruenke, and Matthew and Christy du Mee. They were unbelievably generous with their time and their knowledge. They let me shadow them at a vulnerable, shifting time in their lives. I asked a lot of them.

Abigail Pilgrim always corrected my facile readings of people and situations. Steven Rybicki always kept me informed. David Shaw was always candid and funny. Despite initial suspicion, Ben Adams always took the time to set me straight. Leslie Sillars trusted me to teach some of his classes.

I can't imagine a better agent than Sarah Chalfant. I came to her with an incoherent seed of a thought, and for years she gently guided me in the right direction. My editor, Becky Saletan, passed on her enthusiasm and her close attention to detail. Dorothy Wickenden shepherded my article at the *New Yorker*. Amy Davidson did a critical edit of the manuscript. They all stand as living proof that there is generosity and kindness even among the intellectual elite.

My editors at the *Washington Post* gave me the time and freedom to explore this project. Liz Spayd turned me on to the religious beat. Bob Wuthnow invited me to lecture at Princeton early on, and I benefited greatly from the input of his colleagues and students. Ann Hulbert made suggestions on several stories I wrote for *Slate*, which helped shape my thinking. John Green at the Pew Forum on Religion & Public Life always came up with the right numbers. Michael Cromartie kept me in the loop. Alan Wolfe shared his interesting insights into evangelical culture. Anne Hull provided some critical emergency reporting advice and a model of beautiful narrative writing.

I am lucky to have many friends who are also great writers and editors. Alix Spiegel and Gaby Banks shared their impressions with me. Linda Perlstein was a constant companion in all things book related. Margaret Talbot is the absolute best friend a girl reporter could have—wise and smart and funny and a cheerleader all at once. Meri Kolbrener and Jessica Lazar were like sisters to me in my year of writing isolation. Tonje Vetleseter and Nurith Aizenmann were far away but with me in spirit and e-mail.

My parents, Miriam and Eli Rosin, despite their suspicion of my spending so much time in churches, are an inspiration. They taught me to always be frank, even when it's uncomfortable. They also ground me with their particular brand of Israeli Judaism. My in-laws, Judith and Paul Plotz, defy the stereotype. Every year I love and appreciate them more. Michael and Dalila Rosin, John Plotz and Lisa Soltani, and Nily Jacob make up the most fun and loving extended family. Safta, I wish you were still here.

My children were not so happy about having their mother in far away Virginia every day or holed up in the attic. But they both slept in a bed piled with as many books as pillows. So they eventually reconciled themselves. (MAMA. I CAN NOT WAITE TIL YOU FINISH YOU'RE BOOK! is the sign they made for me, which I will keep forever.) When my children could no longer stay away from the attic, Holy Ramampandrison, our babysitter, found something more fun for them to do. She and Val Tomkins work magic.

My husband, David Plotz, inspires me to religious levels of adoration. He's listened to countless stories about Christian teenagers, cooked countless meals for Patrick Henry students, read countless drafts. What can I say? His existence in my life is the closest I come to knowing for sure that someone up there is watching out for me.

ENDNOTES

With the permission of Michael Farris, I had unlimited access to students in their dorms, classes, at school events, and at their internships. Most of the professors and administrators also made themselves available to me. I spent much of the spring semester of 2005 and the following academic year reporting the book. I accompanied students on several debate trips and visited many students at home, on breaks, and over the summer. Most of the students and other people mentioned agreed to have their real names used in the book. For various reasons, a few did not. The following names are pseudonyms: Sarah Chambers, Mark Shane, Kevin, and Jared.

INTRODUCTION

I first visited Patrick Henry College . . . see Hanna Rosin, "Founders
  Plan Virginia Campus to Train a Christian Vanguard; A College for Homeschoolers," *The Washington Post,* September 26, 1999.

They resembled the overambitious . . . For a discussion of the future Ivy League leaders of America, see David Brooks, "The Organization Kid," *The Atlantic Monthly*, April 1, 2001.

Polls would place them among . . . For the most comprehensive statistics on teenage religiosity, see Christian Smith, with Melinda Lundquist Denton, *Soul Searching, The Religious and Spiritual Lives of American Teenagers* (Oxford University Press, 2005), 40.

At Baylor University in Waco, Texas, . . . A February 27 editorial in the *Baylor Lariat* commenting on San Francisco's decision to grant marriage licenses to gay couples argued that "gay couples should be granted the same equal rights to legal marriage as heterosexual couples" and compared discrimination against gays to racial or religious intolerance. Baylor President Robert Sloan said he was "justifiably outraged" and called the editorial "out of touch with traditional Christian teachings."

a loony Jerry Falwell–style . . . In a September 13, 2001, broadcast of *The 700 Club* Falwell said: "I really believe that the pagans, and the abortionists, and the feminists, and the gays and the lesbians who are actively trying to make that an alternative lifestyle, the ACLU, People For the American Way, all of them who have tried to secularize America. I point the finger in their face and say 'you helped this happen.'"

They are the "Joshua Generation" . . . The book of Joshua opens with Moses's death and God's commandment to Joshua, his chosen successor, to win back the Promised Land. The transference of power is a perfect metaphor for Farris. Moses places all his hopes in Joshua, who proves to be a tough and canny warrior.

Farris loaned me Dallas Willard's . . . Dallas Willard, *Hearing God: Developing a Conversational Relationship with God* (InterVarsity Press, 1984), tries to teach readers how to distinguish between "just me" talking and when a "certain something more was taking place."

CHAPTER ONE
Welcome, Surfer Ninjas and Knights

Twenty minutes before the polls . . . As late as 7:30 P.M. on election day exit polls showed democrat John Kerry ahead by three points in Ohio.

Derek said it to a reporter . . . Dennis J. Willard and Doug Oplinger,

"Power Center Driven by Religion to Reshape Nation," *Akron Beacon Journal,* November 19, 2004.

"Jon Stewart? I've not heard" . . . Many Patrick Henry students are avid watchers of Jon Stewart; a handful has never missed an episode, even during exam periods. This is improbable, as religious conservatives are his favorite targets. The students like to tell themselves that he makes fun of everyone equally, which is not exactly true; mostly he makes fun of President Bush and Patrick Henry types. The best explanation I can give is that they share his sensibility and his obsession with politics, and that the Fox News rip-off of his show is not nearly as funny.

Some have suggested that homeschool . . . Margaret Talbot, "A Mighty Fortress," *The New York Times,* February 27, 2000, writes: "We have arrived, it seems, at a moment in our history when the most vigorous and coherent counterculture around is the one constructed by conservative Christians. That sounds odd to many of us—especially, perhaps, to secular liberals, who cherish our own 60s-inflected notions of what an 'alternative lifestyle' should look like."

When Paul Weyrich, . . . In a February 16, 1999, letter to conservatives, Weyrich wrote: "The radicals of the 1960s had three slogans: turn on, tune in, drop out. I suggest that we adopt a modified version. First, turn off. Turn off the television and video games and some of the garbage that's on the computers. Turn off the means by which you and your family are being infected with cultural decadence. Tune out. Create a little stillness. I was very struck by the fact that when I traveled in the former Soviet Union, I couldn't go to a restaurant or any place else without hearing this incessant Western rock music pounding away. There was no escape from it. No wonder some Russians are anti-American. When they think of the United States, they think of the culture that we exported to them. Finally, we need to drop out of this culture, and find places, even if it is where we physically are right now, where we can live godly, righteous and sober lives."

CHAPTER TWO
Harvard for Homeschoolers

A profile in the **Washington Post** . . . Jason Vest, "Mike Farris, for God's Sake; Does He Have a Prayer of Becoming Virginia's Lieutenant Governor?

Yes—and Some Say That's the Problem," *The Washington Post*, August 5, 1993.

NPR was airing an item . . . Steve Inskeep, "Troubled Classrooms," NPR *Morning Edition,* March 1, 2006.

warning parents about the land . . . Michael Farris, *The Joshua Generation: Restoring the Heritage of Christian Leadership* (Broadman & Holman Publishers, 2005), 12.

God's commanding Moses . . . Numbers 13: 1–25.

Jerry Falwell, founder of . . . Cal Thomas and Ed Dobson, *Blinded by Might: Why the Religious Right Can't Save America* (Zondervan, 1999), 17.

Farris told himself over . . . In this section I have strung together quotes from separate interviews that I conducted throughout the year.

America would soon become . . . Christian Smith, *American Evangelicalism: Embattled and Thriving* (University of Chicago Press, 1998), 5.

In 1909, James Leuba, . . . George M. Marsden, *The Soul of the American University: From Protestant Establishment to Established Nonbelief* (Oxford University Press, 1994), 292.

That same year, Cosmopolitan . . . Marsden, 267.

Like all ruling classes . . . Christian Smith, who seems partial to the young moderates, provides an excellent abbreviated history of the split.

Jimmy Swaggart popped up . . . quoted in Lawrence Wright, *Saints & Sinners* (Alfred A. Knopf, 1993), 79.

They had more pressing enemies: . . . Tim LaHaye, *The Battle for the Mind: A Subtle Warfare* (Fleming H. Ravell Company, 1980), 218.

LaHaye said a prayer: . . . quoted in William Martin, *With God on Our Side: The Rise of the Religious Right in America* (Broadway Books, 1996), 189.

Farris met LaHaye . . . interview with Farris.

"raising an army" . . . interview with LaHaye.

"kill off old people" . . . Mark J. Rozell and Clyde Wilcox, *Second Coming: The New Christian Right in Virginia Politics* (The Johns Hopkins University Press, 1996), 98.

"Jesus Christ was totally against" . . . "Moral Majority and Timothy Leary Tangle in a Debate," United Press International, April 16, 1981.

Nearly everything Farris did . . . Rozell and Farris interviews.

In 1993 he won . . . In the case of Michigan v. DeJonge, 501 N.W.2d 127 (Mich. 1993), the Michigan Supreme Court held that parents who educate their children at home due to their religious convictions have a fundamental right protected by the First Amendment.

In some twenty years, . . . Mitchell L. Stevens, *Kingdom of Children: Culture and Controversy in the Homeschooling Movement* (Princeton University Press), 10.

Farris also organized . . . Stevens, 160.

He called the public-school system . . . Rozell, 91–136.

"Killbaby! Killbaby!" . . . Rozell, 109.

Editorials complained . . . Michael Barone, "In Virginia, Distorted Debate," *The Washington Post,* October 28, 1993. The *Washington Post* covered the race extensively, with many front-page stories, profiles, and editorials.

"leader of the powerful conservative" . . . Peter Baker and Donald P. Baker, "Farris Drops Plans to Challenge Sen. Warner," *The Washington Post,* Dec 1, 1994.

an internship with one of 170 . . . James Guth, a professor of political science at Furman University, tracks the religious affiliations of members of Congress.

John Thune blanched . . . interview with Thune, February 2005.

Representative Mike Pence . . . interview with Pence, February 2005.

Time *magazine published* . . . David Van Biema, *Time,* February 7, 2005.

Skateboarders for Christ . . . For more on Christian skateboarders see Lauren Sandler, *Righteous: Dispatches from the Evangelical Youth Movement* (Viking, 2006), 79–106.

into the "knowledge elite" . . . John Schmalzbauer, *People of Faith: Religious Conviction in American Journalism and Higher Education* (Cornell University Press, 2003), 19.

19 percent of Americans . . . Baylor Institute for Studies of Religion, "American Piety in the 21st Century: New Insights to the Depth and Complexity of Religion in the U.S.," September 2006. This is one of the most interesting studies about religion in America. Instead of using the usual measures of religiosity (church attendance, self-definition) it creates four new categories of belief: Benevolent God, Authoritarian God, Distant God, Critical God, and then breaks down attitudes and behaviors—including reading and movie-watching habits—for those four groups.

Vision 2012, a project . . . President Robert Sloan, Jr., laid out a vision for Baylor that sounded much like Michael Farris's. He wanted to make Baylor a premier research university on par with the University of Notre Dame. He declared a break from the school's fundamentalist "anti-intellectual" past and permitted dancing and hired some Catholics and Jews on the faculty. At the same time he strengthened the statement of faith; applicants were asked, for example, why a Christian would ever need to see a psychiatrist. He also hired a prominent proponent of intelligent design, to the horror of the science faculty. Opposition was too strong from all sides, and Sloan stepped down on January 21, 2005. For a thorough discussion see Michael Hall, "God and Man at Baylor," *Texas Monthly,* October 2003.

CHAPTER THREE
"Elisa Muench, Republican, for Idaho's Senator. She Will Make a Difference."

"Come on, America . . . James Dobson, *Love Must Be Tough* (Tyndale House, 1983), 35.

If a wife works, . . . Tim LaHaye, *How to be Happy Though Married* (Tyndale House, 1968), 107.

wink-wink happy-homemaker . . . Stevens does a fine dissection of Pride and her impact on homeschooling families. Pride's daughter attended Patrick Henry.

Dobson took on an Oprah role . . . While he is insistent that women stay home, Dobson makes a very sensible and astute observation of the isolation, loneliness, and time pressures faced by a new wife and mother in *What Wives Wish Their Husbands Knew About Women* (Tyndale House, 1975), 59–103.

"Don't you enjoy" . . . Mary Pride, *The Way Home: Beyond Feminism, Back to Reality* (Crossway Books, 1985), 39.

Fifty-eight percent of . . . W. Bradford Wilcox, *Soft Patriarchs, New Men: How Christianity Shapes Fathers and Husbands* (University of Chicago Press, 2004), 74–96.

The Christian homeschooling movement . . . Stevens has an excellent analysis of how the homeschooling movement reinvented women's roles to conform to modern expectations.

"Homeworking is the Biblical lifestyle" . . . from the introduction to *Pride: The Way Home.*

"tightened the noose" . . . Raymond Moore and Dorothy Moore, *Home Grown Kids* (Word Books, 1981), 22.

CHAPTER FOUR
America Is a Christian Nation, Capital "C," Capital "N"

'stink on ice' . . . From *History of the World, Part I,* where Brooks plays a royal in the days leading up to the French Revolution.

witnessed mostly "card-playing" . . . Brooke Allen, *Moral Minority: Our Skeptical Founding Fathers* (Ivan R. Dee, 2006), 31. Allen is intent on debunking the Christian right's view of the Founding Fathers. For a more balanced discussion, see Jon Meacham, *American Gospel: God, the Founding Fathers, and the Making of Nation* (Random House, 2006).

He took a razor . . . Meacham, 4.

sociologist Christian Smith . . . Christian Smith, *Christian America? What Evangelicals Really Want* (University of California Press, 2002).

"has twisted the Constitution" . . . Michael P. Farris, *Constitutional Law for Enlightened Citizens* (Home School Legal Defense Association, 2006).

CHAPTER FIVE
Farahn's Attempt to Hid Her Midriff

In conservative Christian . . . For an excellent discussion of prudential rules, see Mark Oppenheimer, "The First Dance," *The New York Times,* January 28, 2007.

Every morning Bush . . . For an excellent discussion of Chambers's effect on Bush's thinking, see Robert Wright, "Faith, Hope and Clarity," *The New York Times,* October 28, 2004.

Senator Barack Obama . . . see Amy Sullivan, "In Good Faith," *Slate,* July 3, 2006.

CHAPTER SIX
"This Is It! Go for Smiles! Go for Christ!"

"nuts" and "goofy" . . . David Kuo, *Tempting Faith: An Inside Story of Political Seduction* (Free Press, 2006), 229.

In a speech . . . On December 11, 2001, Rove was interviewed by moderators Norman Ornstein of the American Enterprise Institute and Thomas Mann of the Brookings Institution: "I will say this, I will say one of the ironies is, is that we probably failed to martial support among the base as well as we should have. If you look at the model of the electorate, and you look at the model of who voted, the big discrepancy is among self-identified, white, evangelical Protestants, Pentecostals, and fundamentalists. If they were a part of the voters of what they should have been if you had looked at the electoral model, here should have been 19 million of them, and instead there were 15 million of them. Just over 4 million of them failed to turn out and vote."

Critics loved it . . . Virginia Heffernan, "Surf's Up! Teenage Hormones Are High," *The New York Times*, August 12, 2005.

Blind unbelief is sure . . . William Cowper, "God Moves In a Mysterious Way," 1731–1800, see *The Handbook to the Lutheran Hymnal* (Concordia Publishing House, 1941), 358.

CHAPTER SEVEN
The Den of Sin

When CNN came . . . "College Caters to Homeschoolers," aired March 7, 2005.

CHAPTER EIGHT
From Humanzee to Liger: A Brief History of Evolution

Soviet researcher Ilya . . . Clive D. L. Wynne, "Kissing Cousins," *The New York Times*, December 12, 2005.

scientists known as baraminologists . . . For more information on baraminology, see Todd Charles Wood and Megan J. Murray, *Understanding the Pattern of Life* (Broadman & Holman, 2003), and Kurt P. Wise, *Faith, Form and Time: What the Bible Teaches and Science Confirms About Creation and the Age of Universe* (Broadman & Holman, 2002).

"God created human beings" . . . Gallup has been asking this question since 1982, and the percentage of Americans who agree has not notably changed.

Instead, they resort to . . . Peter Baker and Peter Slevin, "Bush Remarks on 'Intelligent Design' Theory Fuel Debate," *The Washington Post*, August 3, 2005.

Young-earth creationism . . . For an excellent and thorough history of creationism, see Ronald Numbers, *The Creationists: From Scientific Creationism to Intelligent Design* (Harvard University Press, 2006).

Wise told the story . . . Kurt Wise, "Suggestions for Peaceful Coexistence of Creationists and Evolutionists in the Classroom," paper No. 81-8, Geological Society of America, annual meeting, October 16–19, 2005.

Each year scientific . . . For a summary of the latest attempts by creationists to influence curriculums, see Ronald Numbers and the introduction to expanded edition of *The Creationists.*

"I am not a believer" . . . Stephen Jay Gould, *Rocks of Ages: Science and Religion in the Fullness of Life* (Ballantine, 1999), 8.

CHAPTER NINE
The Fifth Quadrant: Hollywood Finds God

"You get signals" . . . Peter J. Boyer, "The Jesus War; Mel Gibson's Obsession," *The New Yorker,* September 15, 2003.

Gibson used his own . . . Peter J. Boyer, "Hollywood Heresy, Marketing 'The DaVinci Code' to Christians," *The New Yorker,* May 22, 2006.

Disney and its . . . Hanna Rosin, "Can Jesus Save Hollywood?" *The Atlantic Monthly*, December 1, 2005. Additional information came from interviews with Adamson.

Relations between Christians . . . For a good discussion of Christians' relationship to Hollywood, see Robert K. Johnston, *Reel Spirituality: Theology and Film in Dialogue* (Baker Academic, 2000).

Scott Derrickson calls . . . "A Filmmaker's Progress" is reprinted in *Behind the Scenes: Hollywood Insiders on Faith, Film and Culture* (Baker Books, 2005), 163–178.

Dean Batali was . . . interview with Batali.

Yet even with . . . interview with Derrickson.

what A. O. Scott . . . A. O. Scott, "Dancing with the Devil," *The New York Times,* September 9, 2005.

CHAPTER TEN
Today I Met the Boy I'm Gonna Marry

"It's awesome to be" . . . " 'True Love Waits' For Some Teenagers," *The New York Times,* June 21, 1993.

By sociologists' standards . . . Mark D. Regnerus, *Forbidden Fruit: Sex & Religion in the Lives of American Teenagers* (Oxford University Press, 2007).

CHAPTER ELEVEN
Obey, All You Little Children

"Reclaiming America for Christ" . . . This is an annual conference run by Coral Ridge Ministries in Fort Lauderdale, Florida, with a goal similar to Patrick Henry's: to mobilize evangelical Christians for political action to return society to what they call "the biblical worldview of the Founding Fathers."

CONCLUSION

Tim Kaine's victory . . . Hanna Rosin, "Closing the God Gap," *The Atlantic Monthly,* January/February 2007.

Republican Kenneth Blackwell . . . For a good picture of the hopes Christian activists placed on Blackwell, see Frances Fitzgerald, "Holy Toledo; Ohio's Gubernatorial Race Tests the Power of the Christian Right," *The New Yorker,* July 31, 2006.